THE
BIRTH OF
NOW

How the world became rich and free

JAMIE
CAWLEY

Matador
9 Priory Business Park,
Wistow Road, Kibworth Beauchamp,
Leicestershire. LE8 0RX
Tel: 0116 279 2299
Email: books@troubador.co.uk
Web: www.troubador.co.uk/matador
Twitter: @matadorbooks

ISBN 9781785892479 (hardback)
ISBN 9781785891229 (paperback)

British Library Cataloguing in Publication Data.
A catalogue record for this book is available from the British Library.

Printed and bound in the UK by TJ International, Padstow, Cornwall
Typeset in 11pt Aldine401 BT by Troubador Publishing Ltd, Leicester, UK

Matador is an imprint of Troubador Publishing Ltd

To Joe

CONTENTS

.1.

THE QUESTION

I n 1870, more than 4,000 years after it was built, the Great Pyramid at Giza in Egypt was still the world's tallest man-made structure. By 2010, only 140 years later, there were more than 10,000 buildings taller than the Great Pyramid. This book is about what caused this change and what will change next.

The tallest building is not, in itself, a matter of great importance, but it has great symbolism. In the nineteenth century, until 1889, all of the 100 tallest structures in the world, apart from the Great Pyramid, were in Europe and they were all churches, reflecting both Europe's dominance of the world and the power of religion in Europe. Later, from 1930 until 1998, all the world's tallest buildings were in the USA and they were all commercial: an equally fair reflection of the US takeover of world power in the twentieth century and the importance of commerce within America. Currently, early in the twenty-first century, the world's tallest building itself and sixty of the other top 100 tallest buildings, are in Asia. This record itself may not be profound but it does reflect changes in power and influence with considerable accuracy.

On a graph showing the height of the tallest man-made structures in the world through history, the line runs flat for 3,800 years before anything taller than the Great Pyramid is built. Over the following 500 years, until 1870CE, there are a couple of tiny bobbles in the line of our graph, as a few medieval cathedrals are built with spires just taller than the Great Pyramid, reflecting the great culture of the European High Middle Ages. But all these spires fall down, reflecting the way that the memory of that culture has all but vanished since, and the Great Pyramid is left, once again, as the highest. Then, after 1870, the line of the graph takes off, climbing almost vertically, until we get to the present; the Burj Khalifa in Dubai, 828 metres tall, 2,000 miles east of the Great Pyramid and well over five times its height.

The height of buildings illustrates a huge question in history: what turned thousands of years of achingly slow advance into two centuries of dramatically rapid progress? The changes that did happen between the building of the Great Pyramid and a couple of centuries ago took an astonishing amount of time. For example, the first Roman emperor, Augustus, who died over two thousand years ago, had central heating, piped water, a secretariat and a postal system in a world that had vast factories, carefully planned military arsenals with siege engines, a well-organised navy and a substantial merchant marine. Moving 1700 years forward to the Georgian era in Britain and America and it would take a bold individual to claim that their era had surpassed the sophistication of Augustus's classical Romans. Learning had moved forward a little since then but the material position, even of the rich, was virtually unchanged and some would say it had gone backwards – Georgian roads were nothing like as good as the Romans' roads nor were their drains and their largest cities were a fraction of the size of Augustus's Rome. Many aristocrats of the Georgian period around 1750 still *aspired* to the lifestyle of a Roman senator of 50BC and self-consciously tried to imitate the forms of Roman writing they saw as so superior to their own language and style. They built their houses in styles imitating Roman models, but they never managed to include the underfloor heating that the Roman villas of Britain had. The Americans of the period went further and copied not only Roman buildings but also their institutions, like the 'Senate' in the 'Capitol' building.

Over the vast span of history, great men and women have thought and fought, empires have risen and died, temples have been built, destroyed, rebuilt and destroyed again, but all these changes made little difference to the way ordinary people lived their daily lives until 250 years ago. The peasant toiling in fields of 1750 does not seem any better off or any worse off than the peasant who lived 5,000 years earlier. Both peasants, wherever they came from, lived with their families in single-room, earthen-floor huts, working in the fields, with the occasional help of animals, fetching their water from open streams and ponds and subject to malnutrition if the harvest failed. In both periods, the vast majority of the population were peasants or similar small-scale tillers of the soil – something else that was to change drastically after 1800.

This theme runs through many areas of life: 5,000 years with very little progress followed by sudden, dramatic change, starting sometime between 1750 and

1800: technological change, political change and social change. Sometime between 1750 and 1800 some kind of human earthquake started in north-west Europe and a process of continual development and progress began. Economic progress, so centuries of borderline malnutrition became decades of plenty; social progress, from ten per cent literacy to ninety per cent literacy; community change, from village to city; technical progress, from watermill to steam engine to electric car; humanitarian progress, from child labour to welfare state; political progress, from monarchy to democracy. All these started to transform around the same time and in the same places. Since then all of them have progressed together alongside each other, spreading out across the world as they have developed.

A term that has been used to refer to this period is 'The Industrial Revolution'. This term was created by French historians because they wanted to draw a parallel between the French, political, revolution and the British 'Industrial Revolution' of the same period. (It was popularised in English later by the historian, Arnold Toynbee.) But this change was across much more than just industry: it was much bigger than just an industrial revolution. It transformed politics, agriculture, transport, society, finance, education and health as well as industry. Nor did the industrial change come first; it was, as clearly as you can make the comparisons, moving in parallel alongside all the other changes. The changes were profound, multiplying the amount of food and energy consumed per head, even as they enabled the population to increase to seven times the size. The changes were across a very broad spectrum: popular sports were invented, basic education became universal and mass literacy arrived, professions began and science started to be applied to real-world problems. The changes were often benign: slavery, child labour, mass malnutrition and the death penalty were gradually abolished and murder rates dropped to a fraction of traditional levels. The change in industry, the 'Industrial Revolution', was only one part of a much bigger historical earthquake.

As well as being misleadingly narrow, the term 'Industrial Revolution' offers no sense of what caused this huge change. General histories of the period are full of stories of canals and railways, of the spinning jenny and of the weaving frame, figures about how the railways grew by thousands of miles a decade and tales about how the great inventors struggled but triumphed in the end. But this is all 'what' happened not 'why' it happened. A few reasons have been put forward rather tentatively, and we will look at these later, but most histories prefer to simply describe the changes and, slightly awestruck, to leave them unexplained.

But, although few present any theory to explain it, all the histories of the period agree that the speed of change in north-west Europe increased many times over, starting sometime between 1750 and 1800. This view is not dependent on individual facts or figures, or even the exact date, but on the sheer scale of the break between the two periods, one of very slow change over thousands of years, the other of very rapid change over decades.

We can see how slow progress was before the break by looking at Sumer (now central/south Iraq) 5000 years ago. Sumer is the first civilisation that we know of, starting a little before the Old Kingdom of Egypt. A civilisation is an area where towns have developed, not just villages (a town is *civis* in Latin, hence the term 'civilisation'). To be a town, rather than a large village, there must be specialised buildings, such as temples, palaces and markets and clear evidence of defined professions, that is, priests and kings, as well as craftsmen. Sumer is the first area we know for sure that had all these. Sumer was also the first area where we can find written records of society, mostly accounting-type records of ownership and taxes. The best-known towns of Sumer were Ur, Lagash, Uruk, Nippur and Eridu, but later these gave way to Babylon, which lasted for over two thousand years as the capital of the region and was the world's first city of over half a million people. To give an idea of the timescale, the first period of Sumerian greatness was longer before the Emperor Augustus of Rome than we are after him: about 1,000 years longer. Sumer's rise was also nearly 1,500 years before the (believed) time of Moses, 2,600 years before the Buddha, 3,000 years before Jesus of Nazareth and nearly 4,000 years before the Prophet Mohammad.

The Sumerians not only had writing but also arithmetic, astronomy, kings, priests, drains, metals, pottery, mass-produced bowls, sailing boats with long trading routes and trading links over land that meant that they could import decorative lapis lazuli from 2,500 miles away. Astonishingly, there are only four 'inventions' we can be confident were devised in all the time between the period of the Sumerians and the Birth of Now, sometime after 1750: iron smelting[i], which we think started about 2000BCE in Turkey; the magnetic compass, about 200BCE; paper, four hundred years later in 200CE; and gunpowder, sometime after 1000CE, all first recorded in China. The other devices that are first *recorded* after that date are just as likely to go back to the start of civilisation[1] because, before 500BCE, very little was written or pictured about the everyday things of daily life. Items like watermills, stirrups and wheelbarrows do not leave distinctive remains, unlike glass, for example, so although the first windmill to be recorded dates from Persia around 650BCE, the first stirrup around 500BCE and the first water mill around 250BCE, they may all, in fact, date from the Sumerian period or before. Some other 'inventions' seem to be straightforward developments once conditions are right. The plough mould-board, for example, appears in Europe around 1,000CE and has been hailed as a breakthrough 'invention'. But it arrived only after horses, originally bred bigger to carry knights in armour, became large enough to pull ploughs. The plough mould-board was used much earlier in Chinese paddy-fields, where the wet soil is soft enough for oxen to pull it. But, even with every possible post-Sumer 'invention' added in, it is still a challenging task to identify any development that made daily life for the Romans much different to life for the Sumerians and, as we have seen, there is not much that separates the Roman lifestyle from the Georgian…

Drains are a particularly useful marker of

---

1   An invention is a working piece of machinery, not a theory, method, or discovery. So, for example, Pythagoras' theorem, the Alphabet and America are not included as 'inventions'.

development because, where they existed, they were, naturally, underground and so often remain relatively undisturbed and can be found in archaeological digs. The advantages of drains to the people that built them are also considerable in terms of a pleasant and healthy life. To make the point about how little development there was over nearly 5,000 years, the temple of Uruk in Sumeria had drains before 3000BCE but the great Palace of Versailles in France, completed by Louis XIV in 1714CE, did not have drains. With its population of several thousand, the smell was said to be 'unique'[ii].

If a citizen of early Babylon was transported in time to anywhere in the world on a warm day in 1750, he or she would have found little to be astonished about, apart from the fashions of the period (in Europe at the time, rich men wore elaborate wigs covered in white powder). People riding horses would probably have been the biggest surprise, as the Sumerians had little knowledge of horses, because they did not prosper in their hot river valley, although they used donkeys for carrying and horses were already domesticated elsewhere in Asia at the time. Also, the Sumerians did not have cannons or gunpowder but they probably used fire-arrows and clay pots filled with lit tar as grenades – crude oil and tar were widely available in Sumer – although the first actual pictures of fire weapons being used date from later – around 1000BCE[iii].

Even suppose that our Babylonian was transported to one of the great European cities on the cusp of the Birth of Now – London or Paris in 1750 – he would have felt little surprise; by 1500BCE, Babylon had a population of half a million or more, similar to or larger than Georgian London or Paris. All three of these cities were only half the size Rome is thought to have been during its Empire or Chang'an, the capital of Tang Dynasty China, *c.*700CE.

Overall, our Babylonian would probably have found little in the Paris of Rousseau or the London of Dr Johnson that would have been more surprising than people riding horses. There is nothing particular about the houses or palaces of 1750 that can be pointed to as an advance on those of Babylon or Rome. People still ate what food could be grown in the area around the town, they excreted into pots or in public, they communicated only by voice and pen, they travelled by foot or horse, they suffered from disease and died as young and mysteriously as they always had. If the Babylonian were a scholar, there would be information that was new to him – the existence of America, for example[2]. But, in all that learning, there would be little or nothing that made everyday life any different to the Babylonian experience of life nearly 4,000 years earlier. Perhaps there was a tiny hint of what was very shortly to come in London, as even the common folk were beginning to enjoy drinks that came from the far side of the world; tea and coffee, sweetened with that magic substance, sugar, from another far land.

But if the Babylonian was transported to a developed city around 1900 – Paris, perhaps – they would be

---

2   The earth was proven to be spherical and its size measured by Eratosthenes around 240BC although the suggestion that it was spherical comes much earlier. Given the Babylonian excellent astronomy, it was probably considered as a possibility then.

astonished by much of what they saw: trains, gas light, newspapers, self-propelled iron ships, the Eiffel Tower, schools everywhere; the sheer, endless size of the city (around four times its population in 1750). If we take another time-travelling peasant, from much more recent times, in fact, any time right up to 1750, they would have much the same reaction. They would have the same background experience of life as the Babylonian, so they would experience the same astonishment at the extraordinary advances and changes from what they knew. If either traveller was then transported to any major city today there would be no describing their astonishment at the high buildings, the cleanliness, cars, lights, air conditioning, airplanes, televisions and phones. The effect of the changes of the last 250 years dwarf all the changes of the previous 5,000 years put together by a huge amount.

So something started to happen between 1750 and 1800 to transform the human world totally. In our current generation, only 250 or so years after the changes started, the majority of humankind has become city dwelling; the use of human energy to cultivate (planting, harvesting, etc.) has already disappeared from the developed part of the world. Soon we may hope that the job of peasant will follow a long line of dreary jobs into history: labourer, washerwoman, porter, clerk, miner, typist and bookkeeper. Starvation, infection, illiteracy and other grim constants of all previous lives still afflict humanity, but now only the minority suffer and that number is shrinking rapidly. If we continue as we are, without disaster or losing direction, we can hope that freedom from mass deprivation will happen within a current lifespan and that, finally, starvation, like smallpox, will be just a miserable footnote in history.

There is, then, an enormous divide between what we will call 'Then', the period before this change, and 'Now', the period after it. The change to 'Now' was initially confined to a small region of the world in north-west Europe, but it has since extended, rapidly in historic terms, to many other parts of the world. There are, today, still some countries stuck in the 'Then' phase; countries that we call 'developing' or 'Third World', coexisting uncomfortably alongside the growing number of 'Now' societies. The people stuck in 'Then' societies are prevented from escaping by strongly policed borders preventing entry into the 'Now' world. The split between 'Then' and 'Now' was originally a split between two different eras of time; now it is a geographical split between two different kinds of country. Fortunately, the area still in 'Then' is shrinking and, one day, it should finally disappear.

In the period before the change, the constants were hunger, disease, poverty, sudden death, extreme inequality, exposure to the elements, slavery, injustice and cruelty. Sometimes, perhaps for a few years, acute suffering was kept at bay, but it always returned when times were bad. After 'Now' started, shortage of food became unknown in the leading countries, good health started to become an expectation, the law began to strive for fairness, weatherproof housing gradually became near-universal and society aspired towards an ideal of equality and personal respect for all. We will call the start of this change the 'Birth of Now'; the moment or short period when the process started that got us from the old way of living, 'nasty, brutish and short', to the way we live 'Now'.

None of this is to say that the level of development was stationary for the 5,000 years before the Birth of Now: far from it. It is just that it went backwards as well as forwards. For Westerners, the most obvious decline was after the fall of the Roman Empire in north-west Europe: the slump into the 'Dark Ages'. The effect is more familiar and frequent in China. Here prosperous years under a successful emperor or two seem always to be followed by the decline of the dynasty, a fall into internal warfare and anarchy and then a collapse of the country into a primitive state – before a great warlord starts a new dynasty and begins the process again. Periods of development and growth before the Birth of Now are centred on towns and on the wealthy; they bring few changes for the great mass of toiling peasants and what improvements they do provide eventually decline yet again, back to the same, miserable starting level of development.

The suddenness of the Birth of Now is a little disguised because north-west Europe, where it occurred, had been on an upswing in development in the period before it started – not a coincidence, as we shall see. But, apart from the purely intellectual advances of Newton, Descartes and company and the artistic and architectural rediscovery of classical designs, the practical advances are few indeed and bear no comparison to those after the Birth of Now. Mostly north-west Europe, led by the

Netherlands, was just catching up with Italy, which itself had just got back to classical Roman levels of wealth and comfort. For example, London's St Paul's Cathedral was rebuilt around 1700, after the great fire, using a domed format pioneered in Italy by Florence Cathedral, built around three hundred years earlier. Even though it is so much older, Florence Cathedral is three metres taller than the new St Paul's[3], so it is difficult to claim St Paul's shows much progress. But to illustrate again how little progress there had been in the 1400 years since the Roman era, the dome over Florence's cathedral is itself a metre or so smaller in diameter than the classical Roman dome of the Pantheon, a dome that you can still see today, completed in 126CE.

Despite all these examples, our histories tend to assume – without normally justifying it – that earlier civilisations were always more primitive than later civilisations; that there might at times have been one step back, but this was always followed, sooner or later, by two steps forward. Now there is some evidence to be found for this point of view. For example: Mycenae was a leading city of the Greece that, in about 1200BCE, fought in the Trojan War described in Homer's *Iliad*. Its ruins today show that, at its height, Mycenae was much smaller and more primitive than nearby classical Athens, a leading city of Greece that came long after it, flourishing most between 500 and 300BCE. The progress achieved in the 700 years between the two is visible in every way.

But the problem is that Greek Mycenae is also

---

3   The previous St Paul's, which had been completed four hundred years earlier, was also markedly larger than the new one; another reflection on the wealth of the High Middle Ages.

smaller and more primitive than Greek Knossos on the island of Crete, which flourished 500 years *earlier* then Mycenae: that is, until about 1700BCE. This civilisation, in turn, is less grandiose than the nearby Old Kingdom of Egypt, 500 years earlier still, the period when the great Pyramids were built (and which is also quite close by). In terms of buildings and graphic art, the civilisation of the Old Kingdom of Egypt is comparable with empires of a much later period, such as the Han Empire of China, 2,000 years later and the Empire of Charlemagne in Western Europe, more than 3,000 years later.

In contrast to us, Egyptians of the Middle and New Kingdoms saw history as a steady decline, starting from a golden age, through a silver age, to the copper age of their own day. The Chinese tradition is to see history as repeating itself, going round in circles, with the overall cycle unchanging. So the idea that history has a regular direction of progress 'forwards' or 'upwards' is a new assumption with little support before the Birth of Now. Often things seemed to go downhill and sometimes even specific advances were lost: we still do not know what 'Greek Fire' was made of – it was a substance that burned on the water, setting enemy ships on fire. The Roman use of concrete vanished and only returned in the twentieth century. The idea that things become more developed as we forwards in time gains strength only after the Birth of Now, when the extent of progress being made became self-evident.

The rise, decline, fall and rise again in living standards, has happened many, many times in the one part of the world where we have a reasonable written record: the Middle

East, where the Sumerians started it all. The Sumerians were replaced in turn by (simplified list): the Akkadians, the Amorites, the Kassites, locals from Isin, the Aramites, the Aramaens, the Assyrians, the Chaldeans (locals again, sometimes known as the neo-Babylonians), the Persians, the Greeks, the Romans, the Parthians, the Sassanians (a family of Persians), the Arab Rashidun Caliphs, the Umayyads, the Abbasids, the Seljuks, the Mongols, the Osmanlis (Ottoman Turks), the British, more locals and the Americans – the last technically ruling through local leaders. There has been war and peace, bad times and better times, but in all the 5,000 years of recorded history, the only long-term difference has been made in the last 100 years by the introduction of modern technology, washing over from the Birth of Now in Europe. The poet Shelley saw the effect:

> *I met a traveller from an antique land*
> *Who said: 'Two vast and trunkless legs of stone*
> *Stand in the desert. Near them, on the sand,*
> *Half sunk, a shattered visage lies, whose frown,*
> *And wrinkled lip, and sneer of cold command,*
> *Tell that its sculptor well those passions read*
> *Which yet survive, stamped on these lifeless things,*
> *The hand that mocked them and the heart that fed:*
> *And on the pedestal these words appear –*
> *"My name is Ozymandias, king of kings:*
> *Look on my works, ye Mighty, and despair!"*
> *Nothing beside remains. Round the decay*
> *Of that colossal wreck, boundless and bare*
> *The lone and level sands stretch far away.'*

Not all civilisations declined all the ways to basics or bounced back again; some just stayed where they were. The eastern half of the Roman Empire lasted for more than 1,500 years, although in the later period it is frequently known as the Byzantine Empire after its capital of Byzantium (aka, Constantinople, later Istanbul). After Mehmet the Conqueror took over Byzantium in 1456, it was reinvigorated as the centre of the Ottoman Empire, although that empire in turn gradually declined in cohesion, power and influence until 1918. Yet through all the continuity of more than 2,000 years, very little 'progress' happened. The historian of the Roman Empire, Edward Gibbon, points out that, despite speaking Greek, the language of *the sublime masters who had pleased or instructed the first of nations...In the revolution of ten centuries, not a single discovery was made to exalt the dignity or promote the happiness of mankind. Not a single idea has been added to the speculative systems of antiquity...*[4]

Ancient Egypt showed the same spirit, copying the ways of the Old Kingdom and striving to reach its heights for 2,500 years, literally in the case of the Great Pyramid. One of the reasons it is difficult to date Egyptian artefacts is that they imitate the designs and patterns of long, long before. The same is more or less true of China, which also tended to see itself as having declined from the Han golden age of 100BCE. The 'Forbidden City' in Beijing is a giant palace built in the 1400s and largely rebuilt in the 1600s but in the style of the Han Dynasty and using the methods of their period. In China, to become a ruling official you needed to pass examinations: the books that needed to be studied to pass these remained essentially the same from the eighth-century Tang Dynasty, right up to the twentieth century. Despite 'good kings' and, for that matter, bad kings and wicked dowager empresses and eunuchs and revolutions and invasions and dynasties, nothing fundamental changed in China until after the Birth of Now – you have to be a real expert to tell a bronze casting from 1300BCE from one of 1300CE. Equally, although the capital of the area that was originally Sumer and that we now call Iraq[4] moved away from Babylon itself after a couple of thousand years, there was always a major city close to the site. Today's capital, Baghdad, is only eighty-five kilometres from Babylon. Given the length of time, the thousands of years that they existed, why did none of these places make any life-changing advances, technical, social or political – and few enough advances of any kind – until after they were affected by the wash-over from the Birth of Now?

Before the Birth of Now, many of the political events, the wars, the conquests, the growths of empires and their falls, changed only the names and faces on the statues. Perhaps different ceremonial clothing was worn and the location of the capital moved but, like changing the cast in a long-running play, while the faces changed the plot stayed the same. After a time, the new players, in their turn, were subsumed in the next invasion or decline or break-up. The structures of the old regime may have fallen; people, buildings, laws and religions alike, but the rubble formed the foundation of the new

---

4   The name Iraq may derive from Uruk in the original Sumer. The area has sometimes been called Mesopotamia, a Greek word of 2-3,000 years later than Uruk that seems less appropriate.

regime. The lost past repeats itself like the stubble of a crop being ploughed back into the soil to feed next year's growth.

So we seem justified in splitting history into two phases: one of glacially slow change for over 5,000 years from the dawn of civilisation to sometime roughly around 1750 to 1800. Then the other phase starts, with continual and rapid changes taking us through to today. During the first phase, the period that we call 'Then', such advance as there was had little or no impact on the daily life of the mass of peasants. In the second phase, 'Now' in our terminology, everything changed. Typical statistics for the world since 1800 – and there are a number of sources for these, all in rough agreement – are: population has increased by sevenfold, total output of goods has increased by 120 times and energy consumption by sixty times. The scale of change is so huge that the figures do not have to be exact to make the point.

Two questions arise: what made the change from 'Then' to 'Now' happen and why did it happen when it did?

The first issue that arises is that we do not know what sort of change it was. What was the first thing, the bit that started all the other changes going? Coal, for example, was not a new fuel; people had been using it in China for over a 1000 years before 1800 and in England they had certainly been using it for over 200 years before 1800 and probably started using it much earlier in areas where it could be simply picked up from the surface of the land or, as in Northumbria, from the beaches at the bottom of the cliffs. Why was it only in 1712 that the first steam engine was installed, when a working model of a steam engine had been shown 2,000 years earlier by Hero of Alexandria? Alternatively, why did steam power start then, in 1712, and not centuries later? Why that particular period? No definitive answer to questions like these has been agreed so far; indeed, it is very rare for this question to be posed in these kinds of terms at all. 'What caused the Industrial Revolution', is often presented as a story of the right people being around at the right time. Luck then? But, even if some of the stories of individual engineering heroism are true, and maybe some are, they do not explain why they all came about in a rush at the same time. Anyone who put forward the idea that the Roman Empire gained its great size due to a lucky run of brilliant generals would be thought very naive.

The idea that there was a singular turning point in historical development is widely acknowledged as, at least, the 'Industrial and Agricultural Revolutions', but it is then left at that. It is widely assumed – without being specifically stated – that the path of recorded history is one of gentle, if wobbly, progress in an 'upward' direction. We can call it the theory of Constant Slow Progress (CSP). Two steps forward, one step back, maybe; but progress in the long run nonetheless. This assumption has to be unstated as it is quite in defiance of the historical evidence, not only of the one-off step-change of the Birth of Now but also of the many and lengthy development downturns recorded in history – the 500-year Western European 'Dark Age' has to be simply ignored. The assumption of 'progress' was also famously mocked over eighty years ago as 'Whig History', history written by historians determined to find progress, whatever the facts.

What caused the Birth of Now? We want an answer to be something that unmistakably results in effects like those we see at the Birth of Now. Not mysterious pseudo-answers such as a 'change in the spirit of the age', nor a fluke, 'suddenly inventions started to happen', nor a sleight of hand, 'the decline of church dominance that freed the spirit of originality'. We must find a cause that only existed just before the Birth of Now and only in north-western Europe and especially in Britain, the leading area in the Birth of Now. The cause must be known from other evidence to stimulate economic growth and social transformation; the cause must explain how its effects could then spread to the rest of the world. We are looking for solid evidence supporting a well-constructed case. A good murder-mystery does not end with the detective putting forward a hypothesis: he produces the murder weapon; he explains whodunnit and howdunnit, fitting all the facts that were presented earlier in the story. So here we want to find clear, unmistakable evidence – ideally, high-quality numerical evidence – of a single main cause of all the effects we observe at the Birth of Now.

Once the cause of this abrupt change of direction in history is established, it changes the way we see both our own period and our future. Knowing the cause of the Birth of Now will suggest when our current era of continuous change will end and what will come after the period we live in, what comes after 'Now'.

Understanding what made the changes start leads to a better understanding of what will make them stop.

We are running ahead of the story though. The point is to emphasise that some*thing* happened, that there was a definite event, an event that started across a short period – a decade or two at most – a Birth of Now. Despite being the most significant change in history and the only change of era since the dawn of civilisation, we have had little idea what the Birth of Now is and no convincing thoughts about what could have caused it. We shall remain in this uncomfortable position for several chapters. This is not because, like a murder-mystery, the fun is lost if you know whodunnit too early, but because, like a thriller, the ending makes no sense if you haven't followed the plot.

Before we ask what started the Birth of Now, we need to ask why it didn't happen earlier. Many of the devices that are seen as central to the Birth of Now were 'invented' much earlier. A form of printing – stamping – was developed alongside the first writing around 3,000BCE and printing was big business in Song China before 1000CE. We have seen that a steam engine was demonstrated in classical Alexandria around 1700 years before the first commercial steam engines came into use. There are examples of the most elaborate clockwork machinery from ancient Greece – the best known is the 'Antikythera mechanism'. The short-sighted Emperor Nero used eyeglasses to watch gladiators and there are examples of things that look like electric batteries from Parthia around 250BCE[V].

Why did development not take off when Rome

was at its peak? There seems to be nothing obvious in Georgian England, when the Birth of Now did take off, that Rome did not have bigger and better 2,000 years earlier, when it did not take off. There must be some crucial difference we can find. Or the Birth of Now could have lifted off from the wealth and development of Yuan China that so stunned Marco Polo, or it could even have started when the pharaohs built the Great Pyramid, back near the dawn of civilisation? Or Mayan America in its heyday; the High Middle Ages; the vast city of medieval Patna? Why not? Mankind is an ingenious animal that shares good ideas around and seeks to better his circumstances in this world. Why did the millions of people over the thousands of years not start to solve their problems the way they did sometime after 1700? Why did the developments of the Birth of Now not start much, much earlier? What stopped them? What prevented development happening for so long?

.2.

A SIMPLE MODEL

Before the Birth of Now the history of every region of the world has a consistent overall pattern. Its culture and material sophistication rises to something like the point where drains are built, and then either stays stuck there, like Byzantium or Babylon, or falls back into a relatively primitive state, as, for example, much of the Maya civilisation of Central America did between 700 and 900CE or Western Europe in the 'Dark Ages'. Such a consistent pattern suggests that there is a limiting factor, some force that prevents civilisations from developing further. This force or effect allows the development of technology up to waterwheels and the development of thought up to complex belief systems but then stops either process going further and into steam engines or science.

This limiting factor has to be extraordinarily universal. It has to work across all the ages, from before Sumer and the Old Kingdom of Egypt in 2500BCE, until after 1700, when Peter the Great ruled Russia and Louis XIV ruled France. This factor has to apply everywhere across the globe from the Ganges plain of India to the Pacific Northwest of America. This limiting factor works in so many different periods of time and across so wide an area that no specific issue of history, geography, culture or personality can be involved. So we need to find something that both limits development and that applies to every society, everywhere, in every era before the Birth of Now. There can't be many social structures that apply so far and so wide. To understand what it might be we will start with simple Game Theory.

Game Theory is a way of thinking about conflict and cooperation between animals and humans. It is a powerful way to understand how the world works when the interests of different individuals or groups clash. Game Theory was developed mathematically but can be used non-mathematically to illustrate the processes involved in real-life challenges: what the outcomes of a conflict can be and why. Perhaps the best-known non-mathematical use of Game Theory is in helping us to understand how animal conflicts about feeding, mating and breeding play out. Richard Dawkins in his classic book, *The Selfish Gene*, used simplified Game Theory to provide a vivid explanation of how animal conflict can be understood. A similar, simple analysis can shed light on human social issues.

A core concept of Game Theory is the idea of a 'strategy'. A 'strategy' is a simple rule that a 'player' follows in a conflict; rules like: 'Always give in immediately' or 'Fight until you can physically fight no longer' or 'If your opponent is smaller than you fight, if they are larger, run away' and so on. As a rule these strategies are not consciously worked out but come across to us as the character of the individual: we describe them as cowardly or aggressive or, perhaps, full of braggadocio, making aggressive displays but running away if the opponent stands firm. With the strategies defined, we can then list the possible results from a conflict between two 'players', people or animals, following different strategies. Taking the simple example of a fight between two identical animals for a piece of food, there are four possible outcomes for each: win the food, win the food plus get injured, lose the food, lose the food plus get injured. Mathematical Game Theory can find which strategies work best for an animal if it is constantly getting involved in such fights – as many are. But we can use the ideas behind this process to provide an understanding without needing to work out solutions mathematically.

We start with only one kind of 'player': a family unit. Each family unit consists of a man and a woman who started single, merge with each other and have children. All families are treated as identical, except for their strategy and there are only two strategies: 'MYOB', short for 'Minding Your Own Business', and 'Stealing'. MYOB is a simple strategy to collect or grow whatever food the family needs, perhaps helping other families from time to time in return for them helping you. 'Stealing' is a strategy of using violence or the threat of violence to take food from MYOB people.

Let us see how these two strategies play out in a typical group of somewhere between fifty and one hundred individuals; a village or tribe, an ancient form of human social existence. Across history, groups of this size have found three different ways to get food: hunter-gathering, herding and settled farming, the three oldest forms of economic existence.

The simplest thought experiment is with hunter-gatherer societies. Rare today, societies like these probably dominated human history before the New Stone (Neolithic) Age that started around 12,000 years ago. Hunter-gatherer societies are based on groups of linked families – tribes – that live in a food-rich environment. A common pattern is for the women to look after the children and tend the home fire while also gathering herbs, fruit and roots. The men hunt for meat and fish and seek luxuries, such as honey. In these societies only the MYOB strategy works. People don't keep much food, they mostly get it fresh every day or so, and they have little else you could steal. To hunt large animals, the whole tribe – or most of the men at any rate – may have to work together as a team, sharing the kill. Anyway, the food does not keep, so there is little point in taking more than you can eat, even if you were allowed to. So, where the environment is rich enough to support a hunter-gatherer lifestyle – in the rainforest, for example – we would expect to see an all-MYOB, fairly equal society, with most grown-up, mid-life people having roughly the same role and status. The general observation is that such societies, both now and in the past, do, indeed, have quite equal structures between the family units, often using a committee of 'elders' as the group decision makers.[vi]

'Herders', in our thought experiment, are tribes of a similar size to our hunter-gatherers that follow or lead a group of grazing animals – cows, sheep, or camels – animals that provide the majority of the tribe's diet of meat and milk. Herder tribes, too, are diminishing rapidly in numbers, but once they dominated the grass plains of Asia and America, as well as the savannahs of Arabia and Africa, where they still exist today. With herders we get the same outcome as that for the hunter-gatherers: all MYOB and no Stealers. This is the only 'split' that works – but this time it works only within the tribe. You can't steal animals from other members of the tribe without it being completely obvious whodunnit and the rest of the tribe forcing restoration to keep the peace. The need to move to new grazing lands with the herds prevents the development of walls that could shelter the Stealer effectively. However, if you can steal animals from another tribe, it is a serious gain: you get more animals – that is, food or food producers – at no cost to yourself. So we would expect herder groups to have close and equal all-MYOB societies within the tribe and a policy of 'Stealing' as much as they can get away with outside the tribe. This pattern is obviously complicated by the fact that each tribe has the same dual policy, bringing the additional need to protect your own tribe and its animals from other tribes coming to steal. The predicted pattern is found, in fact, to be almost universal in herding societies: strong family and tribal ties, spiced with endless intertribal Stealing and vendettas.

Finally, we come to fixed farmers – farmers who plant and reap their own crops. An MYOB strategy works well enough and, under many circumstances, an MYOB family can produce more than sufficient for their food requirements. There are three snags: they have to remain in the same, cultivable location for a long time to grow the food, they have to store some of the food they grow and locations that are good for agriculture are not generally the best defensively. They need to store food, not only because they need it as seed-corn to plant for next season, but also because nature creates short periods of harvest, where the food all comes at once, so most of the crop needs to be kept back to feed the family until the next harvest. This means there is something for a Stealer to steal and the Stealer strategy becomes viable.

To make a Stealer strategy work, Stealers need to combine with other Stealers, so that MYOB families can be successfully threatened or beaten into giving up their surplus. Stealers need to protect themselves from vengeful or ambitious MYOBers or junior Stealers looking to become top dog. Specialist military equipment too expensive for everyone to possess – swords, castles, armour, horses, chariots – helps consolidate Stealer power. Stealers also need to defend their food sources, that is, they need to defend 'their' MYOBers, from other Stealers. Finally, Stealers need to limit their own theft within their community, leaving enough so that the MYOB people can still live, ready to be robbed another day.

Of course, if a group of Stealers raids a village ruled by another Stealer, the raiding Stealers will not worry about leaving anything at all for MYOBers to live on. This is why MYOBers will tend to prefer their existing Stealers to incoming Stealers, who have no interest in leaving them with anything. The existing local Stealers have to discipline, protect and tend their MYOBers much as a herdsman tends his animals and for much the same reason; to ensure there is something left for tomorrow. As a result, local Stealers provide some social coordination and law in their own districts. This has led some who have lived through times of anarchy to see powerful Stealers as a blessing[5].

So the patterns described above are roughly how societies of these three types are observed to behave. In hunter-gatherer tribes in the jungle or the outback, families have relatively equal status and roles. They are often 'governed' by a council of village/tribal elders – the chief's role being more of a chairman than a boss. Herder tribes, like those of old Arabia and Mongolia, have a similar internal equality with an informal council of sheiks (elders) making group decisions while the tribe is engaged in perpetual raiding and blood feuds with other tribes. Finally, every single settled agricultural society that has ever existed, as far as we can tell, has a split between the farmers/labourers that we have called MYOBers and lords/nobility, Stealers. No tribe, no society, no culture, no civilisation, if based on agriculture, has ever avoided a crystal-clear split of classes between labourers and non-labourers – until after the Birth of Now[6].

So far, so good for our simple model. We now drop the hunter-gatherers and the herders and look in more detail at the group we know leads on to 'civilisation', the settled farmers and their overlords.

Because the MYOB/Stealer split is universal, we don't

---

5   Notably the Legalist school in China and Thomas Hobbes in England, both of whom came up with a very similar support for unrestricted chief Stealers, despite the 2,000-year time gap between them, as a result of living through the grim anarchies of the Warring States period and the British Isles' civil wars respectively.

6   Some claim that the Haudenosaunee federation of North American Indians was an exception that managed to keep a hunter-gatherer-style equality even after many years of settled farming.

generally see it as peculiar. Its grotesque unfairness, with different rules for palpably similar people, together with its one-sided cruelty, are both taken for granted as a fact of life, like the need for water or the long human childhood. We do celebrate, as beacons of the better future to come after the Birth of Now, those few and short-lived societies where the split of the two classes was slightly softened; societies such as classical Athens or Rashidun Arabia. But the almost universal fact of settled societies is the division of mankind into, on one side: Nobility, Boyars, Samurai, Kshatriyas, *Gui zu*, Grandees, *Dvoryane*, the Quality, *Parişadabarga*, Officers, *Manya*, Lords, Patricians, *Aristokratia*, Gentlemen, Junkers, etc. etc. and, on the other side: common folk, the proletariat, *krestyanin*, serfs, slaves, plebeians, the black-headed mob, *ren min*, peasants, hoi polloi, *robotniks*, villains, etc. etc. Over the millennia a great deal of time and effort has been put into glossing over and euphemising the highly exploitative relationship between Stealers and MYOBers. The terms used for Stealers often have positive overtones – Nobility, Gentility, Chivalry – but, even where honeyed terms are used, the split of roles is never totally concealed. People understand the fundamental reason for the split well enough: the use of threats and violence by a few to take the output of others. Certainly, most Stealer societies have made clear that MYOBers who object to the situation will suffer accordingly. To emphasise its simplicity, the process is that Stealers first take MYOBers' surpluses then they take anything else they feel like taking. This has happened in every settled society until the Birth of Now and destroys the possibility of progress.

The critical aspect of all Stealer societies is that there

is no incentive to build for the long term – almost the opposite. If, in a good year, an MYOBer works hard to build up a surplus against the possibility of a future bad year, it will be taken from him. If he improves his house or works to construct additional items of furniture or tools, they will be taken from him. The more attractive or useful the things he creates, the faster they will be taken from him. He may also be beaten up, or face legal penalties and costs in the process of their removal, especially if he attempts to hide his surplus. Or maybe he will be beaten up anyway, just to stop him getting uppity and thinking he can complain.

When you visit a full-blown Stealer society – and there are still plenty of them, easily identifiable by pre-Birth of Now levels of poverty – the overwhelming impression everywhere is of people hanging about, doing nothing. Yet the place is a hideous mess that could clearly produce more if these people did any work on it. But, if they did, a man with a document or a man with a gun would come and take it away and they might imprison or kill someone while doing so. So everyone stands idle. If you obviously have nothing, no one can steal it or torture your children to make you reveal its location. In Stealer societies, MYOB people will go hungry in bad years because there is no provision of reserves from good years. This happens even when storing the surplus of good years is entirely possible within the simple technologies of the society – seed-corn has to be stored anyway, so storing more would not pose a technical problem. But, when the period of hardship arrives, Stealers will take any reserve, so it is pointless to build reserves at all. This is why, again and again across history, there is hunger after just one flood, one hailstorm or one drought and, after two, there is starvation. The reason why MYOBers do not build up reserves is not that they are improvident idiots, but that the reserves would be taken from them if they did; the reason why Stealers rarely build up reserves is that they rarely suffer shortages. Stealers will take enough for their needs and pleasures from their MYOBers, regardless of the harvest, good or bad. If, as a result, a bad year pushes some MYOBers into starvation, then so be it, although, historically, a few chief Stealers have built up stores against future shortages, very much with the attitude of tending their 'herd of commoners'. So the Stealer/MYOB model of society, the model that seems to be the universal model for agricultural societies, unintentionally but effectively works to prevent planning, investment or development. Also, because they are aware of the instability of their position, outnumbered as they are by the MYOBers, Stealers also resist anything that smacks of change, afraid that any change may undermine their privileges.

This is the reason why societies did not start to develop beyond a basic level until the Birth of Now. The universal form of society, where agriculture is the main source of food, is a Stealer society and Stealer societies cannot develop very far because improvements are discouraged and stolen. Not all Stealer societies are the same, they can be crude or sophisticated, vicious or easy-going but, from the first civilisation of 3000BCE up to the underdeveloped economies of today, they all have the same outcome: poverty for MYOBers and stasis for society.

As soon as time and familiarity allow it to be, Stealing is re-branded. Rather than demands with the explicit threat of immediate violence, the transfer becomes rent, tax or traditional dues, all legally owing to the lord and legally enforceable. The harsh edge of Stealing is softened but never lost; the bandit chief becomes the count, the cut-throat becomes the knight. As soon as possible, the MYOBer/Stealer distinction is made sacred by dividing humanity into two separate types. Stealers gradually become a semi-separate species: the Nobility, the Aristocracy, the Quality, the Gentry; special, different people, chosen by the gods for their virtue, strength and skill.

The more protected the Stealers are from revenge attacks, the more ruthlessly they can take from the MYOBers. Around 900CE, in north-western Europe, Stealers developed the concept of the stone castle; somewhere they could be really safe from vengeful peasants. This was the reason castles were built, despite the excuse that they added to the security of the district. Commentators at the time, such as *the Anglo-Saxon Chronicle*, had no illusions:

> *They oppressed the wretched people of the country severely with castle-building. When the castles were built they filled them with devils and wicked men. Then, both by night and day, they took those people they thought had any goods – men and women – and put them in prison and tortured them with indescribable torture to extort gold and silver.*[vii]

(The effect of castles was particularly pronounced in England, where castles were introduced suddenly after the country was taken over by William of Normandy and his cronies in 1066[viii].)

The simple Stealer/MYOB model builds up easily for larger communities, made up of many villages. Each community can be seen as one triangular cell, with a full Stealer, a baron or, in Mafia terms, the *'capo'*, at the top point. Going down the triangle, there is a gang of deputy Stealers, 'knights' or Mafia *'consigliore'*, reporting to the main local Stealer. At the bottom there is a large baseline of MYOBers. Like a house of cards, a series of triangles can be built on each other to form larger triangles and still larger triangles can be formed out of these. At the peak of a largest triangle, based above a large number of smaller triangles, sits a chief Stealer: a king, an emperor or a *'capo di capi'*, who treats the barons rather as though they were his MYOBers.

But the king is less able to skin the local Stealers, the barons, of their surplus than the barons are able to skin their peasants. This is for practical reasons: the geographical distance between the chief Stealer and his subordinate local Stealers is larger and they have a greater ability to hide resources than the peasants do. But mostly this restraint is to do with the relative fighting power of the barons and the king. In many societies, an individual baron has much greater practical ability to resist the king than an individual peasant has to resist the baron, especially if there is a getting together of several barons. Hence, it pays the king to keep the barons sweet by leaving them with some excess.

This balance between local Stealers and chief Stealers changes with developing sophistication and technology. In societies such as the 'Spring and Autumn' period in China or medieval France, fighting was a minimally planned thing. Warbands and armies often set off with no supplies, carrying largely locally-made weapons, hoping to wing it on locally-stolen food. Such childlike simplicity gives the chief Stealer relatively few advantages over local Stealers. This was especially true if the contest was 'played at home' for the local Stealer. He could sit, secure in his castle, while the ill-prepared mob supposed to besiege him faded away looking for food. As a result, a loose, feudal-type structure prevails in unsophisticated Stealer societies, where, in order to maintain his superiority, the chief Stealer needs allies almost as much as his challengers do.

In more sophisticated societies, weapons and military stores are stockpiled in advance. The armies may also be trained and professional, including specialists, such as gunners, engineers and pike men. Such professional armies are normally beyond the capacity of a local Stealer and, competently led and supported, are almost invariably successful against a feudal or a nomadic army[ix]; so military sophistication leads to power moving away from local Stealers and up to the chief Stealer.

The change of relative power brought about by increasing military sophistication can be seen in the consolidation of most pre-Birth of Now empires, from the Akkadian before 2000BCE and including, among many others, the Assyrian, the Roman, the Gupta and the Aztec Empires. In each case, military success was closely allied to their professional approach to military matters, especially in equipment and provisions. In China, the change from a feudal system to a professional military system is noted in the change from the 'Spring and Autumn' period of feudal warfare (771-476BCE), to the more professional wars of the 'Warring States' period. This period ended in 221BCE, with the complete takeover of China by the relentless total-war system of the 'First Emperor', Qin Shi Huang. In medieval Europe, the development of reliable cannons around 1400CE swung the balance in favour of the kings or, in some areas, the larger independent cities. Only these had the resources to make or buy these weapons and maintain their expensive appetite for gunpowder. We see castle-building and independent local armies disappearing in late medieval Europe, as the chief Stealers gradually out-powered their subordinate Stealers.

Senior Stealers in different areas had different types of power structure. There were more or less absolute kings, such as the Umayyad Caliphs, and there were also, at the other end of the scale, carefully balanced hierarchies, such as the one headed by the consuls in republican Rome. Between, there were many mixed forms of senior Stealer rule. Some were formalised as Round Tables or parliaments of nobles, but kings more often consulted informally with leading courtiers, officials and nobles before their bigger moves. Many different formats of Stealer rule can still be seen in the remaining pre-Now countries today. As a general rule, the larger the area in question, the more absolute the monarchy is found to be; the smaller the area, the more likely it is to resemble group rule – an oligarchy. This difference might be explained by the closer personal contact possible between Stealers in smaller countries, compared to the remoteness of the head chief Stealer in a country the size of Russia. But it is difficult to measure the effect or its causes with any certainty.

From the point of view of individual survival or of leaving a larger number of descendants, it is not obvious that being a Stealer is a 'better' choice than being a peasant. Stealing is a high-risk/high-gain strategy. Although leading Stealers can have a rich life, producing and bringing up many offspring, Stealer men also tend to die young and violently as they battle or adventure. Many societies have traditions of killing the children and relatives of a chief Stealer when he is deposed. This was the general practice in China and Ottoman Turkey, for example. While more prone to malnutrition than Stealers, MYOBers are less prone to being knifed and, with luck, a peasant family can go on for years, bringing up quite a number of children. There is also the limit to the number of Stealers a society can support and, if Stealers breed excessive numbers, some must fall out of Stealing one way or another. Despite this, from the MYOBer point of view the Stealer's position looks very attractive. So many MYOBers will seek for 'promotion' by becoming a Stealer themselves.

Some MYOB young women seek to join the Stealers by attracting a Stealer partner and some young MYOB men strive to become junior Stealers. The strategies for women seeking Stealer partners – a prince – form the central topic of many stories. A young male MYOBer, seeking 'promotion' to Stealer status, will typically join in the periodic attempts to steal from other communities under the command of the regular Stealers. These are raiding parties or warbands. Good performance on these adventures may lead to a bold or lucky MYOBer joining the Stealers on a more permanent basis – especially if military success allows the number of Stealers in his band to increase. Every Stealer/MYOB society produces people who are more wretched than mere peasants, in that they have no land, skill or possessions: they live by what little paid work they can get and by begging and petty theft. For young men in such a position, sex is often unavailable so it may be a better choice, from the point of view of leaving offspring, for him to join an army or a gang then to stay at a hovel. The odds of survival, let alone victory and promotion, may be bad but, for a dispossessed male MYOBer, there is often no other plan that will give him a chance of either mating or having enough food or money to live through a bad winter or illness. Violence was, for millennia, the only solution that enabled many young males to leave children, a fact that explains some of the world's issues today.

In a settled Stealer society, in addition to MYOBers and Stealers, there are two smaller career paths: trade/manufacturing and priesthood/scholarship. Roles in trade and manufacturing exist in every society albeit often only for a few. Even very primitive societies have some specialists who knap flints into good shapes for tools and sell them and other specialists who travel and trade goods between different groups. We go on to discuss trade and its effects in Chapter 3, so we will skip it here and move straight onto priests and scholars.

There are two approaches priests can use to get the food and money they need and they generally use both. They can act as Stealers themselves, using the threat of supernatural injury and death to extract food and other things from MYOBers, rather than the threat of ordinary injury and killing, as used by the more conventional Stealers-through-violence. Using this approach priests extract temple tax (tithes, *zakat*) or get unpaid labour on temple lands. In return they help protect the MYOBers from the wrath of the godlets or God. Priesthoods sometimes employ Stealers-through-violence to enforce the temple or church tax, but often the priestly threat of a supernatural attack is enough on its own to get both MYOBers and Stealers to cough up. Skilled priesthoods have managed to become the leading Stealers in some societies, ahead of the Stealers-through-violence. In India, the priests, known as Brahmins, have managed to give the Stealers-through-violence, Kshatriyas, a lower caste status than themselves. The priesthoods of Thebes in ancient Egypt, the medieval Catholic Church in Western Europe and the Magi of Iran from time to time achieved something close to dominance of Stealer power, a dominance the Shia priesthood still retains in Iran at the time of writing. In other cases there has been very little separation between Stealers-through-violence and priests – the Mexica (Aztecs) and Pharaohs combined both roles, as did some Catholic Popes.

In addition to their Stealing activities, priests can also act as tradesmen, selling additional favours from God or the godlets at extra cost. These extra favours are often paid for in the form of sacrifices but can also be in the form of cash payment for prayers. Most priesthoods have offered a personal and flexible service, enabling the wealthy supplicant to gain additional heavenly favour but the western Church in the Late European Middle Ages targeted sales to a mass audience with printed 'indulgences', sold at a fixed price[x].

Scholars were, essentially, those who could read, write and do arithmetic. They are the scribes and administrators that become necessary in any society more complex than the most basic. Scholars have not normally had a class of their own but have been included as part of an existing class. In ancient Sumer and in medieval Europe, scholars were the same people as priests. In pre-Shogun Japan and in Mandarin China, the scholars were, in theory, the same people as the nobility (Stealers). In other societies, scribes are simply craftsmen, skilled professionals generally rated just below the top crafts, such as goldsmithing. Scholarship has never 'broken the mould' of the Stealer society. It has sometimes provided ways in which bookish people could enjoy the Stealer benefits normally reserved for their more violent colleagues, but scholarship never changed the way those Stealer benefits were obtained.

Meanwhile, MYOBers do not just engage in agriculture; they also act as servants to the Stealers, cleaning and cooking and manufacturing clothes, furniture, drink and luxuries. They also construct buildings, both for themselves and for the Stealers – hence the pyramids, the Great Wall of China, temples, castles and cathedrals. The pattern of these activities is the same as with agriculture: the MYOBers engage in low-skill, manual labour, with all the output being taken by the Stealers – unless, as with churches and other communal structures like bridges and canals, what they construct has to be shared.

In these circumstances, Stealers can add benefit to the community as a whole by leading the construction of community projects. In dry areas where there are rivers that bring water from elsewhere, the consistent coordination of the whole of a society to build and maintain irrigation channels brings the huge benefit of plentiful and easily cultivated food crops. In Egypt and Iraq, the discipline Stealers were able to impose on large-scale irrigation projects produced significant benefits to the whole community and enabled the first towns to emerge.

The Stealer society is a highly robust social model, which is why it is so widespread before the Birth of Now. No long-term planning is required; no trust or reciprocation; no writing or structured plan is needed. Whatever the previous social structure, if a society collapses, what arises from the ashes is the simplest and most robust form of social structure: the Stealer society. Societies can fail as a result of a natural disaster or because a chief Stealer fails to maintain his monopoly of violence and the society falls into anarchy. But, whatever the cause of the failure, the outcome is the same. The new Stealer society starts in a crude form – some people are stronger and more violent or they are more devious in manipulating strong and violent people to their ends. These people make a living by forming gangs that steal from others with threats and physical violence, often killing those who attempt to resist.

But soon there is a desire on all sides to put a more pleasant gloss on the situation, to find forms that avoid the appearance of naked theft, personal humiliation and immanent violence with its dangers to all involved. Stealers prefer that the blatant unfairness of their position be glossed over, so as to make it less provocative of resistance. MYOBers prefer concepts that allow them to keep some self-esteem and that may limit or control the rapacity of the Stealers. So the main form of food and money extraction from MYOBers soon becomes called 'rent'. This idea works well because peasants are keen on the idea of fixed property rights, as they can see all around them the desperate underclass of the unpropertied and fear that they might fall into that group. They often have small rental arrangements among themselves, renting land or animals to each other, so the concept of rent has acceptability. After all, you are getting the right to farm the lord's land in return for the rent, so it is a fair deal, isn't it? This is when middle ranks can be introduced: 'gentry', made up of rising peasants and declining Stealers, to swell the numbers on the side of the status quo and allied to the chief Stealers, in the event of trouble with resentful MYOBers.

Stealer societies are stable because they require no special conditions to exist, other than fixed agriculture. Other types of society may require some level of trust between members to work, some degree of planning and some postponement of gratification. But Stealer societies need no such sophistication. It's a strategy that can't be upset by other strategies – at least no one has found a strategy to upset the simple Stealer society at will. The Stealer society is the point of lowest energy, the 'valley' out of which any other type of society has to climb. This simplicity, stability and strength is why, before the Birth of Now, almost every settled society, everywhere in the world for as long as we have records, was a Stealer society – until, after the Birth of Now, when they started, one by one, to vanish.

So before the Birth of Now, every Egyptian and Chinese dynasty, every European, Persian and Indian empire, kingdom, principality and dukedom, every farming African tribe and every Pre-Colombian American empire was a Stealer society. In the last strongholds of the Stealer society today, places in the world where corruption remains a key driver, development remains slow. But when Stealing is reduced, as it has been, country by country, faster development follows. Then economic growth comes, regardless of issues such as tropical climate, minimal mineral resources, or other factors previously held to explain the presence or absence of development. Neither Japan nor Singapore has fossil fuels or the 'Protestant Work Ethic', but both have become wealthy.

Sometimes, more cooperative sharing plans have been tried; the monastic movement in early medieval Europe is a good example of a deliberate attempt to replace Stealer rules. But over time and under stress, they sooner or later fall back into Stealer/MYOB habits – the monastic movement had to keep on relaunching as older disciplines fell into Stealer ways: from Benedictines to

Cistercians to Cistercians of the Strict Observance to Carthusians, each seeking to return to community rule, rather then the rule of power. Whatever the mechanism, Stealing, the social system of least complexity, infects and then replaces cooperative systems when they come under stress.

Stealing becomes softened by tradition in every way: lands terrorised by a bandit grandfather transform into the rightful estate of the noble grandson. The penalty to be exacted by a Stealer if a peasant fails to pay what is required is modified. In newly established Stealer societies, the penalty is likely to go from severe beating to death by living dismemberment. As the society settles down, the penalties tend to become more structured, less haphazard and violent: fines or imprisonment are introduced, although unpleasant forms of death are retained as sanctions when needed. But the decrease in the shock of the violence does not modify the rule that the MYOB surplus, anything beyond the minimum for the MYOB family to survive, goes to the Stealers and from them to associate Stealers and their servants. There are fees for licences, such as for fishing in manorial waters, taxes on inheritance of parental goods, fines to be paid for the wearing of superior clothes and permits required to trade in certain items. But all these niceties, the civilised names for extortion, the 'due process of law', still leave unanswered an underlying question: what is the civilised, acceptable reason why a poor person has to give another, wealthier person the products of their work and money?

One justification for this state of affairs is the claim that Stealers are different to MYOBers because they are descended from a godlet or linked to a godlet in some other way. The pharaoh is made into a living God, an incarnation of Osiris; the Emperor of China commands the 'Mandate of Heaven'; the King of England is the Lord's Anointed, and so on. This can lead to the claim that all MYOBers owe their existence to the magic beneficence of the king-god and they may lose it through disobedience. The pharaoh is a key part of the magic system that created them and sustains them; they owe their very lives to him and they should be grateful for that alone.

Another reason put forward for accepting Stealers and their demands is that they defend the people from the, far worse, Stealers coming in from outside. So skill at fighting is almost always a claim of Stealers and, in theory, kings were the best battle leaders – that is what made them king. The last king of Britain to lead an army into battle was George II in 1743, immediately before the Birth of Now. Stealers often have to prove their prowess in battle and losing a battle normally spells doom for the Stealer in charge. Despite the theory that local Stealers should be better than incoming Stealers, however, it has not always worked that way. It is a feature of Chinese history, at least, that local Stealers were so vicious that the peasantry, again and again, sided with outsider Stealers when they had the opportunity – Hsiung-nu, Mongols, Manchus, British and communists, were all helped assiduously by Chinese MYOBers, plotting the downfall of their existing rapacious lords[7]. The British

---

7 This may also be connected with the use of humans as draught and pack animals in China. Horses and oxen were well known but there was never a period in Chinese history when human power was not cheaper than animal power.

in India were often more attractive overlords than the previous local Stealers, which explains how such a tiny group was able to rule so large an area for so long.

30,000

The final method for explaining and justifying Stealers taking from peasants is to claim that the Stealer race is a different kind of humanity; Stealers are a superior species to MYOBers. Keeping the 'blood' pure, unpolluted by MYOBer input, was an obsession of the nobility of Europe, the patricians of Rome, the *shenshi ren* of China, the Brahmins of India and most other Stealer groups. All these felt that humanity was divided into different categories as a consequence of biological differences, similar to the distinction between a warhorse and a pit pony, a lion and a tabby cat. At times the desire to be separate and to avoid the taint of any 'mixed blood' became extreme. In fifteenth-century Spain, family trees were fanatically inspected and doctored to avoid any suggestion that aristocratic *'limpieza de sangre'*, cleanliness of the blood, was polluted. Even today, the family trees of titled people in Britain and Europe are available in large books called *Debrett's Peerage* and the *Almanach de Gotha*. Most Stealers used a mixture of all three claims, each supporting the other to justify taking from the poor: because they descend from a godlet, they are both a different subspecies of human and they are the only people with the skills to lead in battle.

In Stealer societies, it is quite wrong to expect the 'leaders', chief Stealers, to have the least concern for the MYOBers. Some may care; most do not. They are in power for their pleasure. They can and do steal as much as they want, given the need to keep their MYOBers alive, partially to ensure that their followers (junior Stealers) are kept happy. They may mouth platitudes about the needs of the people and they do occasionally worry if they think they are stealing so much that revolution is in the air. But there is no sense in which their power rests on the consent or 'will of the people'.

On the contrary, Stealers make strenuous efforts to ensure that MYOBers are firmly kept in their place and are continuously reminded of their insignificance and inferior quality. Many Stealer societies have strict hereditary rules, where a person's status is determined by their birth. Any attempt by individuals to 'rise above their birth' is forbidden or, at best, discouraged. People attempting to improve their lot are frequently reminded of their humble origins and punished for their presumption. Serfs and slaves are kept in their place by harsh laws. This is linked to the basic conservatism that comes with Stealer societies. Stealers require stability or people may question their 'rights' to receive rents, taxes and licence fees, so Stealers tend to oppose all new ideas as disruptive. This adds to the difficulty of progress: not only will anything improved be stolen if it can be but, even if it can't be, like a new village well, Stealers may destroy it anyway because it is new and could be a challenge to the fixed structure of society.

In the remaining Stealer societies today, Stealers typically threaten the prosperous trader with regulatory destruction – 'failing a safety inspection' – unless they pay a bribe[8]. Stealer governments multiply regulations

---

8   Unfortunately, the failure of a safety inspection would almost certainly be justified as the wealthy individual has saved money by ignoring safety regulations.

to provide jobs for their families and followers and opportunities for bribery. This has been called a 'licence raj', from its name in India, where regulations requiring an official permit for almost any activity reached a new height before slowly being reduced after the start of this century. The reason why US citizens, for example, require an expensive visa to visit India, but not Thailand, is to fund comfortable jobs in Indian immigration for Stealers. The consequent costs to Indian tourism are not immediately obvious so the enrichment of a few babus this way goes unnoticed.

The Birth of Now took so long to arrive because the Stealer-based society that prevents or destroys development is almost universal before the Birth of Now. Not only did this grim fact keep almost all humanity back for the whole of recorded history until the Birth of Now but also parts of the world have still not made the change away from Stealing and its consequent MYOBer poverty. Somehow a society had to escape from the trap of being a Stealer society and move into a different social structure before long-term improvement was possible. A few societies did rise above the level of the Stealer society, at least for a while. Let's see how the story moves on.

.3.

THE ESCAPE
FROM STEALING

D evelopment is almost impossible in any Stealer society because even the smallest investment in time or money for the future is likely to be stolen before it can be used. Anyone aspiring to improve their fortune looks only to become a Stealer or to climb the Stealer hierarchy or, possibly, to join the priesthood/ scholars. Any other approach or attempt to make changes will result in punishment. All attempts by MYOBers to better themselves, other than by finding a way to join the Stealers, will result in the removal of the benefit by a Stealer. Only two types of long-term projects can survive in a Stealer society: those that go into improving Stealing strength with buildings, weapons and defences, and those that reflect glory on the chief Stealer or the community as a whole, generally in the form of a temple or church.

But there are a few societies from before the Birth of Now that, at times, did not appear to fit the Stealer pattern. For example, there have been a number of 'good kings', efficient and benign monarchs that defy the description 'Chief Stealer'. Do these 'good kings' show that the 'Stealer' society' pattern can be broken? Also, there were some real cities before the Birth of Now, cities with populations of more than half a million people. A more complex structure than the simple 'Stealers-taking-from-MYOBers' pattern seems necessary for cities to get to this size. Finally, there have been city-states, scattered across history without a king at all, run by groups of citizens. Surely these cannot be 'Stealer societies'? We know that at least one society must have escaped from the limitations of the Stealer society: the one that underwent the Birth of Now. So there has to be an 'exit route', some system that can replace the Stealer society and survive. Was it one of these three apparently non-Stealer societies that led to the Birth of Now?

The first of the three challenges to the idea that the Stealer society cannot lead to development is the undoubted existence of 'good kings'. In many cultures there appear, from time to time, to have been some competent rulers who apparently tried to rule for the benefit of their people. Several pharaohs, some of the kings of Babylon and Persia, the Antonine emperors of Rome, the early Abbasid caliphs and the first Song emperors of China are all widely agreed to have been both capable and well-intentioned. All these rulers repudiated the totally selfish behaviour predicted by the model of the chief Stealer; all sought to avoid violence and all clearly had the improvement of their subjects' lives as at least one objective of their reigns. While these 'good kings' are exceptions – most monarchs have been as unscrupulously self-seeking as the Stealer strategy would suggest – we have to see if this kind of behaviour can go beyond the Stealer society or does it fit into the pattern?

There have been several periods recorded in history when a country or region has had the time, peace and luck with nature, to develop a thoroughly pacified society. These societies have had food surpluses because Stealing had become gentler and less thorough; societies where a large number of people have been freed from the need to work the land because the MYOB cultivators produce much more than they need to feed themselves. In some of these benign societies, benign rulers have then arisen. There was a theory, used to justify Russian autocracy that giving one man complete and unrestricted power would mean that he need seek nothing further except the love of his people and so he would rule in their interests. This does seem to be part of the reason why such 'good kings' arose; they simply could not steal anything that could add appreciably to their wealth. Some of them also undoubtedly tried to rule as well as they could to benefit others.

To examine this we can look at the least disputed and most famous case of 'good kings': the Antonine emperors of Rome. The great historian, Edward Gibbon, said of them: *The vast extent of the Roman Empire was governed by absolute power, under the guidance of virtue and wisdom. The armies were restrained by the firm but gentle hand of four successive Emperors, whose characters and authority commanded respect. The forms of the civil administration were carefully preserved by Nerva, Trajan, Hadrian and the Antonines, who delighted in the image of liberty, and were pleased with considering themselves as the accountable ministers of the laws.'*

This period lasted almost a century. Yet we can observe little or no overall everyday improvement in the common lot of mankind. The administration of the Empire was not incompetent; official corruption and theft were well controlled and predictable. There was widespread peace across large parts of the Empire and areas where war was unknown for many decades. The people of the Empire were at a good point and their rulers were almost implausibly well intentioned. But no long-term change at all resulted: the majority of peasants still lived close to the breadline, then and later. In the end, the Roman Empire still declined and fell, just as it probably would have done had the Antonines been more typically selfish.

Technology was not wanting. The great length of Roman aqueducts and the spectacular viaducts along their course show not only Roman engineering and organisational skills but also the ability of that society to plan and invest in long-term improvement. Watermills certainly existed and were used widely. A model steam engine had been demonstrated and was known from written reports, although, for reasons that will become apparent in later chapters, it was never developed into a production tool. Trade and seafaring were prosperous for long periods. Complex cranes were used in docks; sophisticated military catapults were familiar, drains were built and huge cities prospered. Factories existed, some of them employing thousands, producing shoes, clothing, cement, ceramics, iron, books and probably much more. Nor was organisation lacking. The Romans were also famous for their long-term military planning and for their ability to bring disciplined, well-equipped and supplied troops to the point of need. There was a considerable body of well-educated people and discussion was largely free and wide-ranging.

But, despite all this, the peasant or poor townsman was never more than two bad seasons away from serious hunger and, after the last of the Antonines, the state was, once again, never more than two bad emperors from military defeat by unlettered tribes. Benign these rulers may have been but, sooner or later, the simple Stealer society always returned, with civil wars resulting in power returning to the strongest and least scrupulous. Nor were the Antonine emperors the only such 'good kings' of the Roman Empire, although they represented the longest run of them. From Augustus at the start of the Empire, through Constantine and on to some later Byzantine emperors, the experiment of strong, beneficent rule was tried several times with variations; to no long-term effect on standards of living whatsoever.

This same is true for all the other 'good kings' in history. No long-term progress or development was achieved by any of them and little enough in the short term. Some point after the demise of the 'good king', a situation would arise similar or identical to one that had arisen before; a revolt, a tyrant or an invasion. The response to this stress would be exactly the same as before the time of the 'good king'. It would be clear that they had made no difference at all. It is as though they had never been.

But why should there be progress? What would have started the 'progress'? Although a 'good king' may hold

Stealing back, how can he stop it returning when he is not there? The later Roman Emperor, Diocletian, attempted to set up careful political structures to ensure the peaceful succession of benign emperors after his retirement; but they failed almost as soon as he tried to retire. You can prevent water flowing downhill by building a dam but, sooner or later, if it is not maintained, it will break and the water will return to its former path. What could the Antonine emperors have done to start a Birth of Now? We don't yet know ourselves and nor did they. The most a 'good king' can do is to reduce the oppressiveness of the Stealer society while they are in control of it.

The second challenge to the idea that a Stealer society can never develop is to explain how a Stealer society can still be the principle social structure even for a city of over half a million people. There is considerable on-going argument about the population of cities before the Birth of Now but, however it is looked at, there have been only a few cities in the world with anything like half a million or more population before 1750 (and some insisting that these figures are far too high). It turns out that all of these, Babylon, Rome, Patna, Chang'an, Byzantium, etc., were the capitals of great empires when they had their huge populations. They all existed as the nexus for the taxes and spending of the largest chief Stealers. They supplied not only the luxuries of the chief Stealer but also those of his court. In addition, they supplied much of the military equipment, uniforms and other requirements of the state army, who often had large garrisons there. None of them were based, as modern giant cities are, on commerce or manufacturing that might require non-Stealer principles. The extent to which these cities exported only government is shown by a large hill just outside Rome, known as Monte Testuccio that is composed almost entirely of broken amphoras; earthenware containers for cooking oil and wine. Classical Rome in its heyday imported goods but there were no goods to export, so the packaging is still there. There is no reason why such cities, with a base purely of government, cannot be Stealer societies with the same, standard Stealer/MYOB pattern but on a larger scale. These cities have the same structure as smaller towns – money floods into the Stealer's court from taxes and rents and flows out again, through suppliers of luxuries, arms and retailers of food that make up the city. Eventually, perhaps after going through several hands, the money is spent on foods, so sending it back to the country, ready to pay next year's rent and taxes. This is not the complex economic web of large cities today and no new principles are required beyond Stealing – that is tax and rent paid to the chief Stealer and his agents in return for nothing – except 'government'.

So the large cities that existed before the Birth of Now do not challenge or undermine the universality of the Stealer society because they were simply the result of an unusually powerful chief Stealer. The fact that every large city before the Birth of Now was an imperial capital tends to confirm the suggestion that they had the same, simple tax-and-spend pattern of smaller Stealer towns, rather than the complex pattern of modern cities.

But what about the third problem for the universality of the Stealer society, societies without a chief Stealer, societies ruled by a group?

Trade seems an important clue to these. Even the most basic Stealer society has some elements of trade and specialist manufacturing that goes beyond the simple MYOB/Stealer pattern. There is a need for weapons and Stealers are likely to seek weapons that are more sophisticated than just the sticks lying around: owning a suit of armour or a horse (initially with a chariot as well) were sure signs of superiority, nobility or, in our terminology, Stealer status[9] and strengthened the position of Stealers against MYOBers. Stealers also want luxuries. It is a primitive society indeed where the Stealer is satisfied with the excess turnips a peasant can provide. With peace, good soil and other advantages, Stealers, who, naturally, take all the excess, are able to increase the number of non-food items they can buy. This demand supports a small group of artisans, merchants and manufacturing labourers who make or import the items that the Stealers want. This stage, well-settled, peaceful Stealerdom, results in development of towns where the craftsmen live, where small factories are set up and markets are held. The development of such towns is generally seen as the foundation – indeed, the definition – of 'civilisation'. Sumer had many such towns, as did many subsequent civilisations up to the Birth of Now. This 'civilisation' is still very much a Stealer society, but one where the MYOBer agriculture

---

9   In many European languages the word for 'knight' means horseman –
     French: Chevalier, Spanish, Caballeros, etc.

can provide a considerable additional excess that can be used by Stealers to support large groups of servants and craftsmen.

But at this point there is a critical divergence in the pattern: it can go one of two ways and the effect of this small, initial divergence becomes greater over time. The divergence depends on whether the craftsmen or merchants are principally *servants* of the Stealer(s) or outside *suppliers*. Are they totally dependent on the Stealers and are paid a wage for their work or are they independent and paid for the goods they make and supply to Stealers? Does the king get his armour from his own armourers or does he buy it from an independent armourer? Do the ruling elite send their servants to buy goods abroad or do they buy the foreign goods they want from an independent merchant? The distinction is vital, because, if the tradesman is independent, he can make and retain a profit. With this profit he can build an independent power base in a way not open to people who are just Stealer servants. The independent supplier can build up, from small beginnings, a base of wealth that does not come from Stealing. Often the independent tradesmen and manufacturers can also join together to form guilds or fraternities in collaboration with others and these can gain considerable collective wealth and power. A form of power not based on Stealing has arisen. Over time, and with luck, the town can be fortified and the suppliers and their guilds can build up their own town government, leaving the Stealers (nobility) largely outside the town on their estates. The town can then gain some delegated powers in the form of grants and charters of rights and privileges from the chief Stealer. Eventually some of these towns become fully independent.

Smaller countries tend to have power shared among a number of leading people or families; larger countries tend more to single, absolute monarchs; so smaller countries will naturally tend to have more independent suppliers, simply because there are several important customers rather than just the one. With very small states, successful tradesmen can quickly overtake the power of the original landowning Stealer aristocracy to dominate both the city and its hinterland. The classical Greek states of Athens, Corinth and others and Italian medieval states, notably Florence, Venice and Milan, are well-known examples of places where this happened.

We will use the term 'Suppliers' (capital 'S') to refer to these independent merchants, craftsmen, artists, manufacturers and the like: mostly they combined at least two of these aspects in their work. The great Amsterdam artist, Rembrandt van Rijn, is a good example of an independent supplier of this type. He sourced his the raw materials for his painting, pigments and canvas. With his assistants, he prepared them – grinding and mixing pigments and binders to make paint, stretching and pre-treating his canvases. Then he painted the picture, sometimes with employees painting the boring bits, and displayed the finished works in his showroom, selling them alongside other artists whose paintings he also displayed and traded. Even when he was approached with commissions, he was not only an artist but also an independent trading businessman, agreeing the deal, buying the materials, employing assisting staff, etc. All this can still be seen in Rembrandt's house in Amsterdam. More generally, goldsmiths were one of the first trades to set up in many civilisations and almost always combined retailing and manufacturing, often with a little lending on the side. It was not until after the Birth of Now that the distinction between manufacture and retail became common with the growth of specialist 'factories'.

A chief Stealer who moves his place or residence often will tend to create independent suppliers, simply because it may be very difficult for some types of Supplier to move their businesses. Large smithies or ports cannot move easily with the king and so their operators tend to be independent of him. Medieval European kings moved their courts constantly, encouraging independent Suppliers to grow up, Chinese emperors not so. Towns may also supply several chief Stealers from different areas; typically a port town may do so. This can build a powerful and independent merchant class, such as was found in Venice or Amsterdam. It can also be that Stealers are split between Stealers-by-violence and priests, both buying luxury or specialist goods. This again tends to lead to independent Suppliers, as it did in late medieval Italy, where the Pope was a leading customer, as well as local princes.

By contrast, where only one king, chief Stealer, exists and is closely in contact with the city, it is difficult for craftsmen or merchants to maintain separate businesses. Any profit they make, above the amount they would expect to get for their personal work, is seen as money embezzled from the King. The Emperor's goldsmith in China may make goods for senior mandarins as well as the Emperor: but only at the Emperor's pleasure. In this pattern, the arsenal, the factories making armour and uniforms, the iron works and mines are all the property of the state, temple or king. Employees of the chief Stealer run them, not independent businessmen, and they cannot build up their own power base. In the thinking that prevailed over much of history in China or Russia, it made no more sense to farm out the arsenal or state iron mines to independent management than to farm out military command to independent management. They were central to the role of the king/ state. Besides, trading was held to be the lowest form of human activity, certainly in China.

In areas where the development of independent Suppliers does happen, it might be wondered why Stealers do not steal the capital Suppliers build up, especially if any of it is available in the form of gold or similar money-like material. The answer is that they do always, sooner or later, attempt to steal it. But sometimes Suppliers could resist the theft. Sometimes Stealers delayed stealing from a craftsman or merchant because the merchant was providing an important service that the Stealers did not want to disrupt. Often Suppliers concealed their wealth, to avoid attracting the Stealers' attention, until they had defences in place. Given time, Suppliers found ways to defend themselves against the Stealers. They formed the guilds and fraternities that combined their wealth and clout. Sometimes these guilds employed their own thugs and mercenaries – either individual guilds or collectively as a town – although mercenaries had dangers, as they could easily see the town or guild as the 'mother lode' for money and simply rob them instead. Where they could, Suppliers built walls round their towns and formed municipal corporations – mayors and councils. In China there were periods when such towns existed, especially during the southern Song and Yuan Dynasties from around 1000-1300CE and the same may have been true of India for long periods (although there is little written record of India until much later). In Europe, late medieval London stands as an example of such a town where the King trod carefully if he disagreed with the lord mayor and corporation. One of the many causes of the English Civil War (1642-1651) was London's refusal to let the King remove its independence without a fight. Geographical advantages could lead to fully independent Supplier towns, such as the towns on the islands of Tyre, Bahrain, Penang and Zanzibar, the swamp-towns of Venice and Amsterdam and the mountain-girt cities of ancient Greece. However, such independence was a fragile thing and often lasted only for limited periods.

The process whereby Suppliers took advantage of the little bit of leeway granted them by Stealers to build defences is vital. It is largely in the guilds of industries, or the fraternities associated with specific churches, that we see the ideas of (limited) democracy being first put into action in a civil society. In the classical Athenian experiment in democracy, this was strengthened by the small scale of the country, the relative weakness of the original aristocracy and fuelled by apparently endless money from the silver mines at Laurion (see below in the section on money). Guilds developed in countries as widely different as Novgorod (now part of Russia) and Qing China, as well as Western Europe. They also developed, for their members only, ideas of social security, insurance and standards of trust and commercial behaviour. In a few places, Suppliers, and their guilds or fraternities, got the upper hand and started to impose Supplier values on the broader society they lived in. These included the 'inviolability' of property – the idea that something, legally obtained and legally held, could not be taken away by a Stealer without sanctions being applied to the Stealer.

The guilds were also important in enshrining the hallmark of Supplier societies: reputation. Early Supplier societies did not have a sudden development of civil law. What made trade possible, and still makes it possible in developing societies today, is the development of reputation. With a good reputation, trade credit can be extended, terms of business can be taken on trust and the quality or authenticity of the goods accepted without prior checking. If a dealer later feels he has been mistreated in a deal, he points it out to other dealers who will start to question the reputation of the person who has mistreated him until the matter is sorted out to their satisfaction. As a result, traders in Supplier societies took fanatical care of their trading reputation, since it was often their most valuable asset, smoothing all kinds of transaction: allowing delayed payment, payment on promise of later delivery, receipt of goods before agreeing a price and accepting goods without quality or weight-checking each one. In many cases, trading is almost impossible without the parties trusting each other and everywhere the simplification of transactions that follow from a good reputation make a trader's life very much easier. Guilds or fraternities sometimes undertook to underwrite the good behaviour of each of their members to gain the advantages of reputation, so the guild would agree to pay the debts of a defaulting member or to compensate a buyer if an inadequate product was sold to them by a member.

This illustrates a critical difference between a Stealer society and a Supplier society; in a Stealer society a reputation for fighting brings success; in a Supplier society it is reputation for fair play that succeeds. The development of a successful reputational system is what takes a Supplier society forward, rather than the official 'rule of law' which, in practice, lags far behind. In a few cases, the wealth and power of leading Suppliers became so great that even Stealers sought to become Suppliers. A small number of towns grew up where Suppliers had the grip on power, where individual Suppliers exceeded Stealers in their wealth and guilds could be as powerful as minor kings[xi].

There are two ways an individual can get money – or its equivalents – from others outside their family: they can take the money by force or the threat of force or they can sell them something they want at a price they are willing to pay. While both ways of making money exist in all societies, Stealer societies are dominated by taking, Supplier societies by selling. Stealer societies are dominated by the threat of violence, Supplier societies by trust born of reputation. While there are some overlaps – monopolies for example, often combine aspects of both Stealing and Supplying – the two systems are fundamentally opposites: Stealing discourages development, Supplying needs to develop to keep ahead of competition.

It seems, however, that independent Supplier states could not outgrow their original city size by much: they stayed small or, for one reason or another, reverted to Stealer rule. Sometimes this was just because Supplier societies are more fragile then Stealer systems and can break under stress. Sometimes a Supplier state reached a size where it needed a full-time professional army, rather than a part-time citizen army, and, at this point, it was inevitable that the army commanders would seize power for themselves. Rome, in its early city-state days was ruled by an oligarchy of senators but the senate was reduced to an ornamental role as the size of the state grew and the emperors took over, formalising the Stealer structure in law to match the reality of the Stealer structure it had ended up with.

A list of the best-known such Supplier societies shows that, although small and often short-lived, there were quite a few of them. The earliest we know for sure to be Supplier states were around 1000BCE: Tyre, Sidon, Byblos and the other trading cities of Lebanon (Phoenicia). It seems likely that Bahrain (Dilmun), Aden (Eudaemon) and other stopping points on the Gulf and Red Sea trade routes may have preceded these, but we lack conclusive evidence. These were followed by classical Corinth, Athens and several other Greek city-states, then by Carthage before it became an empire. These were followed by, most famously: Mecca at the time of the Prophet Mohammad, Penang (Malaysia), medieval Novgorod (Russia), the Hanseatic League of Baltic and North Sea trading towns, as well as Venice, Genoa, Amalfi, Pisa and several other city-states of Italy and Dubrovnik (Ragusa) during the medieval period, going on to Zanzibar (an island off southern Africa) and the states of the Netherlands from around 1600. There are many more small Supplier city-states in each period that are less well known. Pre-Colombian America probably had them as well, for example, on the island of Marajo, in the mouth of the Amazon. These oligarchical or democratic city-states have long been appreciated as the catalysts of change, and the forerunners of the kind of society that emerged after the Birth of Now.

Supplier societies vary officially between being oligarchies (rule of a few families) and democracies. In reality, all are somewhere in between. The official 'democracies' always limited who could vote, reducing the franchise down to a narrow group. For example, in famously 'democratic' classical Athens the vote was restricted to free men who were born in the city and over the age of thirty and to those who actually lived in the city itself – perhaps one in six or one in eight of the population. In practice, a few families have often dominated what were, by structure, apparently democracies. On the other side of the coin, the states that were apparently ruled by a few families ignored the views of the mob at their peril: the riff-raff might not have the vote, but they were often capable of expressing their views with vegetables or harder substances if they disapproved of the decisions of the oligarchs (and, in city-states, there is no separate army to bring in from outside to put down the mob).

Most of these Supplier societies were characterised by great instability, which prevented any kind of long-term development. The well-documented 200-year history of classical Athens between the start of its democracy and its final demise as an independent state, involved varied wars, evacuation of the city, victory, defensive union, empire, colonisation, defeat, tyranny, war, conquest, defeat, etc. etc. This makes for interesting reading but poor soil for social and technological change.

In Europe, the period before 1500 threw up two larger-than-usual Supplier states: Venice and Amsterdam. Venice, a few other Italian city-states[10] and the free states of the Netherlands are exceptional in that the conflicts between different factions and oligarchs did not destroy them, nor did invasion and conquest. They remained Supplier societies up until the time of the Birth of Now (when they were, both of them, taken over by Napoleon's revolutionary France, a paradigm Stealer state).

Venice's location had three huge advantages. It was very well positioned to bring exotic imports from the East to the rich hinterland of northern Italy and to the whole of northern Europe. It was situated in a highly defensible position, in a shallow lagoon/marsh that made attack by both land armies and conventional ships effectively impossible. Finally, it was largely out of the

---

10   Fans of Florence (Firenze) may feel their city should have a separate mention, possibly ahead of Venice but it is not always clear the extent to which it was always or even often a Supplier state, always seeming to teeter on the edge of reverting to full Stealerdom under the Medicis.

way of trouble from the main power blocks – away from France, the Ottomans and the Austrian heartland of the ('Holy Roman') Empire; easier to bypass, rather than attack. With its trade, it also developed a number of specialist industries, the most famous being glass-making, but its arms, musical instrument and naval supply industries were also outstanding.

Venice's glory days started from the profits of the Fourth Crusade. In 1204, having supplied the Frankish crusading army with ships to get them to the eastern Mediterranean, the Venetians diverted the Crusaders into a surprise attack on the immensely wealthy, if inconveniently Christian, city of Byzantium. Largely because the attack by fellow Christians was so unexpected, Byzantium fell for the first time since it became capital of the Empire, 900 years earlier. It was thoroughly plundered by the Frankish knights, who returned much of the profit to Venice. At its height, in the fourteenth and fifteenth centuries, Venice was the richest city in Europe, although some of its Italian competitors, Florence and Milan, were close to it in wealth. It had a substantial overseas trading empire, including much of Dalmatia, the Ionian Islands, Rhodes and Crete and included the whole province of the Veneto, with the smaller but important Supplier towns of Padua, Treviso, Verona, Vicenza and others. But after 1600 it suffered many years of decline, the reasons for which we will consider later.

Amsterdam also enjoyed multiple advantages. Like Venice, it was a successful port, with the Rhine River giving it access to much of central Europe and a market large enough to develop specialist industries. Also like

Venice, it was defended by shallow waters and swamps, which proved effective in hindering armies attempting to attack it. It was also surrounded by similar, if smaller, Supplier cities; Delft, Rotterdam and Gouda are probably the best known and Amsterdam often worked in league with them. These cities had also developed specialist manufacturing industries and, while the most important industry was weaving and cloth finishing, there were many others[11]. In its heyday, the Netherlands also had an important trading empire including Cape Province (South Africa), much of the East Indies (Indonesia), Manhattan and some sugar islands and trading posts in the Caribbean.

The lottery of inheritance in the medieval period had made the Netherlands part of the Duchy of Burgundy and, as the cities of the Netherlands became wealthy, they had become increasingly resentful of their overlords. At the same time, they used their wealth and influence to gradually gain privileges and some degree of independence from the dukes. In 1566, open conflict with their overlord broke out. By dynastic twists, their ruling duke at the time was also the King of Spain. The following eighty-plus years of war were a period of extraordinary growth for the Netherlands, culturally, economically and politically. Later, long after that war ended but before 1700, they went into a decline that looks similar to the depression suffered by Venice after

---

11   These cities and their surrounding states we will refer to as the Netherlands. Properly they are the 'Northern Netherlands' that went on to become independent and that we often call Holland. The Southern Netherlands remained subject to the Habsburg Spanish and later Austrian monarchs and eventually became Belgium.

its glory days. Some elements of this golden age of the Netherlands certainly fed into the Birth of Now; but the Birth did not start there. Indeed, the period 1700-1800 sees the decline of the Netherlands from world leader to a ho-hum state, picked up by Napoleon in 1795, without either party, the Netherlands or Napoleon, thinking much about it[xii].

We have focussed on Venice and the Netherlands with its surrounding cities because, of all the many cities that became Supplier societies, from Tyre and Sidon in 1000BCE, to Penang and Zanzibar in the seventeenth century CE, these two seemed to have had the best chance to progress further. But neither did. The decline of Venice is generally ascribed to the loss of its valuable spice trade to the seafarers of the sixteenth and seventeenth centuries. The new ocean mariners after 1500 were able to sail directly from Portugal and Spain around Africa to the Spice Islands, cutting Venice out of the delivery chain. To a lesser extent, Venetian mishandling of its relations with its crucial trading partner, the Ottoman Empire, is also blamed for its decline. This may be so, but still leaves the similar Dutch (Netherlands) decline a mystery. Moreover, Venice had ridden with strength through many other blows over the three centuries of its pomp; you would not have expected this new competition to have reduced its resilience so much. The sense of failure was strongly felt in both places, the Netherlands after 1700 and Venice after 1600. Bewildered citizens often ascribed their perception of a terrible decline to the failure of the current generation to match the strength and intelligence of their forebears.

Even now, the reasons for their declines are still not agreed, historians recording the fact sadly but without attempting a definitive explanation. We shall suggest one later.

We also have to explain why it was that the Netherland's historical stepchildren – Britain, north Ireland and the Southern Netherlands, or Wallonia – provided the location of the Birth of Now. These areas inherited Supplier traditions and know-how from Amsterdam and its surrounding cities and copied much of the Netherland's laws and practices. But they must have added something else, something that triggered the huge changes of the Birth of Now. Let's have a look at the ideas that have been put forward as explanations.

.4.

JUST BEFORE THE BIRTH

The simplicity, robustness and historical dominance of the destructive Stealer form of society held back human development as long as it existed and it existed almost everywhere before the Birth of Now. However, there is an escape route from the Stealer society when, occasionally, circumstances allow trading-based Supplier societies to arise. Although Supplier societies arose many times over several thousand years, none led on to the Birth of Now until Britain, north Ireland and Southern Belgium (Wallonia) sometime after 1750. So something still held back previous Supplier societies, although they had escaped Stealing. Perhaps something more needed to be added to them before they could take off, something that Britain, north Ireland and Wallonia had that previous Supplier societies did not have.

Even as late as 1700 there was little that was remarkable about Western Europe compared to previous civilisations or to its contemporary competitors. Two hundred years earlier it had the enormous luck to 'discover' a new continent, America, and accidently kill a huge proportion of the population through disease, allowing the New World to be exploited for gold and silver. But by 1700, the benefits of America to Europe were almost entirely in the past. The gold and silver had been largely worked out and, while Spanish and Portuguese rule in South America still remained, it brought little gain to their 'mother countries', which had gone into a serious decline. Only a few sugar islands showed a profit, mainly for the Netherlands and Britain. The North American colonies had small but growing populations but barely broke even. Eastern Europe had been seized by the Turkish Ottoman Empire and was to remain dominated by them for another century. India was dominant in cotton cloth – demand for it in Britain kept on rising, even as tariffs were raised in an attempt to protect the domestic wool business. China was blossoming under Manchu imperial rule and its advanced technology, particularly in porcelain, was stunning Europe. Europe led only in shipping – the carriage of its own imports and in piracy and protection rackets in the Indian Ocean, where a few small enclaves harboured its bandit ships. Indeed, its inability to export anything to China, India and Indonesia was starting to drain the continent of the silver it was using to pay for its imports from them[12.]

After 1800 everything changed. Western Europe dominated the world, quite literally, as towards the end of the next century it claimed to rule most of it. Together with the USA and other largely European-led cultures, Western Europe's trade, its manufactures and its finance were totally dominant until at least 1950 and its culture and its traditions still dominate the world today. The

---

12   Much of the silver originally came from America and some was still being sent across the Pacific direct from Mexico.

Birth of Now came in the century between 1700 and 1800 in Western Europe and one of its first effects was to cause this turnaround in the relative power of Europe. Specifically it started in Britain, north Ireland and Wallonia, now part of Belgium and we need to know a little about the background to these three areas between 1700 and 1800.

BRITAIN 1700 – 1800

Before 1700 there had been a long, slow changeover in England and Scotland from a Stealer society to a Supplier society. This change came step by step over more than 100 years and needed a great deal of help from the Netherlands. It started from almost zero Supplier influence during the Stealer reign of Henry VIII, the King of England and Ireland who died in 1547 but, by the time the first 'German George' arrived in 1714 as a semi-absentee king, Britain was almost completely Supplier-dominated.

Henry VIII had been a classic chief Stealer. After his death, the monarch's absolute power started to lessen. Initially, this was because Henry's son, Edward, was a minor when he became king and died young, aged sixteen. Then Henry's two daughters, first Mary, then, when she died, Elizabeth came to the throne. They had their power slightly limited because of their gender – so, for example, they did not lead armies themselves. Elizabeth's reign was followed by the arrival of a foreign king, James of Scotland. James's power in his own country was already much less than absolute. For many years as a child he had been controlled by a regency council and the religious complexity of Scotland at the time limited his room for manoeuvre. The existing English government bureaucracy carefully managed the handover of power to James on Elizabeth's death, taking care to retain some control of the key levers of power. James avoided serious confrontation with the existing English establishment – more by luck than judgement[xiii] – and it became, informally, accepted that there were limits to Royal power, notably on the issues of religion and taxation.

James's son, Charles I, tried to reassert the King's absolute power, but prompted instead a civil war. The influence and money of the merchant class were very significant in defeating Charles, who was removed from power and executed. The leading merchants and the London guilds were also critical in the decision, some years later, to invite the son of the executed king back from exile to become King Charles II – with conditions and on the understanding that his powers were to be further limited in practice. This second Charles was wily enough to work within these implicit constraints but his brother, James (the Second of England and Ireland, the Seventh of Scotland), who inherited the throne and a great deal of goodwill from him, was fool enough to try to reassert the King's power in unpopular causes again. So, in 1688, shortly before our period starts, the English and Scottish parliaments voted to replace James with his daughter, Mary, and her husband, Willem of the Netherlands, as joint monarchs[13]. Willem was already used to receiving his powers at the hands of Supplier committees in the Netherlands and agreed to a

---

13 This decision was much helped by Willem and Mary being Protestant, while James was Catholic. Plus Willem had invaded Britain and James's army had deserted to Willem. There was some doubt whether Scotland would follow England's lead in accepting Willem, but James wrote a deeply foolish and arrogant note to the Scottish parliament that swung it to Willem's side.

great many limitations on Royal power in return for the throne. Willem also imported a number of people from the Netherlands to act as advisers, growing the already strong Netherland's Supplier influence in England and Scotland. However, while the American states had followed the English and Scottish decision to replace James with Willem and Mary, Willem had to take the southern part of Ireland from James in war. This helped perpetuate a Stealer culture there, in contrast to the developing Supplier society in the rest of the British Isles. In 1702, on Willem's death (Mary died earlier) the throne passed on to James's other daughter, Anne.

At the beginning of our period, in 1700, the islands of Britain and Ireland were home to three independent kingdoms, England, Scotland, and Ireland (Wales is, technically, a principality of England), although they shared the same monarch. The same monarch also ruled over Barbados, Jamaica, a few other West Indian sugar islands and the American states (colonies). Despite sharing a monarch, all three countries and each American state had their own, separate, government, each with their own distinctive history, laws and traditions.

In 1707, amidst considerable opposition and distrust on both sides, the English and Scottish parliaments agreed to merge their countries together. The new, combined kingdom was called the United Kingdom of Great Britain (referred to here as 'Britain'[14]). It

---

14 In France the region known as Brittany in English is called by the same name as the island of Britain – they are both known in French as 'Bretagne'. To make the distinction clear the island is called 'Grande (Big) Bretagne' in France. This was translated into English as 'Great Britain'.

succeeded beyond expectations in actually forming a combined country, whose unity was barely questioned for 300 years.

On the death of Queen Anne in 1714, by prior arrangement, the Duke of Brunswick-Lüneburg (commonly known as the Elector of Hannover) was made King George I of Britain, of Ireland, of the American states, etc. The new King could neither speak English nor display any real interest in Britain, once he had got his hands firmly on the title, the money and the additional clout the title gave him 'back at home'. When he became king, George I relied on his English-speaking wife and British chief minister, Robert Walpole, almost entirely. For the rest of the century, Britain and the other lands were blessed with George I's descendants, some of the stupidest kings possible, whose infrequent attempts to take back powers for themselves never came to anything, as they were easily baffled by their opponents.

So, by this stage, the pomp and trappings of monarchy were matched to the reality that power was largely shared between an oligarchy of leading families and powerful merchant interests, influenced by popular sentiment. The Supplier society was dominant and any overt Stealer behaviour by the king, or any other grandee, would result in their removal. It had taken 170 years or so for England to go from a unitary, Stealer – king's absolute rule in 1547, to a largely Supplier society, strongly modelled on the Netherlands and only technically under the rule of a king who could not speak the language and spent around a quarter of his reign at home in Hannover. Over the period, two monarchies, Charles I and James II & VII were terminated and four were appointed by the oligarchy with ever tighter conditions, James I & VI, Charles II, Willem and Mary, and George I. So the superficial constitutional turbulence leading up to our period was, in reality, the opposite. It reflected a consistent popular desire for social and religious stability and the ability to get it, even if it meant replacing kings when they looked like rocking the boat. The result in Britain was an extremely resilient system that, over the next 300 years, evolved step by step into a modern democracy, without a revolution or major political breaks.

The constitutional breaks that did happen after 1700 were outside the island of Britain. Late in the century, in 1783, after a war, thirteen colonies in America became the independent United States of America – gifted by Britain from their inception with the structure of a Supplier society (in much the same way as Britain had received it from the Netherlands). Then, in 1800, appalled by the savagery of the Irish civil war that had started in 1796 and thinking to repeat the very successful merger of Scotland and England a century earlier, the British Government merged with the Irish Government, forming the United Kingdom of Great Britain and Ireland (UK). This was again supported by a majority vote in both British and Irish parliaments[15]. The change from three countries in 1700 to one after 1800 explains why the terms used for the countries and their inhabitants vary, although it makes little difference to the issue of the Birth of Now itself.

---

15 There was undoubtedly a lot of bribery and coercion in these votes. But that was equally true of the merger of the English and Scottish parliaments.

Britain, Ireland and the 'Colonies' were, between 1707 and 1800, minimally governed from the centre. Their separate governments raised money mostly by taxes on specific goods[xiv] to spend almost entirely on defence and trade protection; for Britain that meant the Navy. The areas the government was seen as *not* responsible for are worth listing: education, health, support for the poor, the elderly, orphans or the disabled, weights and measures, policing, immigration, roads, rivers or harbours (except for those used by the Navy). The idea that there is something called an 'economy' had not yet arrived let alone the idea that the government could influence it. Although the government did issue coinage, its value was almost entirely dependent on its metal content. Banknotes were issued throughout the period by the Bank of Scotland (the first to do so), the semi-independent Bank of England and by some commercial banks, all convertible on demand into gold held in their vaults. The governments made a small gesture towards the administration of justice by providing judges and a court system but only for the most serious criminal cases and the very rare civil cases. Everyday criminal justice was entirely in the hands of local gentry, who held the position of magistrate or Justice of the Peace. The care of the needy, if any was provided, was also in local hands, those of the parish councils, semi-church, semi-municipal bodies of local worthies. So minimal was the influence of the British Government in America that the attempt, later in the century, to introduce the most basic form of external rule and taxation into the American states was regarded by some Americans as quite unacceptable and was one of the causes of the War of Independence. America then crystallised this vision of minimal government in writing. In the US Constitution, the (Federal) Government is rigorously defined as existing only to provide for the united defence of the States and the regulation of interstate commerce (although its powers have extended somewhat since).

Religion in Britain, which had caused so many deaths the previous century, was politically quiet, although people had to profess the state religions to hold any government office or qualification. This excluded 'dissenters', as they were known, from the professions or political power but, otherwise, alternative religious views were tolerated, if they kept politically quiet.

Trade prospered with the colonies in the West Indies and America, both before and after the US War of Independence, which made no difference to trade between the parties, once the war was finished. The East India Company was doing well in India – so much so, that trade barriers were erected to prevent imported Indian cotton destroying the British clothing industry in the first half of the century.

At the start of the century, taxes were relatively low compared to the later norms – they seem to have amounted in total to less than one tenth of the national income – although they were high compared to other countries of the time. By far the most important taxes throughout the century were sales taxes, known as 'excises'. As the century progressed, the frequent wars led to an increased need for revenue and to new categories of goods being taxed, often at higher levels. It helped that both Britain and Ireland are islands, and so were able to keep sales taxes at higher levels than most other countries could maintain. While the pressure of war raised levels of taxation to previously unprecedented levels during the course of the century, there is little record of serious resentment about tax demands. The money was clearly seen as necessary for the wars, which themselves were widely supported – or, at any rate, felt to be unavoidable – with the exception of the American War of Independence, which split the opinion of the country. Writers who objected to the relatively high levels of tax at the time saw clearly that they were caused by popular support for wars and wished Britain was less assertive. Because the wars were partially financed from borrowing, even when there was peace taxes remained high compared to the perceived norm in an attempt to reduce the level of national debt. This did not work but, fortunately, after tidy and efficient bonds called 'Consols' were launched in 1751 the government was able to borrow all it wanted at low interest rates. At the end of the period, in the desperate days of the Napoleonic Wars leading up to 1800, the costs of war were enough to bring about the invention of a variety of new types of tax, including income tax. Even then, there seems to have been a widespread acceptance that the taxes were raised for a purpose and were largely used for that purpose, with few suggesting alternative ideas, other than less national belligerence.

This popular acceptance of Georgian governments and their taxes is surprising, since the monarchs were widely despised, the electoral system was obviously risible and it was known and accepted that more or less all members of government were to some degree corrupt. But, at the time, no one seriously believed that an alternative system of government was possible for Britain. The possibility that a different system could work in an existing kingdom was raised by the French Revolution but the idea's attractiveness rapidly declined as the revolution turned into a bloodbath. Most important in keeping popular support was that, eccentric as they were, both government and parliament were aware of the popular mood and sometimes responded to it. There was wide freedom of speech, with satirical attacks on the kings and members of the government reaching levels of viciousness that can still shock – the cartoonists Hogarth and Gillray had few problems portraying the Prince Regent literally shitting policies onto venal members of government. But for all their stupidity, no alternative to the King Georges was at all acceptable to the vast majority of the people, partially for religious reasons, partially because any alternative would have added complications to the international position.

Most parliamentary seats had few voters, so local aristocrats determined who would have the seat, many of which were uncontested. Most MPs were clearly members of the oligarchy, the brothers or cousins of aristocrats, who had their own House of Parliament, the House of Lords, with considerable power. Ministers were expected to enrich themselves and appoint their relatives and acolytes to remunerative posts. So long as this was done with discretion and the resulting amount of money that vanished was not abnormal, it was accepted. But, from time to time, there were scandals as some fund was found to have been plundered to an unacceptable extent or some scheme came apart due to the embezzlement of its budget. This changed completely, however, at the end of the century, as corruption of any sort became unacceptable under the pressure of the Napoleonic Wars and died away.

Many Members of Parliament did not bother to turn up much but, then, there was normally little business of importance. A lot of time was spent on passing acts in favour of rich individuals, such as allowing the enclosure of previously common land, the rare divorces (each of which needed an Act of Parliament), patent extensions, canal permissions, etc. However absurd the system seems to have been on paper, it is clear that the government had some regard to popular sentiment and, almost because it was so unrepresentative, tried to avoid actions that would inflame popular opinion. Part of its success was that, in contentious issues, such as the ongoing subsidies demanded by George III's wastrel sons, Parliament felt as the people felt and clearly expressed popular anger. This was also reflected in the strongly expressed differences towards the American War of Independence, where, as far as we can tell, Parliament seems to have reflected the mixed opinions and swinging mood of the country very well.

The merger of the Scottish and English parliaments was successful for two main reasons. The first was this same lack of government generally; in practice, the effect of the merger on English and Scottish individuals or institutions was minimal. The second reason was the considerable effort that was put into making the merger successful, the careful support of Scottish institutions, such as its law system, its Presbyterian Church and its contribution to the army, ensuring that Scottish military officers got senior posts[16].

Until the Napoleonic Wars at the end of the century added the cost of huge subsidies to continental allies, the government still spent almost all its money on only three items: the Navy, which frequently accounted for 80-90 per cent of all expenditure, Royal Court expenses, including sinecure jobs for relatives of the ruling class and, during wars only, an army. Until the Napoleonic Wars at the end of the century, the majority of the King's army was stationed outside Britain and made up of soldiers from the King's other realm, Hannover. These included the troops from the neighbouring area of Germany, the Hessians, who made a well-remembered impact in the American War of Independence. The disorders of the previous century, with its long and bloody civil wars, meant that the peacetime army in Britain (but not in Ireland) was restricted to a miniscule size – hence the extraordinary lack of arms to resist the mob supporting Bonny Prince Charlie – see below.

The primary business of government was protection of British strategic and commercial interests and, in practice, it occupied itself with little other than international relations and the protection of trade.

---

16   There were never enough army posts for the Scottish gentry, who did not have access to the church as a career for younger brothers. Scottish officers became leading generals in both Russia and Ottoman Turkey, amongst many other posts abroad.

Between 1700 and 1800, Britain was officially at war for forty-three years and expecting war or winding down after war for much of the rest of the time; but, despite this aggressive record and the threat of invasion on a number of occasions, there was very little war and minimal destruction in Britain itself. Throughout the whole century 1700-1800 only four small battles were fought on British soil: Preston and Sheriffmuir in 1715, Prestonpans, 1745, and Culloden, 1746. They all happened during attempts by two descendants of King James, his son in 1715 and his grandson in 1745, to regain the throne. Despite some hysteria in Britain at the time, neither attempt was at all realistic; the numbers involved on both sides were small – in the low thousands – and nor did they have much impact on British life in general.

The whole episode of 'The '45', the second and marginally more serious rising, illustrates the minimal government of the time. The Catholic claimant to the throne, known as 'Bonnie Prince Charlie', landed in the largely Catholic Western Highlands. He was able to collect a force of around 2,500 highlanders and, with just this force, 'take over' all of Scotland. The British establishment forces in Scotland had turned out to consist of 2,300 hastily raised men. The highlanders defeated this meagre force at the Battle of Prestonpans, near Edinburgh. 'Bonnie Prince Charlie' then advanced as far south as Derby in England, his force never more than 5,000 strong. No local militia, army attachment, duke, lord or town authority stood in his way – showing how far Britain had come from being a Stealer society! Having got to Derby six months after his first arrival in

Britain, he turned back towards Scotland. It had become apparent that he was profoundly unwelcome, that French support was not going to arrive and that the British authorities were, finally, summoning troops to match him. After this remarkable delay, the establishment was finally able to collect an army, still small, but larger than Bonnie Prince Charlie's, better organised, better supported and led by the King's brother. The rebels were completely defeated at Culloden.

So, although Britain was often at war 1700-1800, the warring did not seriously disrupt society, lessen the Supplier society or give any assistance to a return to Stealer ways. This long Supplier period gave at least the opportunity for the development of the Birth of Now; it provided an environment in which the Birth was not snuffed out by Stealers from the start.

The intensity of the wars against France late in the century led to a crucial change in the nature of British Government: it drove out corruption. In Britain, the start of each of the wars of this period had been marked by a howl of public rage as the impoverished state of the Navy was uncovered, 'rotting at its anchors'. During the years of peace, official corruption meant that much of the Navy's funding had been effectively stolen. Corruption is a community activity; any corrupt deal involves several people directly and more can indirectly guess that it is happening. So corruption can only happen as long as it is quietly acceptable. When it is not widely accepted, word of a corrupt deal gets out and the corrupt individuals are removed or arrested. During wars, corruption becomes less acceptable and, during wars of community survival, it becomes completely unacceptable. The USA, for example, was born in a tight struggle and so started with the unusual advantage of a largely uncorrupt government.

Britain was often under serious threat during the long Napoleonic Wars and, during this time, institutionalised corruption largely vanished. It could not be afforded in that desperate struggle. Britain went into these wars with an almost entirely part-time and amateur government, with ministers often working to feather their own nest. It came out of the wars, twenty-three years later with a largely professional government, showing pride in their professionalism, led by full-time government officers and politicians. The war went on long enough for institutionalised corruption to become a faded memory to the individuals in government. Consequently, even when the war stopped, the government remained basically uncorrupt: governing had become a serious profession, no longer a route to quick personal gain. After about 1790, the momentum of the Birth of Now was greatly helped by Britain's reasonably professional government. It made decisions that, while not always successful, were reasoned and it became largely unnecessary for entrepreneurs to bribe officials. Indicators of this change are that, for the first time in over a century, a senior administrator was impeached for corruption (Lord Melville, in 1805) and, ironically, muckraking exposés of corruption started to be published. The *Black Book or Corruption Unmasked* of 1819 sold over 50,000 copies. Corruption was no longer accepted as normal practice but had become a shocking abuse of office. In fact, by 1819, there was very little corruption in the British Government and the *Black Book* was shown to be almost entirely fictional.

Britain spent the majority of its war budget on its navy during the wars of the eighteenth and nineteenth centuries. Navies were unlike armies of the period in that much more was spent on equipment and supply, rather than just on pay. This also meant that the vast majority of the money was spent at home. So Britain's emphasis on the Navy kept much of its war chest at home and fed technical development. Marc Isambard Brunel's line for manufacturing naval pulley blocks in 1802 was the first production line in the world[17]. The huge growth of the iron industry prompted by the naval demand for cannons and munitions – by 1800 the British Navy had around 50,000 cannons – made capacity available when the railways were planned.

The ethos of the Navy was also important. Navies require a degree of professionalism in their officers that armies of the time, at least British armies, seemed happy to do without. An idiotic ship's captain was much more quickly and certainly disastrous than an equally idiotic regimental colonel. The British Navy became a byword for professionalism, allowing only a very limited amount of aristocratic promotion peddling[xv]. This professionalism had a cultural impact on government and business as well. The same was not always true of the army, which felt it had to ensure that its officers were committed to the status quo

---

17 His son was the even more famous engineer, Isambard Kingdom Brunel. Marc Isambard Brunel was nearly bankrupted by his highly successful pulley-block development. He was only paid eight years later.

and allowed the purchase of officer ranks, so that senior officers were always from a wealthy background. While the immense length of the Napoleonic Wars temporarily weeded out many idiots, sale of rank did, at times, lead to some memorably inept officers – leading a British general of the time to say, on being shown a list of his new officers, 'I don't know if they will frighten the French but, by God, they frighten me'.

Finally, the British ended the war with their navy completely dominant in the world. This meant that, for Britain at least, there were minimal blockages to trade, political or military. Consequently, once war with France was concluded in 1815 and the 1812-15 war with the USA ended, trade flowed easily. This peace in Europe lasted longer than any previous peace, which also helped trade.

Other than defence, the only area that was seen as the central business of government was religion. The government saw its task as the defence of Protestantism and, within that, support for the official Episcopalian Churches of England and Ireland and the, quite different but equally official, Presbyterian Church of Scotland. This was central to the role of government and remained so until the early 1800s, well after the Birth of Now. As the century went on, however, there was a change in the nature of government involvement in the church. Early on, continuing from the religious wars of the previous century, there was an evangelical feel to the support for the established (official) churches: Britain was the 'modern Israel' of true faith, battling against the wickedness of Catholicism (and misguided non-conforming Protestants). Later on, as Britain's strength grew and especially after France abandoned official Catholicism after the Revolution, it became a complacent defence of the rights and privileges of the established churches and their vast incomes. By the end of the Napoleonic Wars, the ruling classes had all but abandoned any sectarian fervour, although it took several bills and over several decades to get laws past parliament restoring all civic rights to non-established church members.

Turning to society in general, the population of Britain was very religiously devout throughout this period. Despite the decline in *political* Christianity, personal Christianity remained strong – there were few middle-class people who did not try to go to church twice on Sunday. From the middle of the century the growing cities led to movements, such as the Methodists, to renew Christianity in this new environment. However, towards the end of the period, sceptical ideas were beginning to be spread or, at any rate, to be openly talked about amongst intellectuals.

An important difference between the British (and most north European) populations and any preceding population was the number of people who could read. More than half the men, and just fewer than half the women, could read and slightly fewer of each could write. In almost all societies before the Protestant Reformation, which started in 1519, reading and writing had been a professional task for a professional class of scribes and priests or reserved to the ruling class. But in north-west Europe, people were taught to read because it was seen as desirable for religious reasons. Moreover, this was a period when the main spoken languages were used for writing. Until 1700, most serious writing in Britain had been in the scholarly language of Latin; after 1700 English became the universal tongue for works published in Britain. So, for example, Newton's work that defined and founded modern science, the *Principia* of 1687, was written in Latin. One hundred years later it was inconceivable that the work that defined and founded modern history, Gibbon's *Decline and Fall* of 1776, would be written in Latin (although Gibbon's Latin was fluent).

Britain was notably prosperous during the whole of the 1700s in comparison with all other European countries except the even richer Netherlands and some states of Italy, and it became more so as the century wore on towards the Birth of Now. By the middle of the century, the basic pay for labourers was significantly higher in Britain than in most of Europe, around double that in France (measured in the quantity of silver that could be bought for the average wage). This can largely be attributed to four Supplier society factors: internal peace, the rule of law, sound money and no internal tariff barriers – France, in contrast, had hundreds, blocking or complicating trade along every road and river as Stealers sought to grab what they could. The good overall level of political and economic calm also helped the economy, despite worries about Bonny Prince Charlie in 1745 and the 'South Sea Bubble' economic crash of 1720.

This absence of disruptive factors in Britain's economy allowed systems to become more productive. For example, the 'putting out' system allowed increased production efficiency, even before the development of machinery. This system was to distribute to villagers a basic raw material, such as wool, for spinning and weaving in their plentiful, quiet times, picking up the finished product months later. This practice, which is only possible in a stable, law-abiding society, blossomed during this period, to the modest enrichment of many. Regular supplies of food and good markets enabled specialists to focus more exclusively on their work and become more expert and efficient. Coal was easily accessible in many areas and had become the main fuel for heating, enabling the available wood to be used for construction and for building the Navy. Coal transport, mostly by sea from north-east England to London, had become a major business. All these elements helped create relative prosperity and social calm. This prosperity has been called 'Smithian', after Adam Smith, an influential philosopher of the period, now mainly remembered for his contribution to economics. Smith pointed out how much more efficient it was when people are able to concentrate on doing one task well, rather than attempting to do many, gaining efficiency from the 'division of labour'. The peace and approximate lawfulness of the period in Britain allowed trade to prosper and so also allowed people to concentrate on doing something well, a concentration that was responsible for much of the country's prosperity.

Although Britain had an aristocracy, a Stealer remnant, aristocrats were very few in number. During the century there were never more than a couple of hundred people sitting in the House of Lords and there were no private armies (apart from a marginal exception in the Highlands of Scotland). Titled people made up 0.00857 per cent of the population[xvi], if you include all lords, baronets and knights. This compares to between 1 per cent and 2 per cent of the population in France with aristocratic titles and exemptions. Although the few aristocrats that existed were often very wealthy, they were subject to, and largely respected, the rule of law. The social atmosphere was dominated by a Supplier society feel, with only a light addition of old Stealer habits, a condition that had much to do with the influence of the Netherlands.

Towns were largely self-ruling, insofar as there was any formal rule at all, and were dominated by local oligarchies. The population overall grew steadily and probably doubled over the century, despite high levels of emigration to America. This was accompanied by the growth of 'enclosures', a process whereby traditional peasants were dispossessed of the land they farmed, which was then generally turned over from arable farming to stock rearing. This was one of the factors pushing people into emigration – which many did, predominantly from England during this period, forming the base population of what became the USA. (The major Scottish and Irish migrations were in the next century.) Population growth and rural enclosures also created a pool of unemployed labourers[xvii], many of whom drifted into towns, mining and the early mills. The country saw itself as prosperous and frequent attention was drawn to the greater wealth and meat consumption of English labourers compared to French or Irish labourers.

Despite the relative prosperity, the poverty of the poor was grievous and everyday levels of suffering and cruelty are beyond our comprehension. Children were expected to work, if poor, from the age of seven, including cleaning chimneys, which killed them before their teenage years, or down the mines or in ships. Soldiers and sailors were routinely flogged, occasionally to death, and held in service against their will. Unwanted babies were exposed and killed. Even when the first 'Foundling Hospitals' started to receive babies, they did not feed them milk, so they almost all died anyway. Many sold themselves or their children as 'indentured labourers', slaves in all but technicality, to work, unpaid, in the colonies and, almost inevitably, to die there. Prisoners were also transported to the colonies of America and the Caribbean for use as slave labour. Animals were routinely tortured for sport. The list of barbarities is endless and only explicable as the inevitable lot of the less fortunate everywhere since the dawn of civilisation until the Birth of Now.

Returning to the specific century, however, there were no drastic weather events or natural disasters during the century – except in Ireland, 1740-41, which suffered especially badly from Europe-wide freezing temperatures. Nor were there any plagues over the period, although there was also no effective medicine. The disfiguring and often deadly diseases of smallpox and syphilis (the 'great pox') were widespread and dreaded.

Looked at from our society today, Britain 1700-1800 was desperately poor, deeply corrupt, fantastically unequal, perpetually at or close to war, quite violent, undemocratic, inefficient and absurd. Looked at compared to any previous society it was rich, free, peaceful, attentive to the voice of the people and largely law-abiding. These characteristics it shared only with the Netherlands, north Ireland and Wallonia.

WALLONIA AND NORTH IRELAND

It would be easier if we could ignore Wallonia and the region around Belfast in Ireland as unimportant complications, keeping our story within Britain. But it would be misleading, as it would imply that it was the peculiarities of Britain that made the Birth of Now happen. That it started in other countries as well shows that it was not. If we are to understand the cause of the overall change, even in this short story, explaining Wallonia and Belfast is an essential.

Wallonia is the current name for the southern, French-speaking area of Belgium. Unlike Britain and Ireland it is not an island but very much in the centre of Western European politics, war and commerce. It had, after the long wars of the previous two centuries, remained largely Catholic and under the rule of the Hapsburg Empire, unlike the independent, Protestant Netherlands to its north. What is now called Wallonia was, for most of this period, known as the Austrian Netherlands to which we can add some medieval leftovers, such as the Prince-Bishopric of Liège. This part of the Netherlands had come under Austrian rule in 1714, but was of little interest to its Austrian rulers, whose more or less only policy for the area was to try to swap it for some area of more use to them. So, like Britain, its rulers were largely inconsequential. So the area was mostly left to get on with things itself. The Austrian Netherlands approach to getting on with things itself was, again, like Britain's, mainly learned from the northern Netherlands, with a fairly open oligarchy and low levels of interference in daily life.

Like Britain, Wallonia had enjoyed the backwash of the boom in the northern Netherlands during the 1600s. Wallonia had boomed less than the northern Netherlands before 1700 but slumped less later – again like Britain. What made Wallonia distinctive were three things: its rich coal and iron fields, its excellent water-transport links and its proximity to so much of the fighting during the century. This meant that, from the start of this period, it had a highly developed iron and arms industry, one that increasingly sold across Europe. This led to the domination of the region by commercial and manufacturing Supplier interests.

For war and peace, the first half of the century to 1750 was fairly typical for Wallonia as 'the cockpit of Europe', with armies tramping back and forth across it and the occasional serious battle in or close to the region. The wars of Spanish Succession (1701-14) and Austrian Succession (1740-48) largely centred on the area. It is difficult to assess the impact of these on the people and local industry, although the general impression is that the destruction of war was to some extent balanced by the money brought into the region by the armies fighting it. The area itself was rarely involved heavily on one side or the other, it was just that the southern 'low countries' of Flanders and Wallonia became almost inevitably where the battles of European powers were held – a pattern that largely held until 1945.

In the second half of the century, however, there was a pause as the Seven Years' War (1756-63) was largely held elsewhere but, with the French Revolutionary wars at the end of the century, Wallonia and its near neighbour returned to the centre of the action at least for a period after 1792. Again, the people and economy and local politics seem remarkably undisturbed by the odd army passing through and occasional battle. The fact that the Birth of Now started in part in Wallonia is convincing evidence that it does not require a cradle of peace, an island or several other features sometimes claimed as essential.

The British and Walloon mild approach to government, carried on with popular indifference and general support, was not shared by Ireland. During this period, Ireland was a separate country to Britain with its own parliament, although the British Parliament sometimes tried to claim, as they tried to claim in America, some sort of superior power. But Ireland was divided into different and hostile religious groups. Most people in Ireland were Catholic by religion and were forbidden to hold office or vote. Another group, particularly in the north, were dissenting Protestants who were almost as badly disadvantaged. As a result, the country was ruled and dominated by a small clique, known as 'the Ascendency', who belonged to the Church of Ireland and were the only people allowed into public office or to vote.

Over the course of the century, Ireland became economically divided between two areas. In the north of the island it followed – even led – the British and Walloon pattern, becoming a Supplier-dominated society. As the century closed, the burgeoning linen (and, for a short while, cotton) industry led to the rapid development of Belfast, the main city in north Ireland, in a way that closely resembles the growth of Manchester in cotton and Leeds in wool. It was in the north of Ireland that the first modern canal, the Newry Canal, completed in 1742, was built to carry coal to Belfast, the model for all later British canal developments.

In contrast, most southern and western areas of Ireland continued in the Stealer pattern. The island's Ascendency, less than 20 per cent of the population, as with so many similar minorities with unfair advantages, abused their position and (we are told) missed no opportunity to grind down on the disadvantaged majority, who, as Catholics were barred from office[18]. However, the population of Ireland, like Britain, more than doubled over the century, which implies that times were not too bad.

At the end of the century, with the Birth of Now in full flood, there was a revolt in Ireland, a revolt very much inspired by and following the successful revolt of the American states a few years earlier, looking to create a more rational society based on Enlightenment ideas of progress and equality. The authorities quickly controlled the first outburst of the revolt, led largely by Enlightenment idealists in the northern areas. But it restarted elsewhere as a tangled swamp of discontented uprisings, fuelled by

---

18 The Ascendency was as Irish as anyone. All Irish groups had some links to and sometimes emigrated to England temporarily or permanently; none was English.

Catholic and Protestant nonconformist resentment at the Ascendency dominance and corruption – although the Catholic Church itself was entirely on the side of the authorities throughout. The revolt staggered on for several years, backed by Napoleonic France, who landed troops to support the uprising in Ireland in 1798. There were, as always in Ireland, reports of remarkable cruelty on all sides but open acts of rebellion were more or less snuffed out by 1800 and legends about the revolt later became nationalist myths. In practice, the revolt(s) made very little difference to the Birth of Now in the north of Ireland: Belfast developed alongside British cities and the south stagnated – a split that has taken some 200 years to become economically insignificant.

Belfast's development in north Ireland and Wallonia's in the south of the Netherlands, together with the British experience, shows that politics, specific location or religion had relatively little to do with the Birth of Now. Whatever it was and whatever started it worked in all three areas, regardless of their very different geography, political and religious histories. So let's move backwards a little in time to review the candidates that have been put forward as causing the Birth of Now.

EMPIRE

Empires can be defined as large areas of land, inhabited by many different peoples and ruled by one person[xviii]. Traditional empires were built up through military power, sometimes helped by political marriages. The 'empires' acquired after 1500 outside Europe by Western European countries have sometimes been credited with causing the Birth of Now. These are often misleadingly called 'colonial empires', probably because the small 'empires' of the classical Greeks were often based on colonies and classical examples have dominated analysis. In fact there were four very different ways lands came under Western European control after 1500, all of them sometimes called 'empires', only one of them based on colonies.

The first type, the 'conquest-and-exploitation' empire, was similar to the traditional concept of empire and similar to several other empires being built up elsewhere at the time. The Western European conquest and exploitation empires were in Central and South America, the Caribbean and North Asia.

The actual 'colonial' empires, where Europeans intentionally moved to make a new life in largely empty lands, were in North America and South Africa. Australia and New Zealand were also colonial but were only developed after the Birth of Now.

Some Western European countries built up a network of small trading posts. These are sometimes referred to as 'empires', largely because, long after the Birth of Now, they became the basis for nationalistic empires.

'Nationalistic' empires also came after the Birth of Now and consisted of declaring large parts of the world, for example in Africa, to be part of an empire, often with little effect on the people or politics except to prevent some other European nation from doing the same.

It is oversimplifying, but a good way to remember the pattern of European 'Imperialism' is as four successive and almost unlinked events:

1500-1600	Traditional Conquest Empire: Spain and Portugal take over Central and South America
1600-1800	Trading Period: Portugal, the Netherlands, France, Russia and Britain build up a chain of trading posts: sugar, spices, tea and coffee
1650-1800	Colonial Period: Britain, France, the Netherlands in North America, Spain in Central and South America. US independence
1800-1945	European Nationalist Imperialism: many areas claimed as parts of European empires European culture dominant elsewhere (incl. US and the, now independent, South American countries)

Conquest-and-Exploitation Empires

Between 1500 and 1650, five large, traditional-type conquest-and-exploitation empires were built up. In approximate order of population size these were:

- The Turkish Osmanli (Ottoman) family empire was built up to include all the Middle East, North Africa and south-east Europe, reaching up to Vienna by 1629.
- The Jurchens of Manchuria built an empire in and beyond China around 1644.
- The Turkish/Mongol Mughals built up an empire in India from 1556.
- Castilians conquered Central and South America for the Kings of Spain[xix] in 1521 and 1572.
- The Safavid family built an empire in Persia by 1502. At the same time, Russia extended its influence across Siberia and central Asia, reaching the Pacific in 1639.

The creation of all these empires in this period form a pattern that suggests that, from about 1450, a new 'Age of Empire' had begun. There have been several previous Eurasian 'Ages of Empire', when some factor seems to allow the consolidation of independent areas into larger units, most notably before 1100BCE and in the period of Han/Roman/Parthian dominance from 200BCE to 200CE. In this case the arrival of gunpowder and the logistical efforts needed to make practical use of it seems to have swung the balance away from smaller kingdoms or the temporary horse-based conquests of the Mongols to the large groupings we call empires.

Because Spain is in Western Europe, so somewhat closer to where the Birth of Now started than the other empires of the time, the American Empire has sometimes been linked to the Birth[19]. The driving force of this empire was to extract the precious metals of gold and silver from America and to send them home to the King, although, as time went on, some Spaniards did seek to bring Christianity to the local people. It differed from other empires of the time because a huge proportion of the previous population died of the diseases introduced by the invaders, fundamentally changing the society and culture. To plunder the area, a small number of Spanish people had to live in the empire, but, initially, almost all of them expected to return home to Spain. The Portuguese Empire in Brazil, and the Dutch, French and British rule in the 'sugar islands' of the West Indies were also conquest-and-exploitation empires in a similar way to the Spanish Empire, albeit much smaller. These 'empires' largely depended on agriculture, mainly growing sugar for their profitability. But their objectives were as purely exploitative as the Spanish Empire's. Indigenous people and indentured labour from Europe were initially used as agricultural labour to extract as much money as possible for use at home. Then, when these largely died off, more tropically robust slaves were imported from West Africa to continue the process.

---

19 It was not a Spanish empire, nor even a Castilian empire. It belonged personally to the man who was King of Castile and other areas. The money from America was his private revenue. This fact is vitally important, as we shall see.

The New World empires had very little impact on the political system in Western Europe. Certainly they are not associated with the kind of advance we see in the Birth of Now. The vast influx of American gold and silver helped the King of Castile (Spain) to fight his wars in the Netherlands and caused Europe-wide inflation as the supply of gold and especially silver increased. But these revenues had startlingly little impact on Castile or the rest of Spain – it is difficult to point to anything in Spain, even the palaces, where it can convincingly be said that they would have been very different if American gold and silver had not existed. So much of the money was exported that, from around 1627 and for the rest of the century, Castile was in constant financial crisis, with debased currency and default. Despite this, Spain and Portugal retained their empires through their long relative decline in importance and wealth after 1600, their imperial rule over lands in America and elsewhere unable to make any difference to their shrinking power and wealth. There is no visible link between the Spanish conquest-and-exploitation Empire in America and the Birth of Now, any more than there is a link between the Ottoman conquest-and-exploitation Empire in Europe and the Birth of Now. Both these empires were in decline before 1700, while the Birth of Now started well after 1700. Gradually the Spanish and Portuguese conquest empires turned into colonial empires as the permanent population from the 'home countries' became larger and more settled in their conquests.

However, the South and Central American Empires had two important side effects. The first was the direct boost the empires gave to European development of ocean sailing simply because ocean travel was needed to get to them and get the gold back – and for privateers and pirates to steal it as well. The second was that the conquest of the American empires generated huge amounts of gold and silver and this was a vital fuel to European trade with Asia between 1600 and 1800. Europe sold very little to Asia but bought from it tea, porcelain, cotton cloth and spices, especially pepper, in vast quantities, as well as smaller commodities, such as rhubarb and opium. All this had to be paid for and silver, much of it originally from America, was the vital fuel of this trade. Without this silver there would not have been enough trade to justify the trading posts that became, later, the ground for nationalistic empires. So the loot of the Americas was a key enabler of the later European empires.

Colony 'Empires'

Colony 'empires' are the lands people moved to from a number of European countries to start a new, self-sustaining life. In the 1700s the most significant of these colonies were in North America, although South Africa and Siberia were also important. After 1800, Australia and New Zealand also became important areas for colonisation.

The principle emigrants to America at the time were from England, mostly as voluntary settlers, but some as transported prisoners, to be used as slaves, or as 'indentured' labourers, near-slaves. More emigrants came from France, the Netherlands, Ireland and Scotland. Towards the end of the period, many came from Africa as slaves. Where voluntary, these emigrations were largely attempts by individuals from crowded and restricted lands to set up in the more favourable circumstances of a land left largely empty by the annihilation of its previous population by disease.

In the history of the British American colonies we have an elegant test of theory that a colony empire brought benefits. The North American colonies were by far the largest part of the 'British Empire' before 1775 and after 1781 they mostly ceased to be part of the 'British Empire', so if a colonial empire made a difference we should see that difference vanish after the American War of Independence[20]. Neither before nor after the War of Independence were the British or federal Governments in America burdensome – or even noticeable – for most of the American population. In practice, such governing as happened in America was almost entirely at the state level. Before 1775 the British Government was frequently irked that it had no influence in and gained minimal benefit from the American colonies. The sole theoretical benefit was that all trade with the colonies was supposed to go via Britain, in return for which Britain was continually being asked to help defend them, at a considerable cost. Although the political ideas of the Enlightenment were the principal long-term cause of

---

20 It seems that the colonies were actually independent states before the War of Independence with no legal links to Britain, other than sharing the same king. In practice, as with Ireland, which had the same status, the British Government sought more clout than the legal position might suggest. It never succeeded, though, in either case, until Ireland was merged with Britain in 1800.

the struggle for independence, it was an attempt to limit defence costs by limiting the expansion of the colonies to the west and recoup some of the cost through taxes that triggered the revolt[xx]. (While the attempt by Britain to exert power and raise tax was minimal at the time, if the principle had been established that the British Government could oversee and tax the states in America, taxes would undoubtedly have risen and the control increased over time.)

Ironically, almost as soon as the former colonies became fully independent as the USA, they became the key suppliers to Britain's best-known boom industry during the Birth of Now: cotton processing. This trade became immensely valuable to both Britain and the US and, except for a short period of war (1814-16), trade was wholly unaffected by the fact that the US was no longer officially a colony. It is difficult to see how it could have done so: before 1775 the British Government had no practical power over the states of America, and, while afterwards it technically had less, it is very difficult to think of any noticeable difference this made. In practice, the states in America that remained part of the 'British Empire' and that later together formed Canada, were no more ruled by Britain than the US was, although they did not have an independent foreign policy for many years. In the long term, the foundation of the USA was a hugely significant event but it made very little difference to Britain at the time. Britain was more chagrined that it had lost a war to France, who had come in on the side of the USA. Although trading with America became important, this 'empire' was lost to Britain at almost the exact point of the Birth of Now and the fact that it had earlier in some way been part of an 'empire' could have had little to do with the Birth.

Trading-Post Empires

Starting in the sixteenth century, several Western European countries, led initially by the Portuguese and Dutch, started to take over small trading posts around the world to enable them to trade over long distances (copying the earlier example of the Venetians). Typical examples were the Portuguese trading posts at Goa in India and Macao in China, the Dutch posts in Ceylon and Malacca, the British at Bombay and Calicut. These were all initially intended to be as small as they could be to resupply and provide anchorage to ships while defending themselves and their warehouses from raids and theft. We do not need to cover the history of these in detail, just as it relates to the question: did these 'empires' cause, in part or whole, the Birth of Now? This means that we need only look at the history of these empires before the Birth of Now. We can take the date of 1800 as the last we need to consider here; the Birth was well under way by then.

At the start of our period, in 1700, six European countries had competing chains of trading stations: the Venetian empire in the Mediterranean, the Russian chain of trading posts in Siberia (and later north-west America), and the Portuguese, Dutch, French and British chains of ports. Many of the Dutch and British trading posts were run by their East India Companies – they had split the Asian trade between them when they were both under Willem, the Dutch getting the East Indies (now Indonesia), with their spice trade, and the British getting the Indian trade, mainly in cotton cloth (calico). However, none of these can be called 'empires', as they consisted only of small trading posts and their immediate hinterland was held as a protection against attack. There was no attempt to rule or conquer larger areas until the European wars and struggles for supremacy intervened.

These wars of 1700-1800 complicated the situation. The European countries involved sought to attack each other's trading posts, forming alliances with local kings and chiefs to achieve this aim. During the Seven Years' War (1756-63), Britain, the Netherlands and France fought over their West Indian sugar islands, their colonies in North America and their trading posts in India and South East Asia. In each war, local allies were involved: Native American tribes and (Asian) Indian rajas in their respective areas. For example, the Nawab of Bengal allied himself with the French and sought to attack the British trading post of Calcutta. The British East India Company, using almost entirely local troops, defeated him and the Nawabs became puppets of the company, which from then on effectively ruled Bengal, an area of India with a population similar to that of Britain itself. This extension of rule was not popular in Britain. It was widely regarded as, at best, a distraction and, at worst, a collection of endless liabilities undertaken by individual chancers on the make. These became known disparagingly as 'Nabobs' – people who were seen as making themselves wealthy at the country's risk. They did not see how Britain would make money out of these places, other than from the trade that was going on anyway and did not need rule to help it. But the argument was that if another European country had been allowed to take over the trading bases they would have excluded Britain, so the acquisition of territory was always justified as preventing the area from being acquired by another European power.

European rule in India was accepted easily and continued, often uneventfully, for many years because the local rulers they displaced had been very much in the chief Stealer mould and consequently unpopular, and the Moghul emperors were seen as no more Indian than the British[21]. Very few British, Dutch or French citizens were involved and no tribute or tax was expected to flow back to the homelands. Indeed, Bengal's success in exporting cotton goods to Britain, via the British East India Company, was so great that they had to be taxed and restricted to protect Britain's pre-Birth of Now textile industry.

But even after the acquisitions of the whole century, it is surprising how small the area 'ruled' by Britain was before 1800. The only large areas were the territories that later became Canada. These were all very thinly inhabited and developed and, even in its few towns, rule from Britain was completely notional. The first Australian settlers, 775 prisoners and their guards, only arrived in 1788, so it can hardly be counted. The 'Empire' also included a few sugar islands in the West Indies, the largest being Jamaica, together with the Bahamas and Bermuda. Finally, there

---

21   The belief of nationalism had yet to be invented.

were the trading and naval stations, kept to a minimal size: Gibraltar and Minorca in the Mediterranean; Senegal and the Cape Colony in Africa; Bombay, Madras, Calicut and Surat in India, Penang in Malaya and a few, tiny others. The only substantial population was in Bengal, ruled, as we have seen, by a puppet of the East India Company. The actual area of rule was minute, although the influence of the British Navy was widely felt at sea. This picture is often confused with the vast areas of the nationalistic British Empire around 1900 that included much of India, theoretically great areas of Africa, islands galore and a powerful influence in the Middle East and China. But all this was to come after the Birth of Now and is irrelevant to the question of what caused it.

But the empires were not central to supplying the 'mother country's' needs. Take Britain as an example: between 1700 and 1800, some of Britain's key trading commodities were sourced from within its empire but many were not. Most of Britain's sugar and cotton (until 1780) came from within British-controlled territory in the West Indies or India. But tea came entirely from China until after 1800, and timber, iron (largely imported from Sweden before 1750), coffee and cocoa came from outside the empire as did cotton after 1780.

The claim that owning the trading posts was necessary for a country's trade was not an excuse – each European nation did exclude the others where they could. But even this was only intermittently successful. During Britain's long wars with France, 1792-1815, Britain needed all the merchant transport it could get and licences for foreign vessels to break the Britain-only rules became very common. Once the attempts to limit trade to one country's merchant marine diminished, after 1815 trade of all types occurred widely across all categories and it is impossible to say – at the time or now – what was, for example, the benefit to the Netherlands of the Dutch East India Company ruling large chunks of the East Indies (Indonesia).

We can use this example to illustrate how unimportant 'empire' was to anything other than pride. During the Napoleonic Wars, the British seized the East Indies from the Dutch, who were under Napoleonic rule and so enemies of Britain. (This seizure was not a bloodless process; minor battles were fought. The locals, apparently, could not have cared less and did not get involved.) The British 'ruled' the area from 1811, a task involving, at the most, a few thousand British soldiers and administrators, before simply handing the whole 'empire' back to the Dutch in 1818 after the war ended. As far as can be told, none of the parties, Britain, the Netherlands or the locals, gained or lost anything more than pride, if that, from this exchange.

So, while trade may have been important to the Birth of Now, much of this trade was not linked to these 'empires'. It is true that, without crucial trading posts, much of the long-distance trade would have been impossible, but these ports were not what later became perceived as 'empire' and were often ruled only reluctantly to prevent them falling into the power of another European nation or from being plundered by local warlords. The pomp, the pride, the racism and even calling them 'empires' all came much later, long after the Birth of Now and the development of the nationalist belief in the nineteenth century[xxi].

Slavery in the European empires has been linked to the Birth of Now. This approach starts with the cotton mills of Lancashire that are seen as a critical element in the industrial part of the Birth of Now[22]. These were fed by cotton largely cultivated and harvested in the United States, principally by slaves of African origin. Without the capture, transport and mistreatment of slaves, it is said the British cotton-processing industry could not have grown as fast as it did and the Birth of Now would have been at least very different and might not have happened. We should inspect this possibility, noting that the British cotton-processing industry started with Indian cotton, with American cotton taking over as the main supplier only later in the century. Had America not been there, Indian and Egyptian supply might well have grown to meet demand.

It is a quirk of history-telling that the story of slavery is dominated by the transatlantic African slave trade from around 1650 until its after-effects faded in the late twentieth century. This focus is understandable, in that it was a huge and very wicked business, with around three-and-a-half-million slaves transported. It is also relatively recent and its political consequences in the USA are still raw. Slavery was the 'original sin' of the USA, the issue

---

22 As made clear elsewhere, the cotton trade was not essential to the Birth of Now. In textiles alone, the growth in the UK linen and wool trades may have been as large, or larger, than that in the UK cotton trade. However, they do not involve imported materials and so their growth was not measured and historians are forced to use figures for the growth of the cotton textile business because they have no others.

it denied its creating principles on, a sin punished by the brutality and bloodletting of the US Civil War.

Putting a context on it, however, the condition of slavery had been taken for granted in every culture until the Birth of Now[23]. There is no condemnation of it in the Bible, the Qur'an or any other religious writings before 1750. The Bible's New Testament is unequivocal in approving slavery.[xxii]

In the context of the savagery of the times, slavery did not stand out as especially bad until after the Birth of Now[xxiii]. Although the life experience of a slave on a sugar or cotton plantation may have been far from pleasant, it was probably better that that of, say, a sailor in Nelson's fleet. They, like the slaves, were often seized against their will (by the 'Press Gang', although some did volunteer under more or less duress), they were not free to leave the ship, they were subject to extremely poor living conditions – the space for a sailor's hammock (with the sailor in it) was eighteen inches high – wretched food, the hardest and most dangerous work and discipline of extreme severity, including flogging and the death sentence for insubordination – and that when not fighting or dying of scurvy! So slavery did not then stand out as unusually cruel.

The key reason why US slavery and its slave-trade precursor stand out so strongly is that they perpetuated these pre-'Now' standards of life and justice into the era after the 'Birth of Now'. Unpaid labour in grim conditions without any rights had been an unfortunate

---

23 It was declared illegal in England in 1772. There had been a number of previous legal bans on slavery in other places but none had any long-term impact and most were completely ignored.

but normal experience of life before 'Now'. Carried on into the post-'Now' period, it was a horror of cruelty and injustice for which there was no necessity whatever, only tolerable by pretending that humanity could be divided into two unequal species and it was OK to maltreat one of them. Our revulsion is, in part, at being exposed in a modern context to the sight of how unpleasant pre-'Now' life often was.

Slavery before 1800 had also been big business across the Mediterranean and in what is now southern Russia for centuries. The reason why villages were built in hills on the Mediterranean islands was not to keep their gold from pirates – they had none – but to keep their children from slavers. Millions had been captured by slavers and sold in the markets of Amalfi, Dubrovnik, Istanbul and elsewhere. After 1500CE Muslims from North Africa dominated the slaving business in the Mediterranean. They were only put out of business when Britain abolished the slave trade in 1807 and enforced its abolition on the seas.

After the Americas and the West Indies were discovered, sugar became a hugely valuable crop there and labour was required to grow and process it. (The absence of local labour was due to the wiping out of the indigenous people by European diseases accidentally introduced after Columbus' original voyage.) Originally, much of the labour required came from Britain and Ireland, from two sources: the transport of prisoners as slaves and a system of 'indentured labour'. Indentured labour was very close to slavery in all but name: the desperate signed up to work for a period of years, unpaid

– effectively for their food and drink. They were, like slaves, advertised for sale in the islands when they arrived. Unfortunately, British and Irish slaves and indentured labourers were poor value because of their appalling rate of death: around half in the first year and a significant proportion of the remainder every subsequent year.

The Portuguese had started the sugar business by growing cane on the island of Madeira, just off North Africa, and had found the locals on the nearby African shore keen to sell them slaves. This had proven a huge success for the Portuguese and the sugar business got under way in Madeira with local African slaves doing the cultivation. The Portuguese then carried both the sugar cane and slaves to Brazil. Here again, almost all the locals had died from European diseases and labour was needed, so African slaves, the same solution as for Madeira, seemed obvious. From there the idea of importing Africans, who were much less likely to die, spread to the colonies of other countries. In the West Indies they traded at much higher prices than slaves or 'servants' of European origin[24].

While the transatlantic slave trade was appalling:

- Europeans turned to African labour mainly because they could not keep Europeans alive long enough. Racist distinctions only came later when the

---

24 Generally European indentured labour or prisoners were referred to as 'servants' as it was not clear whether it was allowed to make Christians slaves. This rarely made any practical difference – the treatment of 'servants' or 'slaves' depending equally on their master. Female European transportees in the West Indies were encouraged, sometimes strongly, to have children by African men, as the offspring would be more robust and of higher value...

overwhelming number of African slaves on some islands was felt to need special measures to maintain the system of mastery.

- Europeans directly enslaved nobody, but paid for slaves from the African locals, although the demand they provided undoubtedly increased supply. The abolition of the slave trade caused severe disruption to the West African economy. Seventy years later, local chiefs in the Gold Coast (Ghana) were still lobbying for its restoration[xxiv]. Widespread slavery continued in Africa for at least a century after the British abolished the sea-born slave trade.
- The death rate of slaves on the passage across the Atlantic was appalling at about one in seven. However, the death rate of the (European) sailors was worse, at more than one in six.[xxv]

Slaver traders were wicked and cruel men and the slave trade was wicked and cruel. But, until the Birth of Now, the world was a wicked and cruel place and they fitted in. The abolition of the slave trade, in 1807, was the first step in the progress of humanitarianism that is one of the key features of the Birth of Now.

However, it is true that the abolition of the slave trade was but one effect of an, otherwise appalling, attack of smug superiority that hit the British at this period. Following the Birth of Now, the British and Irish middle and upper classes developed the absolute conviction that they were a superior people – a bit superior to continental Europeans and much superior to the peoples of other lands. To be fair to them, the facts at the time seemed to support this, with Europeans able to stroll around the world, dictating whatever they wanted to the local peoples – the Mongols had felt the same when they conquered all before them. The negative side of this was a haughty contempt for non-European cultures: the positive side, a feeling of responsibility for looking after these people; people who were felt to be less able to defend themselves. The abolition of slavery was a good side effect, racist arrogance a bad side effect. Another side effect was the development of missionary societies, which often seemed as much about promoting the superiority of the European people and way of life as about Christianity.

This hauteur reached its peak as late as 1899, as expressed in Kipling's poem 'The White Man's Burden':

> *Take up the White Man's burden-*
> *Send forth the best ye breed-*
> *Go, bind your sons to exile*
> *To serve your captives' need;*
> *To wait, in heavy harness,*
> *On fluttered folk and wild-*
> *Your new-caught sullen peoples,*
> *Half devil and half child*[25]

The resentment and embarrassment at Victorian 'Imperialism', so prominent in the late twentieth century, can be attributed far more to Marxist ideas combined with fury brought on by this insufferable attitude, than to the actual ills experienced[xvi].

---

25 The poem was written to encourage the USA to develop its own colonial empire in the Philippines.

Taken as a whole, it is difficult to see any form of empire as connected with the Birth of Now. No mechanism pushes itself forward as an obvious contribution of world-changing effect. The original American exploitation empires encouraged ocean sailing and provided the silver for the European trading posts in Asia but these made no contribution to the Birth of Now that we can discern. Even taking the most straightforward part of the Birth of Now, the Industrial Revolution, 'empire' made little contribution. Cotton was important but there is plenty of reason to believe that, if wool and linen were the only fabric base stocks, the industrialisation of the British fabric business would have been much the same. They, too, need spinning, carding, weaving, dyeing and finishing. In the early phases of the Industrial Revolution cotton came from (largely non-Empire) India, Iran and Egypt and America only took over because it became a cheaper source, not because it was the only source.

Before 1800, the only traditional empires ruled from Western Europe were in South and Central America and they were getting on for 250 years old and in decline by 1750. The colonial states of North America had traditional economies based on agriculture and remained dominated by agriculture, long after the Birth of Now. The chain of European trading posts fringing Asia and Africa was tiny, with the exceptions of the Spanish Philippines, the Dutch influence in parts of Indonesia and the British in Bengal, the last two both acquired reluctantly in the process of defending trading posts and enforcing mercantile monopolies. Political involvement in both was considered at the time to be a liability, rather than an asset, reluctantly taken on to enable trade.

Only after the end of the Napoleonic Wars were Europeans able to dominate any part of the world they chose to and this was as a result of the Birth of Now. There was a race, especially after 1850, to grab any land and declare it part of a European empire: the nationalistic phase of European imperialism. But nationalistic imperialism was a result of European, and especially British dominance, resulting from the Birth of Now, combined with the nationalistic belief that dominated European thinking at this period. If 'empire' made any contribution to the Birth of Now, it was only minimal.

ENLIGHTENMENT

The term 'The Enlightened', '*Lumieres*' in French, was first used in 1733 by some French writers to describe themselves and the people they admired. Since then, 'The Enlightenment' has come to mean writing of this period in science and mathematics, in political philosophy and in literature – allowing the stature of the scientific and mathematical advances of the period to rub off on its ethical and political writing. The ideas included under the heading of the Enlightenment were diverse but had two principle things in common: rejection of God or religion as a source of science or ethics and a belief in social progress and the improvability of mankind[xxvii]. In reality, the link between ideas from the sciences and those of the humanities was mainly through a few remarkable individuals, who each made lasting contributions to both mathematics/science and philosophy/literature. It is figures like Leibnitz, Descartes, Franklin and Goethe, whose genius crossed many disciplines, that provide some substance to the overall label 'Enlightenment'.

The most immediately influential aspect of the Enlightenment was its moral and political philosophy. Writers and thinkers like Hobbes, Spinoza, Locke, Rousseau, Paine and Kant developed a new approach to moral and political theories. These did not use God's will, or even his existence, to explain what was right and what was wrong. The idea that religion, specifically Christianity, could guide political thinking had been extensively explored over the previous two centuries. The ensuing bloodbath had persuaded many that looking to the Bible or church for political guidance was problematic. But this left an uncomfortable gap: if the rules of religion only guide our personal conscience, what can we use to guide our common, community decisions? What guidance is there for political morality?

Enlightenment thinkers came up with a number of ideas, including the concepts of the equality of humankind, the existence of rights and freedoms and the idea of 'nation-states' and the belief of nationalism. These were initially presented with much reasoning in support but, as the eighteenth century wore on, they came to be seen as self-evident, as the US Declaration of Independence puts it or, in Kant's version, compelling on us by their very nature. It is these beliefs that, more than any other factor, led to the United States War of Independence (1775-83). US citizens were not any freer or richer after the War of Independence than they were before. Nor were they freer or richer than the still 'colonial' Canadians. But the fact of independence in itself was a success for the principles of Enlightenment. A new state without a king or an aristocracy had been built, a state based on rational principles, a state that had shown that ideals could work in practice and that they seemed to work well. European thinkers were galvanised. Fired by the American success, Enlightenment principles led to three other major political developments before the end of the 1700s: the French Revolution of 1789, the Polish Constitution of 1791 and the Irish Revolt of 1796.

The French Revolution was the result of Enlightenment ideas affecting the French parliament, known as the 'Estates General'. Elections to this were finally called in 1789, after a gap of 175 years, to address the French King's perennial money problem. The idea that every aspect of life could do with a makeover of pure rationality swept through the assembled members. Cutting the story short, the ensuing shambles led, after some years and much loss of life, to a military *coup d'état* and a dictatorship under Napoleon. In the wars that followed, the philosophical principles of the Enlightenment were reduced down to simple gut nationalism. When Napoleon overreached himself by attacking Russia and was finally defeated, the older monarchy was restored, albeit very weakened. But the French Revolution happened in France well after the Birth of Now was already in full flood in Britain and Wallonia. Far from being linked to it, the French Revolution appears to have been an alternative to the Birth of Now. Both were the result of the changes over the century since religious wars ended, both changed the structures of power, although only temporarily in the case of the French Revolution.

The same idealism that fired the French Revolution inspired the writing of a grand, new Enlightened constitution for the Polish-Lithuanian commonwealth in 1791. This great state had long been a leader in European political thinking and the new constitution was a triumph of rational thought. But this liberal document united the chief Stealers of the area, the neighbouring monarchs as well as the Polish grandees; in a way nothing else could have achieved. An unheard-of combination of the Tsarina of Russia, the King of Prussia and the Kaiser of Austria, combining with the larger Polish aristocrats, worked to destroy not only the new constitution but also the country itself. It was split in three and the bits swallowed up by Russia, Prussia and Austria in 1795. Here again, no link between the effects of Enlightenment and the Birth of Now can be seen.

The same idealism, a desire for a rationally organised, non-sectarian state, arose in Ireland. Thinkers in Ireland saw their position as very similar to that of the American states – Ireland, like each of the American states, was only legally linked to Britain through having the same king, an increasingly notional concept. They felt that the British Government was increasingly trying to control and tax them and looked to follow the American success in shaking off the British government's pretentions. They hoped the French would support them, as they had supported the Americans, especially as Britain was already at war with Napoleon's France during the period. Open revolt broke out in 1796, supported by the landing of Napoleon's troops in Ireland in 1797, before being put down by the Irish Ascendency with great harshness and fizzling out into a more or less separate agrarian guerrilla campaign. The rebels had underestimated the power of the Ascendency in Ireland, the key role of religious issues – initially the revolt had been as anti-Catholic as the existing government – and the determination of the British Government, which was fired by already having to fight for its life against France.

Despite this, the British Government was appalled by the atrocities of the Ascendancy and the risk to British security their unpopular rule had brought to light. Thinking to repeat the successful merger of Scotland and England in 1707, Ireland and Britain were merged by votes in both parliaments into the United Kingdom in 1800. But abolishing the local rule, however benign the intention, at the dawn of the Europe-wide nationalist fervour that burst out after 1800, turned out to be a typical example of the misfortune that seems always to affect well-intentioned policies in Ireland.

So there were attempts in America, France, Poland and Ireland to turn Enlightenment ideas into realities of law and power. In France, Poland and Ireland, traditional forces largely overcame the new ideas. America, which was the Enlightenment pin-up, remained economically dominated by agriculture until well after the Birth of Now, not catching up with Britain's industrial development until after 1850. It also retained old habits, including slavery and very limited voting rights for many years, so Enlightenment ideas only went so far even there and seem unlinked to the Birth of Now.

On the contrary, it would appear, the Birth of Now started in countries that conspicuously did not invoke Enlightenment ideas. Britain was fiercely against Enlightenment ideas, in theory at least, and fought against governments that professed them in the USA and in revolutionary France. But the change from Stealer societies to Supplier societies had already largely occurred in the Netherlands and Britain (and Wallonia and north Ireland). These countries were already moving in the direction of greater social equality with very little theoretical consideration. The ideas of equality and the universality of human worth were not exclusive to the Enlightenment. Many saw these ideas as long-standing Christian religious ideals. The great explosion of Victorian philanthropy after the Birth of Now, for example, was motivated almost entirely by Christian, not Enlightenment, principles.

This was not the first 'Enlightenment' in history. The Arab Enlightenment of 750-*c.*900CE was an extraordinary burst of development and creativity in science and learning. When the caliphate, the rule of all Muslims, was taken over by the Abbasids in 750CE, it fired the Arabs and Persians with excitement. They saw the Abbasid family, related by blood to the Prophet, as true Muslims, finally replacing the cynical – and dubiously Muslim – Umayyad clan as leaders of the Faithful. In the ferment that followed, almost every aspect of learning was developed. A massive project of translation was started, with leading families competing to see who could claim the most distinguished record of sponsoring translations of Greek and Persian classics. There are many great names of literature and science in this period of Enlightenment. In mathematics, Indian numerals were adopted and used to develop new problem-solving techniques, an achievement recognised by our continuing use of Arabic names for 'zero', 'algebra' and 'algorithm'. Chemistry, itself a word of Arabic origin, was developed and we have Arabic terms like 'alcohol', 'aniline' and 'alkali' to illustrate the advances they made. Medicine, optics, astronomy, philosophy, religious scholarship and jurisprudence all took a huge leap forward. It was in this period that the foundation of the European revival of knowledge, 600 or so years later, was built. The Europeans got much of their knowledge transmitted through the Muslim kingdoms of southern Spain, who kept this Enlightenment tradition of scholarship long after it had expired in Iraq and long before it gained a foothold in Western Europe.

But all this enlightened thinking and writing was to have no practical effect in its home of Iraq: there were no lasting changes. The sack of Baghdad and killing the last Abbasid caliph in 1258 by the Mongols is normally blamed for the death of the Arab Enlightenment. But, in its centre, in Baghdad and in Iraq itself, it died much earlier than that. From around 900CE, a sense of profound decline and ruin set in, alongside political fragmentation, as the provinces became effectively separate kingdoms ruled by their Turkish governors. So bad was the decline that, long before the Mongol invasion, the irrigation canals of Iraq were no longer maintained, a failure of rule or society that had not happened there for over 2,000 years. Pure knowledge, 'enlightenment', had changed nothing, it seemed: civilisations collapse just as thoroughly with an Enlightenment as they do without one. (We will discuss the mysterious cause of the decline of Baghdad later, alongside other mysterious declines of rich and enlightened societies.)

But we may be taking too narrow a view of 'enlightenment', limiting it just to the period that proclaimed itself as such. Some date the start of the

European path to the Birth of Now much earlier, to the fall of Byzantium, in 1453. The fall of this great and old city, the capital of the last remnant of the Roman Empire, to the Ottoman Turks, caused a flight of Greek scholars to the west, bringing their ability to read the Greek classics with them. It is sometimes said that we can see the end of the Middle Ages around this time and a steady stream of European achievements, leading step by step to the modern world. This picture is of a longer Birth of Now, starting slowly after 1500, perhaps accelerating from 1750, but certainly a significantly longer process than the one we have been considering so far. Change, in this vision, started around 1500 with the combination of the 'Renaissance', the 'Reformation' and the 'Voyages of Discovery'.

Taking 'Renaissance' first – this word, which means the 'rebirth', was not introduced until the nineteenth century, long after the Birth of Now and, apart from art history, where it has a clear meaning, referring to the style and subject of paintings, it is unclear what was 'reborn'. Thinking did advance and there were a number of great men in Europe over the period of the 'Renaissance' before the thinkers claimed by the Enlightenment discussed above: Luther, Erasmus, Galileo, Kepler, Francis Bacon, etc. – as you would expect, across a whole continent and over a period of 250 years. But knowledge advanced also in medieval Europe through thinkers like Thomas Aquinas, Peter Abelard, Duns Scotus, William of Ockham, Roger Bacon, etc. Unlike art, it is not obvious that the style and subject of thinking underwent any major change. There was, however, a distinct change in north European architectural styles after 1620 or so, when Italian and Roman classical designs became fashionable. There is a connection between the revival of Roman ideas in both politics and architecture, but all this is really just the early days of the Enlightenment we have discussed above. Perhaps the idea that the world went round the sun, an idea developed during the period before the 'official' Enlightenment, also helped original thinking by changing the view of God, making him more distant. But, as we saw, the Enlightenment thinking built on this does not itself seem linked to the Birth of Now.

There was, however, a clear, if slow economic and cultural advance between 1500 and 1700 in Western Europe. But its highest achievement – outside pure scholarship – was only to return to a level of development and civilisation similar to that of the Roman Empire of 1,500 years earlier, although with fewer drains. Or to a level that matched the sophistication, if not the power, of the Ottoman Empire of the time under Suleiman the Magnificent (1494-1566). This small advance is best seen as a slow recovery from the constant disruption caused by the feudal system and from the impoverishment resulting from the Black Death, which recurred a number of times after its initial burst around 1350.

This very small advance (in comparison with the Birth of Now) was assisted by the economic growth caused by the flood of American gold and silver brought to Europe over this period. Perhaps also advances in the quality of cannon casting helped by swinging the balance of power away from local Stealers to chief Stealers, bringing more political stability. But before the

Birth of Now there was nothing special about European technology. Europeans were still trying to catch up with Asia in 1700 – to learn the technology of porcelain from the Chinese, for example.

The 'Voyages of Discovery', the second of the three reasons put forward as an earlier point of change before the Birth of Now, added new lands to the European picture of the world, much as the stories of Marco Polo's travels to China had around 1300. These discoveries were pioneered around 1500 in Portugal and Spain but neither of these countries was linked at all to the Birth of Now 250-300 years later. Indeed, by the time of the Birth of Now, both countries had fallen back badly in economic terms and were regarded as very backward by the standards of their northern neighbours, a position which was not to change for 200 years. The only perceptible link between these geographical discoveries and the Birth of Now is that they may have helped people to see the ancient thinkers as less well-informed because they did not know of these lands. This, in turn, may have reduced the awe they felt for them, encouraging wider thinking. Any other link between the 'Voyages of Discovery' and the Birth of Now, centuries later and in very different countries, is mysterious indeed. (The various encouragements these discoveries made to trade have been discussed under 'Empire', above, but did not link to the Birth of Now either.)

Finally, we turn to the Reformation. This is the name given for the split in the church in Western Europe between many varieties of Protestants and the Catholics, a change that allowed new ideas into religion. Many consider that the freedom to think independently of the Churches was essential to the Enlightenment and to the Birth of Now. They have the view that churches in Europe have always been conservative, especially in regard to science and technical advance. Two examples of this are often given. The first example is the 1612 papal declaration that Copernicus's theory that the earth went round the sun (published 1543) was heresy. The second example commonly given of the churche's anti-science stance is the religious objections, made in the second half of the nineteenth and in the early twentieth centuries, to Darwin's *Theory of the Origin of Species by Means of Natural Selection.*

However, these two examples are the *only* significant stories of a major group of Christians officially being anti-science[26] – although there are always a few 'fundamentalists' and tiny cults whose views on many topics, among them selected scientific ideas, are odd. Both cases show the Church against a theory, not against a technology. Both Copernicus's and Darwin's theories can be seen as diminishing or refuting God's role in the world. Although most believers did not see them as such, they can appear to be direct challenges to the importance of God in a way that a steam engine is not. Despite this, only a few churchmen ever attacked

---

26 In the Victorian period, there were many arguments about the age of the Earth that involved religious claims but these arguments were between different geologists, some of them churchmen. The churches themselves were not officially involved. As the evidence for an ancient Earth cumulated in the late 1800s, the short ecclesiastical dating was dropped without much of a fight.

either theory – many leading Christians accepted both theories with few problems, finding ways to fit them easily within their religious framework – as the Catholic Church itself did for seventy years after Copernicus (until Galileo started a direct fight about it with the Pope). So, yes, factions of some churches have reacted rather simple-mindedly against what they saw as theories directly attacking revealed faith. But there is only this very limited record of church opposition to scientific *theories* and none of mainstream Christians being anti-technology. There is no reason to think such opposition would suddenly have arisen had the church been more politically powerful around the period of the Birth of Now. The Christian Churches, while socially conservative in general, have never been broadly against technical progress. It is a remote possibility that, had the Churches been in a stronger phase at the Birth of Now, they might have declared the steam engine, for example, to be a product of Satan and encouraged destruction of machinery where it could be found. However, there is no reason to think this at all likely.

The Reformation certainly allowed new religious and philosophical ideas to be tried out. But it is fair to say that experiments with religious ideas in Europe from 1519 had stopped by 1698, when weariness with the endless slaughter of 200 years of religious wars became overwhelming. Politically and religiously these wars had changed very little.

But the decline of political Christianity after 1700 did have a powerful effect. Before 1700, issues of public morality had been unquestionably the business of the

Church. Attitudes to war, care of the needy, provision of education, etc. had been seen as very largely the Church's business, whether it took its role actively or not. This was one of the reasons why government at the start of the 1700s was able to be so minimal. But, even as the Church let it drop, there remained a demand for a public morality. Initially Enlightenment ideas filled the demand for a moral system but the failure of the Polish Constitution, the Irish Revolt and, above all, of the French Revolution, discredited political idealism, certainly in British eyes.

So the 'Renaissance', the 'Reformation', the 'Age of Discovery', the Enlightenment and the decline of political religion seem to have made only small contributions, if any, to the way the Birth of Now developed. But perhaps the longer-term effect of the Enlightenment, the development of a culture of science was its critical contribution to the Birth of Now?

The foundation of modern science as we know it, the creation of the structure on which all subsequent scientific development was built, is seen as part of the Enlightenment. Newton set up the possibility that the world could be comprehended scientifically, through calculation, hypothesis and experiment. Descartes refined the system for understanding the world mathematically. Linnaeus provided a structure for understanding living things and Lavoisier laid the basis for scientific chemistry. Brilliant as these achievements were, it is worth remembering that these were jewels, selected retrospectively, from a large pile of not-so-glittering scientific material and that the clarity of modern science arose only slowly as these achievements were built on over an extended period.

Apart from the use of geometry and clocks in navigation, science made little or no contribution to practical matters before the 1850s, well after the Birth of Now had started. While there was considerable overlap between those involved in manufacturing and transport and those interested in science, they were seen as very different activities. The celebrated Lunar Society of Birmingham, a monthly dining club that mixed leading scientists and industrialists of its day (1765-1813), had a spectacular membership of luminaries from both worlds. Yet there seems to have been no direct cross-fertilisation from science into industry at all but rather frequent mutual contempt between the practical men of industry and the academics of science. The early iron bridges and steam engines were built without engineering calculations. They had to be. The strength of the materials used was unknown and probably inconsistent, the ability of the joints to handle complex stresses unsure. Subtle calculations are pointless if the basic parameters are unknown. Like the soaring cathedrals of the Middle Ages, early bridges were designed on an engineer's judgement, including a guessed-at safety margin. Also, like the Gothic cathedrals, they occasionally fell down. There are a few early examples of mathematics applied to engineering but they are rare exceptions until well after 1800.

The same rules of expertise applied to practical chemistry. It was not by calculation and scientific understanding that gunpowder was made, but by applying expert experience to traditional processes. This was the approach to all chemical processes of the time. When large-scale steel-making processes were developed, an iron-master assessed the moment to turn off the air that was blasting through the molten iron, using the change in the colour of the flame to perfect the steel. We still use such processes widely in areas such as cooking, winemaking, distilling, ceramic manufacture and so on, where the complexity of the system requires a skilled judgement that is difficult to completely replace by scientific analysis of the contributing factors.

Although the scientific investigation and understanding of electricity progressed greatly in the first half of the 1800s, its only commercial use was in treating people for illness, a process championed by Franz Mesmer (1734-1815). It is now believed that these cures were entirely placebo and hokum. The first electric motors were, indeed, products of scientific research but they were not developed and put into industry until the 1870s, something like 100 years after the Birth of Now had started.

After 1850, links between academic scientists and men of business gradually started to have an impact on industry. An early example of the crossover – possibly the first example – was the academic development of mauveine (1856), an artificial purple dye that caught the eye of the fashion world and made its discoverer, William Perkin, rich and famous. Although he was later held as an exemplar of the best mixing of science and industry, Perkin initially left his academic job where he had discovered the dye, disgraced in academia by the grubby touch of commerce.

So, once the Birth of Now was well under way science took development forward. But it was not present at the Birth itself[27].

We have looked broadly at all the effects of Enlightenment without finding any direct link to the Birth of Now. It may be that the Birth of Now could not have happened in a society with rigid structures of religion and hierarchy, but these are the stamps of a Stealer society and that kind of society would have prevented the Birth of Now for other reasons as well. Supplier societies are inevitably looser then Stealer societies, with a wider spread of power and a more flexible social hierarchy. Such a looser society allows for both the development of intellectual ideas, such as the Enlightenment, and, independently, for the Birth of Now: but it is difficult to find any evidence that one caused the other or that there is any causal link between the Enlightenment, however widely considered, and the Birth of Now.

---

27 The frenetic development of electronic devices today is similarly unconnected to academic or traditional forms of science, although the key tools, the triode/transistor/silicon chip and the laser are based on scientific developments of the 1950s.

GEOGRAPHY

It has been suggested that both the Netherlands and Britain benefitted from good transport links by water and that these were crucial to the Birth of Now. The presence of almost limitless supplies of coal and plentiful iron ore has also been hailed as the critical ingredient in the 'industrial revolution' part of the Birth of Now.

Before the Birth of Now, land transport over any distance was exceedingly expensive. The only method normally available for carrying goods was by packhorse, as the roads were generally too poor for carts to travel any distance. In practice, it was unaffordable to carry anything overland this way except light and expensive goods, such as spices, fine cloth, precious metal objects and ornaments. Heavy goods, such as coal, wood, cement, bricks or stone and all but the smallest iron objects, had to travel by water. If water transport was not available for these, local materials had to be used instead. Because of these restrictions to land transport, some believe that access to water transport was essential for the industries that developed during the Birth of Now. For example, the ability to send coal to London by sea allowed the Northumbrian coal mining industry to develop in a way that would have been impossible had there not been a simple, navigable water connection between the two.

There are two reasons why water transport cannot have been crucial to the Birth of Now: Britain did not have better water-transport links than most of Europe and key industries of the period developed in areas with poor water transport.

The Netherlands and Wallonia did have an excellent water-transport network – partially man-made – but the same did not apply to Britain before the Birth of Now. The accessibility of Britain from naturally navigable water is not better than the accessibility of, say, Scandinavia, Italy or Greece from water. Before the river improvements and canals built during and after the Birth of Now, central England, where Birmingham was a key industrial hub, was completely unconnected to water transport. Yes, London, Belfast and Lille (in Wallonia) were ports, but so were Copenhagen, Marseilles, Hamburg, Istanbul and many other European cities that were not involved in the Birth. Early industrial towns like Manchester, Birmingham and Leeds were not ports and during the Birth of Now had, at best, access to only small rivers with virtually no capacity to carry goods. One of the effects of the Birth of Now was to radically improve water access to these industrial hubs as part of the ongoing process of improvements in all aspects of the economy. Water transport did then greatly help the further development of these towns, but they had to get started without it.

The early cotton mills of Lancashire, seen as the epitome of the 'Industrial Revolution', were largely in the Pennines, which had water*power* from fast-moving hill-streams but again had no water transport until it was brought in later. The nearest port to these towns, Liverpool, was around forty miles away, a very serious distance before rail, canals or metalled roads. Lyon's silk industry, an early French manufacturing business, is also landlocked. Although the Rhône river gives theoretical navigation access to and from the Mediterranean, it used to take three hard weeks of pulling for a barge to do the upstream journey from the sea to the city. In all these cases, if water access had been essential, the industries would have developed elsewhere. So good transport links cannot be an essential cause of the Birth of Now nor do they give a reason why it was focussed in Britain and Wallonia.

But the best network of water transport at the time was in the Yangtze Delta, where the main river links to multiple smaller delta streams, as the Rhine does in the Netherlands, but also to the Grand Canal, going all the way up to Beijing. The delta had a large population, excellent agricultural qualities and good transport links to fertile and productive areas. It also had a long history of development and, at this period, a stable and peaceful government under the Qing Dynasty at its peak. Exports were more or less prohibited but the size of the internal market in China, probably two or three times that of Europe, was enormous. Finally, there was ample coal, not in the immediate delta but in Anhui province, easily accessible up the navigable Yangtze River, and as close as, say, Newcastle is to London.

The Ganges/Brahmaputra Delta in Bengal also had excellent transport links, a substantial cotton processing industry – much larger than Britain's in 1750 – a large local market and excellent international links, although it lacked political stability. It, too, had easy access to coal just up the navigable Ganges River, an easier transport challenge than the sea passage from Newcastle to London.

It was unquestionably helpful to the Birth of Now that coal was readily available in huge quantities in Britain and Wallonia and a little in north Ireland. Were it not for ample accessible coal, England would have experienced a severe energy crisis as early as 1600, as wood for heating became scarce. This need not have been a complete show-stopper – for example, although Venice had no coal and little wood itself, it was still able to get close to the Birth of Now – but it would have posed a problem; but, then again, not too severe a problem. There is only a little coal near London, yet London was undoubtedly present at the Birth of Now. London's coal mostly came from hundreds of miles away, carried by sea from the Newcastle area. This coal could have been imported, with less convenience no doubt, from another country if necessary. After all, the coal of Wallonia is closer to London than the coal of Newcastle is anyway. Shortages of even essential and heavy materials were overcome during this period. The shortage of wood in Britain, for example, led to a shortage of the charcoal (baked wood) that was needed to make iron in this period. So iron was in short supply in England before 1750 when the coke (baked coal rather than wood) iron-making process started to increase iron production in Britain again. But this simply meant that, for several decades, large amounts of iron were imported from Sweden, which has endless woods available to make it with charcoal. Similarly, every ounce of cotton, seen by many as the fulcrum of the industrial Birth of Now, needed to be imported. This totemic industry, cotton processing, did not need coal any more than it needed access to water transport. The industrialisation of cotton textile production was done using waterpower, long before it switched partially to coal after 1800.

Coal had been available in Britain forever, so was hardly a trigger of the Birth of Now. Coal was also widely available and had long been used in countries that were completely uninvolved in the Birth of Now – China, for example, and China's economy had to catch up long after the Birth of Now in Europe. So the existence and availability of coal by itself is hardly a trigger for development. During the early phases of the Birth of Now, the role of coal, apart from providing domestic heat and heating ceramic kilns, was negligible. Coal could not be used at the time for many industrial processes needing heat, such as the brewing of beer or making iron, because of its pollutants. Power was supplied almost entirely by water and wind until well into the Birth of Now, with steam power coming in as part of the developing process itself, rather than a cause at the start. The earliest date at which it can be said that steam engines made a significant contribution to the power needed for industrial output is 1800 when it supplied around 10 per cent of industrial power in Britain. By then the Birth of Now was already in full flood.

Ample supplies of coal were undoubtedly helpful

as the Birth of Now progressed but, at the actual Birth, sometime between 1750 and 1800, the few steam engines that existed were used almost entirely for pumping water out of the coal mines themselves. So the presence of coal and iron ore was not a cause of the Birth of Now in Britain. Had neither been easily available locally, they would have been imported, as iron was until after 1850 and cotton was throughout the Birth of Now.

It is intriguing to speculate on what would have happened if Britain had been resting on a sea of oil, as Sumer/Iraq is, rather than coal. Oil shale deposits in the southern British county of Dorset have been used as fuel in Britain for centuries in a small way, but their remoteness from the main industrial centres, combined with the unpleasant and toxic smoke they gave off when burned, meant they were little used, although gas produced from the oil shale was used for town lighting as early as 1836[28]. Alternatively, what if the gas, later found near Britain under the sea, had been more widely accessible on land? Natural gas was known very early on in China and the Middle East and was exploited for cooking and heating in China more than 2,000 years ago. Perhaps there would have been claims of the essential contribution of oil and gas to the Birth of Now. But we digress.

Coal and iron were much more important for Wallonia, which was largely dependent on a single-industry iron economy. Almost as important was the excellent transport available with Wallonia's good river links to the Rhine and North Sea. It was iron, and the demand for arms

---

28   The oil shale was used in early manufacturing, to make alum in the
     1620s (until it was stopped by holders of the English alum monopoly).
     The area is now the site of Europe's largest onshore oil well.

made from it and transported to customers by water, that led to Wallonia's wealth at the Birth of Now. These two geographical factors, easy mineral and water access, coupled with the demand from incessant European wars, are the reasons why it was Wallonia, not any other region, that accompanied or followed so shortly after Britain and north Ireland in the Birth of Now.

Although the availability of plentiful and strong waterpower in the Pennines of England was an important step in the development of cloth-processing machinery, it was not essential. There is very little waterpower available in the fairly flat area of Wallonia and the Irish linen business developed very largely using handmade materials. Machinery capable of spinning good-quality linen came long after and was adapted from cotton processing machinery. The Birth of Now would not have been stopped by the absence of the Pennines.

But, more fundamentally, the thinking about coal, iron and water transport and waterpower as primary causes is based on the presupposition that the Birth of Now is the same as the Industrial Revolution; that is, the start of the change was the move from hand processes to machine processes in manufacturing. It also rests on an exaggerated view of the contribution of the cotton processing industry to the Birth. While cotton processing did grow hugely, so did many other less well-recorded businesses. Cities like Birmingham, Glasgow and London grew just as vigorously as the cotton capital, Manchester, despite having little, if anything, to do with cotton processing. These purely industrial developments in coal, iron, waterpower and transport seem to be an effect of the Birth of Now not its cause. Experience would suggest that, in general, manufacturing growth and manufacturing innovation respond to demand, rather than lead it. It would, for example, be unconventional to suggest that advances in pneumatic-tyres manufacture led to the twentieth-century boom in automobile sales, rather than that demand for vehicles led to growth in tyre sales and the development of improved products.

The final aspect of geography that is mentioned as a cause of the Birth of Now is that Britain is an island and, as a direct consequence of this, suffered virtually no destruction from wars in the 1700s. But many other countries did not suffer war damage either – Sweden, for example. Nor did most of France suffer any war damage before the French Revolution in 1789; only the very north-east of France suffered from war on its land. Wallonia, on the other hand, suffered armies crossing it with something close to frequency during the century. While the relative political stability of Britain built confidence that helped the long-term investment needed to build canals and factories, it was not a unique condition. Being an island was not a cause of the Birth of Now – although, as we will see later, the combination of Britain being an island and being at war, did keep many of the developments made during the initial period of the Birth isolated during the Napoleonic period as the Birth of Now developed.

Because Britain and Ireland are islands, there was a concentration in defence expenditure on the hi-tech Navy rather than a low-tech army. This also helped keep defence expenditure within the countries' economies. While this, too, could be a contributory factor helping the Birth of Now, it is not a mechanism for starting it.

There appears to be nothing unique in the geography of Britain, north Ireland and Wallonia that can be put down as the cause of the Birth of Now. There were some undeniably convenient factors in water transport, coal and access to waterpower, but these were available elsewhere in the world in only slightly different mixtures; some elements better, some not so convenient. Geographical factors helped and shaped the development of the Birth of Now but did not cause it.

INVENTION

Few myths are more embedded in our culture than the legend of 'The Inventor' and his 'Inventions'. The legend is that brilliant – and sometimes maverick – individuals drive progress by devising new ideas for practical devices: inventors make inventions.

Many people believe, loosely, that inventions by individuals were a key part of the Birth of Now, possibly its single most important cause. Children are taught lists of the inventions that moved mankind into the modern age: printing, the 'spinning-jenny', the steam engine, internal combustion, flight. Each invention is presented as the beginning of a new chapter in the story of development and their inventors as heroic figures: Gutenberg, Abraham Darby, Watt, Compton, Edison, the Wright Brothers and more. But, most emphatically, inventors are presented as the heroes, the men (they all seem to be male) who 'won' the Industrial Revolution, rather as a general is said to have won a battle.

But, studied with care, no major 'invention' has arisen from a process anything at all like the classic 'invention' story. Every 'invention', on examination, turns out to be a development driven by external events and by changes in demand[29]. This also means that every 'invention' turns out to have several people or teams working in parallel on solving the same problem or meeting the same demand. It also means that the 'invention' is made, sometimes in slightly different forms, by several of these teams or individuals at around the same time. The choice of whose name goes down in legend as the 'inventor' is often due to flukes of recording or to one individual, sometimes someone minimally involved, scheming to get the credit or patent revenues. These two factors, chance and PR, have had more effect on the decision about who ends up being named as 'the inventor' then the importance of the contribution they made to the 'invention'. But these are challenging assertions and an affront to a much-loved popular belief so we need some strong support to justify it.

Because it is impossible to go through the history of every 'invention', we will look only at the stories and the histories behind what can be seen as the four 'biggest-ever' inventions: the wheel, printing, the steam engine and the light bulb. First, we will review the legends that are commonly linked to each of these 'inventions', and then we will look at the actual history of each 'invention'.

The Wheel

In legend, the 'invention' of the wheel is seen as an anonymous, but crucial, step towards civilisation. It is said

---

29 The word 'invention' is used here to mean a complete, new working device. Theories are often devised by single individuals (Newton, Darwin, Einstein, etc.) and small advances and improvements on existing machinery are also often developed by one person.

that the wheel was a breakthrough development, moving on from the earlier use of tree-trunks as rollers. Rollers were used, for example, in moving the stones that built Stonehenge and the Pyramids – the wheel not having been invented at this stage. The Incas and Aztecs of Pre-Colombian America did not 'invent wheeled transport' and this shows how backward their civilisations were compared to the Europeans; a backwardness that explains why they were so easily defeated by the more advanced Spanish. These are bits of the legend we need to examine.

In reality, wheels are of little use in transport without a fairly smooth surface to travel on – a good road. Anyone who has bicycled over rough ground will be able to confirm the difficulty. On top of this, most draught animals can actually pull less weight up a steep hill than they can carry on their backs. Even on gentle hills and with a good surface, they can have problems because of slipping. Bringing carts down hills also presents considerable problems and dangers using unsophisticated braking systems. So, for much of history, carts – and their wheels – have had only a limited use. Goods transported across land were carried on the backs of pack animals. Carrying people in carts or carriages was difficult and appallingly uncomfortable over anything but the, very rare, smooth road. Anyone who could manage it walked or rode a horse or, for short distances, used a Sedan chair carried by two coolies or footmen. In addition, many alleys in towns were too narrow for carts, so they were limited to the main roads.

So, until the railways and the improvements in roads that followed the Birth of Now, wheeled vehicles were only important in large towns and their surroundings and only then when times were prosperous, the town was in a flat area and there were enough good-quality roads to be found. Frequently, poor road surfaces meant that such carts as existed could carry only a limited weight and needed huge wheels to enable the animals pulling them to get over the ruts and stones in the few places where they could be used at all. Often the main benefit of a cart, compared to a pack mule, was that it was easily loaded and unloaded for local city deliveries. Wheeled vehicles were very important in ancient Sumer and in classical Rome, but they almost vanished during the darker ages of Europe and the Middle East. By the sixteenth century, however, town growth and prosperity in Europe meant that vehicles once again became important in the cities, but even as late as 1698 there were only three stagecoach routes in England. The idea of regular coach travel only got under way after the mail coach was started in 1785, around the period of the Birth of Now.

So the wheel does not represent a breakthrough but an idea that had a limited, specific use; a use it was put to in every situation where its benefits could be applied – not, for example, in moving the vast stones of Stonehenge across rough country, where rollers were far better. The idea that the wheel is a difficult concept to envisage requires the creation in imagination of a super-dull race of humans. These imaginary dullards never stuck a twig through the middle of a large leaf and twizzled it or rolled it along the ground. Only in this context can the wheel be seen as an 'invention'.

Pre-Colombian Americans did know about the wheel, as numerous remaining, beautifully-made toy animals on wheels and calendar wheels from the region show. But several factors made carts (even) less useful in the civilisations of America than Eurasia. There was no horse or ox in America to pull them; the llama is the largest Native American draught animal. The principal civilisations of pre-Colombian America were based in the high Andes, with its stepped roads, or in the watery lowlands. In both these environments, the cart could be of minimal use. So the likelihood is that wheeled carts were not much used, not because Pre-Colombian Americans were an intensely dim people, but because they were not much use there.

The wheel is an obvious concept with very limited use until smooth paved roads and powerful traction is available, not a breakthrough 'invention'.

Printing

Legend holds that the 'invention' of printing by Johannes Gutenberg (or at least his use of moveable type) ushered in the modern world of learning. He used his invention to print the Bible in 1455. This was a central contribution to both the artistic Renaissance and religious Reformation (which started only sixty or so years later) because, for the first time, ordinary people got to read both the classical authors and the Bible for themselves.

Turning to reality, the idea that printing was, in any

practical sense 'invented' at all requires us to ignore the obviousness of the concept of printing. We have to call on the same race of super-dullards that failed to envisage the wheel and, it turns out, they still do not exist. Using an object with a raised or incised pattern to repeatedly impress/emboss an image or place ink on a substrate and mass-produce a pattern is a simple idea to anyone who has put a wet foot on a dry rock.

Seals, for just such use, creating endless repeats of words and patterns, were common as far back as the first writing itself. Some of them, 'cylinder seals', were rolled onto a flat surface, exactly as a modern gravure-printing cylinder is. We have collections of them from the early years of Sumeria, simultaneous with or possibly even pre-dating the first freehand writing. They continued to be used in all the ancient empires of the Middle East, the Assyrians and the Persians, thousands of years before Gutenberg. Rather than using ink to make marks in a contrasting colour on paper, they embossed writing repeatedly onto soft clay tablets that were then hardened by drying or firing; but that's how they wrote everything in that region.

Moreover, printing with moveable type on paper using ink – exactly what Gutenberg is credited with inventing – was common in China and Japan from the eighth century onwards. The Chinese made much less use of moveable type than the later Europeans, simply because it worked less well with Chinese script, with its thousands of characters, than with the twenty-six letters of the Latin alphabet; but they did use some. The role of printing was not trivial either. The Empress Shotoku of Japan had a million copies of four prayers printed in 770CE – quite a few of them still in existence. It was a substantial industry during the Chinese Song Dynasty around 1000CE, including printing paper money. So not 'invented' several hundred years later in Europe, then.

The story in Europe is of the period of recovery from the devastation of the Black Death of 1350CE. This caused substantial social changes and helped loosen both aristocratic and religious authority. Together with the dislocation brought by the 'Great Schism', the split of the Western European Church into two, each with its own pope, the economic recovery took a more middle-class turn, less church-and-chivalry, than the earlier period of the High Middle Ages. A gradual increase in literacy led to the growth of writing in local languages, not just in Latin. At the same time, papermaking began to be developed in Europe – paper had been unknown there earlier. The technology of papermaking was brought slowly from China, via the Moorish kingdoms of Spain. Affordable paper is critical to making printing commercially viable and, as it became more accessible[30], printing could develop. Initially, printing used woodcuts to make multiple copies of pictures but increasing sales, more written material and more publications made it desirable to reuse individual letters, rather than recarve them every time – again a development hardly requiring an inspirational bolt-from-the-blue. All

---

30   By a quirk of fate, printing was more difficult in Europe than in the East. Paper in the East was developed for brush writing, and so was soft and absorbent. An inked stone or woodcut pressed onto it by hand makes a clear impression. The harder, less absorbent paper, developed in Europe for pen writing, required hard printing pressure – generally with a screw-press – to make a clear impression onto it.

these developments supported each other from about 1400. One of the areas where printing first got under way in Europe and where much of the process was developed and streamlined was in the mass-production of 'indulgences'. These were bits of paper the Church got printed that could be bought to reduce the time in purgatory between death and being allowed into heaven. Gutenberg, who had earlier made money as a printer of indulgences[xxviii], was very much out of the developing mainstream of printing in his financially ill-advised attempt to print the whole Bible, which was still vastly too expensive for all but the wealthiest people and churches. The mass-market for print was driven by large-scale sales of small, cheap, often scandalous popular works – pamphlets, small sections of the Bible, summaries and excerpts of classical writers, etc. – sold at street corners by lairy types who could avoid the authorities by running off. We still call the more respectable type of bookseller a 'stationer' because they used to have fixed (stationary) premises and were unable to sell the subversive, libellous and pornographic pamphlets that the street-corner boys could. Sadly, this picture is too complex to compress into a quick and satisfying tale and Gutenberg, who first got the whole Bible printed in one edition, is selected and remembered as the 'inventor of printing', rather than as an unsuccessful publisher. Such a simplification of the process and selection of one individual as the 'inventor' also comes in the legend of the development of the steam engine.

The Steam Engine

The story of the invention of the steam engine has several levels of sophistication, starting with the child's story of the infant James Watt being inspired by watching a kettle lid bounce up and down as it boiled. This is wrong in every possible way. But there are much more sophisticated versions of the steam engine invention legend.

Probably the most sophisticated legend starts with the story of Hero of Alexandria, a Greek-speaker who lived, according to different sources, around 400BCE, 60CE, 100CE or 400CE – it doesn't really matter which[xxix]. He developed a steam-powered spinning toy that never got beyond a novelty because, it is said, the Greeks had slaves and so did not need mechanical power. For some reason it was not for at least another thousand years that the idea of an engine powered by steam was revived. The first serious step was with an idea for a steam-powered pump, developed and patented by Thomas Savery (1698). Several examples of this were built but it was limited and unreliable. Thomas Newcomen, the legend continues, built the first real, working steam engine, in around 1710, using it to lift water out of Cornish tin mines. Power was produced from the vacuum you get when a cylinder filled with steam is condensed by a spray of water. The vacuum can then suck a piston up or down and that is where the power comes from.

Newcomen is politely sniggered at for missing at least one obvious point. Some people feel that

Newcomen missed the point that, when you boil water in a container, it generates a *pressure* that can provide more power than any condensation vacuum (and you can still use the condensation vacuum afterwards, in addition to the pressure power). Others realise that, with the limited technology of the time, a pressure engine would be sure to explode sooner or later, whereas a vacuum engine limits the stress on the machine – it cannot create more stress then normal atmospheric pressure provides. Furthermore, if it fails, it implodes (breaks inwards) not explodes. These people feel that Newcomen boobed in not having a *separate condenser.* Every injection of water in Newcomen's design cooled the cylinder, which wasted a huge amount of the heat, and the engine was hideously inefficient. James Watt was the man who realised – in a flash – the benefit of a separate condenser when he was a young lab engineer repairing a model of the Newcomen engine at Glasgow University (he told this story himself). He forged a partnership with the Birmingham iron-master, Matthew Boulton, to produce his design of steam engine. Watt's genius was such that he developed many other related inventions, such as the 'Watt governor', spinning balls that raise a safety valve if they spin too fast, the 'Watt linkage', etc. as well as doing research into heat and power that built the groundwork of the science of thermodynamics. This mechanical genius was combined with Bolton's money and connections and the Industrial Revolution was born!

Turning to the actual history of the steam engine, we

can see that there was little need for steam engines before 1800. Far from animals being the only source of power in Britain, watermills were widespread. *The Domesday Book*, listing the properties of Britain 700 years earlier, lists 5,624 watermills or about one for every fifty people in England. These were often sophisticated devices, including tidal mills in low-lying areas. Windmills were also known but, being less reliable and powerful, were used mainly in flat areas or chalk hills that had no streams.

In addition to their most famous task of milling flour from grain, watermills were used for every industrial process, including hammering ingots into sheet metal as well as powering lathes and other industrial machinery. Long before the Industrial Revolution most larger-scale power in Britain came from non-animal sources. The cotton processing industry arose largely in east Lancashire, not because of coal, but because the high rainfall there, combined with the steep Pennine valleys, made for plentiful waterpower. In 1800, eighty-eight years after the first industrial steam engine started working, it is estimated that more than ninety per cent of the non-animal power generated in England was still provided by water and wind[xxx]. Even today, you can see the line of mills along the stream at the bottom of the valleys in many Lancashire Pennine towns.

However, the need for a machine to pump water out of mines in the 1700s was acute and, as demand for coal for heating rose, so the need for pumping increased. On top of the need to remove water, these coal mines had a problem by-product – small coal fragments and dust, known as 'slack', which they could not sell. This just piled up near the mine-head, so any machine that burned the slack and lifted water out of the mine was going to be attractive. As the slack was waste anyway, efficiency was not an important consideration. So there was no doubt about the commercial potential for a 'fire engine' if one could be made to work.

But the technology of the day was not accurate enough to allow a metal piston to work in a metal cylinder. Bad fit and rough finish meant the piston was either too loose and let the vacuum escape, or it was too tight, and the piston stuck, immoveable, in the cylinder. Savery's earlier steam pump (for which he got a patent Newcomen had to license from him later) had cleverly avoided the need for a piston by applying the vacuum directly to the water to be pumped, but it was too limited to be of much use[31]. There were also several other one-off attempts by other people (including the ever-present Leibnitz) to build a working steam engine and some of these may have worked in a limited way. The principle of a steam engine was easy and obvious: making it work commercially was the challenge Newcomen overcame. He used the vacuum created by condensing steam in a cylinder as his approach to power generation, as any pressure-based device would certainly have failed explosively with the technology of the day. Newcomen then solved the problem of sealing the cylinder – apparently after a great deal of research – by surrounding the piston with a leather seal, kept soft with water. Keeping the seal wet

---

31   A directly applied vacuum can only lift water about ten metres.

meant keeping the cylinder itself cool and wet, so the water injected to create the vacuum was also necessary to keep the seal wet. In 1712 Newcomen was able to install the first working steam engine at a coal mine in the West Midlands. Newcomen was no fool; he solved a very tricky problem and his engines were widely used for many decades. Gradually, as they became reliable, standard equipment, they started to be bought by people mining things other than coal, including some of the tin mines of Cornwall, and by one or two mills. At these locations, the issue of their poor efficiency started to become important because the coal to power them had to be brought from elsewhere at considerable cost. (The idea that the first use of steam engines was in Cornish tin mines appears to derive simply from the fact that Newcomen came from the neighbouring county of Devon.)

So Newcomen solved a difficult technical problem and created a safe, working machine with the crude technology available and was very far from a fool. On the other hand, it could be argued that James Watt *was* a fool. His idea of a separate condenser theoretically saved a lot of energy but it meant that the power cylinder was kept hot, preventing the cylinder seal from staying wet and it needed to stay wet for the leather to seal the cylinder. The idea of a separate condenser seems as obvious as the reason why it would not work. Newcomen's engines had been extensively adapted and improved over the previous fifty years, but no one had built a separate condenser system, because, as Watt was to find out, it stopped the engine working. The alternative explanation is that all the engineers, on all the Newcomen machines, in all the fifty or so years they had been around, had all been descended from the same intellectually challenged group as the pre-wheel and pre-printing crowd. Despite the problem of the cylinder-seal not working, Watt managed to get substantial backing for his idea of a separate condenser (1765) from an ever-optimistic Glasgow industrialist called John Roebuck, and was able to build several test rigs. But his engines failed to work because he could not get their pistons to seal.

Watt then gave up on steam engine development and became a surveyor and civil engineer to provide himself with an income. But, despite having no working machine, he and Roebuck had spent a great deal of money in London and had got a patent on the idea of '*a new method of lessening the consumption of steam and fuel in fire engines*' in 1769. In his patent he did not provide drawings and avoided specific descriptions, so covering a huge area of possible innovation. Such a wide and vague patent would not be allowed now for multiple reasons.

Three years later, the Birmingham iron-master, Matthew Boulton, accepted Roebuck's two-thirds' share of this patent in lieu of a debt Roebuck owed him. Bolton's friend, John Wilkinson, had a new development of a cannon-boring machine that could be adapted to create much smoother, tighter cylinders that did not need the water sealant/lubricant for a piston to seal. This new development made the previously dud idea of the separate condenser a working possibility and with Watt, still the owner of the other one-third of the patent, Boulton set up a joint venture to make such machines.

There was a long-established market for (Newcomen) steam engines, some of them now far away from coal mines. These were crying out for more efficiency and the separate condenser engines used around a quarter of the coal for the same power output as a Newcomen machine. Boulton and Watt's first separate-condenser commercial machine was installed in 1776, eleven years after Watt's 'invention' of the separate condenser.

Boulton and Watt spent a great deal of time and money persuading Parliament to extend the patent up to 1800. Watt also spent a great deal of time on preventing others (including Wilkinson) using a separate condenser, since, now that it was possible to make such machines work, several people wanted to progress the idea. (Watt was much more aggressive than Boulton in seeking the prosecution of 'infringements'.) With their monopoly they tried to extract huge profits by charging customers a royalty to use their engines, rather than selling them. This is why Watt did so much work on energy efficiency – so that he could change his customers a proportion of the cost of the coal they saved using his machine, not for the benefit of mankind. Boulton and Watt did not develop the crucial next stage; the use of steam pressure. This was a far more important development than Watt's earlier adaptation of the, by then, traditional Newcomen vacuum engine. Newcomen-type vacuum engines had to be vast to be at all efficient and got even bigger with Watt's adaptations. Steam-pressure engines could be much smaller and lighter than vacuum or 'atmospheric' engines, so they could be used to power locomotives and ships, bringing on a complete new phase of development. Watt prevented his chief engineer, William Murdoch, from pursuing this line of development and injuncted Richard Trevithick, who did pursue it, for breaching his wide patent. As a result Trevithick and others were only able to market a pressure engine after Boulton and Watt's patent expired in 1800[32].

Watt never claimed to invent the centrifugal 'Watt governor'. It had been in use in watermills for at least 100 years[xxxi]. However, Watt did benefit from an extensive biography by one JP Muirhead published in 1858, long after everyone who knew him had died. This cast him, in two-volume detail, as the patron saint of steam power and possessed of every known virtue. It has been used as the source on Watt's life ever since.

The invention of the steam engine is the key symbolic idea of the Industrial Revolution. But it never happened. The idea of the steam engine was, literally, ancient. Before Newcomen, a number of limited working models had been made. The steam engine was developed in stages, prompted by rising demand and facilitated by collateral improvements in materials. The demand for the engines arose for the first time with Britain's runaway demand for heating coal, coal which had to come from increasingly deep and wet mines. This demand was met by Newcomen's

---

32 The pressure engine became possible at about this time because the advances in metallurgy etc. made it less certain to explode. Trevithick was simply the first to produce such a machine; others were very close behind. They did still explode from time to time.

solving the problem of the piston-seal. After fifty years, and many incremental improvements to Newcomen's original design, Wilkinson's cannon-borer made a dry-seal possible and so a hot cylinder and separate condenser. Watt's premature development of this concept had failed but he had a patent and he was able to manipulate this to get an extended monopoly on the more efficient engine this made possible. Later it became possible to use the increasingly high-quality iron available to make a pressure steam engine, again a concept that is obvious in theory but difficult to make safe. This was efficient enough, and light enough to be used in transport, creating another step in the revolution after the Birth of Now.

Getting the publicity right has often been important in getting the credit for 'inventions'. In the early days of the Birth of Now, the one bit of writing that clearly identified the 'inventors' was the patent. Many of those presented in histories as 'inventors' were those who were first granted patents. But the process of patenting was in its infancy, and patents were granted to applicants who were prepared to pay; there was then no checking that concepts were either original or could work. Patents were also allowed that were so loosely described as to cover a wide range of possible ideas – Savery's patent was for '*A new invention for raising of water and occasioning motion to all sorts of mill work by the impellent force of fire*' and had no further description or diagrams! Watt's was similarly vague.

Between 1700 and 1780 fewer than eleven patents a year were issued in England, many of them completely flawed by later standards, but they remain the clearest written record. At the time there was much debate as to whether these patents justly rewarded ingenuity or provided destructive monopolies for often unoriginal and, sometimes, stolen ideas. The jury is still out on this.

That 'invention' itself does not stimulate industrial revolutions can be seen in the example of knitting. In 1589, 200 years before the Birth of Now, William Lee of Nottingham attempted to get a patent on a knitting machine that greatly speeded up the process of knitting stockings[33]. But Lee's machine did not, at the time, lead to any industrial revolution and his business failed. The knitting frame continued to be used in his native East Midlands, however, and over the years, improvements were made to the design. But it was not until 200 years later, as the Birth of Now got underway in Britain that this, now ancient, device, with several key but largely anonymous modifications, powered the growth of the industry and populations of the great knitting towns of Leicester, Nottingham and Derby. After 200 years, the Birth of Now had put power behind the machine, not the other way around.

The Light Bulb

Another master of publicity, Edison, is often credited with the 'invention' of the very symbol of 'Invention',

---

33   There is evidence that several stocking-knitting frame ideas were around in Nottingham and elsewhere at the time but William Lee is credited with its 'invention' because he presented it to Queen Elizabeth in his attempt to get a patent.

the light bulb. This story has been debunked several times recently but it is worth summarising. Thirty-eight years before Edison was even born, Humphry Davy had demonstrated that running electricity at a high enough current to arc across a gap between carbon rods produced an intense light. Carbon arc lights were used long before Edison in special places and as novelties. But their intense brightness, fragility and short life made them impractical for everyday use.

People quickly discovered that a thin wire heats up and glows when electricity is passed through it – every time a short circuit is made in error, this tends to happen. The problem is that the heated wire melts or burns almost immediately. The idea of getting a thin wire (known as a filament) made with a high melting-point substance so it would not melt and putting it in a glass bottle of inert gas so that it would not burn as it would in air, came to many people, equally quickly. That such a product would have a market to replace candles and the relatively difficult, dangerous, smelly and very hot gaslight was just as obvious. But it proved challenging to make a light bulb that would last. Carbon has the highest melting point of any element and a carbon filament bulb was demonstrated in 1840 – still well before Edison was born – but lasted for only a few, carefully managed, hours. Decades later, and several teams were still on the case, including those of Joseph Swan in England and Thomas Edison in the USA. Both arranged demonstrations of the products their teams had developed, Swan in Newcastle in 1878 (or early 1879), Edison in New

York later in 1879. Both still used carbon filaments, as did the bulbs of several other teams. For all their efforts, both only achieved a few extra hours of life for their bulbs – forty years after the initial demonstration of a carbon filament bulb – and neither bulb was ready for everyday household use, although some wealthy households and stores adopted them. Edison had spent huge sums of money but failed to achieve his objective of a widely useable, domestic light bulb – or even to improve significantly on an idea that was demonstrated before he was born. But Edison was a superb huckster, so is on the record for many people as the 'inventor' of the light bulb[xxxii].

The everyday, practical light bulb arrived with the development of the completely different filament made of a high melting-point metal, Tungsten, originally produced by Sándor Just and Franjo Hanaman in Hungary in 1904[34] - not that this stopped the (U.S.) General Electric Company getting an American patent for the tungsten filament bulb in 1913, although it was withdrawn later when challenged.

The 'inventions' we have looked at were selected on the basis that they are the best known and seen as the most important 'inventions'. Yet they all turn out not to depend on any individual, brilliant or not. It seems that this is, indeed, true for all 'inventions' and inventors. If the particular well-known name had not somehow got attached to a device as the 'inventor', there are generally five or more others,

---

34   This, in turn, depended on the separate development of the process of 'sintering' which enables fine wire to be produced without having to melt the metal.

close candidates, often with better claims to making original contributions.

In mathematics and science there *are* individual breakthroughs, but these breakthroughs are in ideas and theories, not 'inventions' – they are not gadgets that work. Einstein made several individual breakthroughs in 1905 but they were all theoretical; the working device that one of these papers pointed to, the atomic bomb, required forty years and a huge team to create it.

'Inventors' and their 'inventions', then, are legends, with as much relationship to reality as most legends. 'Inventions' are not the reason for the Birth of Now; or for anything else.

TECHNICAL DEVELOPMENT

If the idea of the single maverick inventor is a myth, then surely the inventor story is easily replaced with the more complex but no less powerful story of step-by-step technical development? Was the Birth of Now principally caused by the acceleration of technical development? Perhaps it just needed to tip over a point, like a roller coaster at the top of its climb, to run away on its own. After all, since the Birth of Now, development has continued, feeding back on itself again and again. After thousands of years with very little innovation, it seems that a button is pressed or a point reached, then development starts and never stops. Innovation is not confined to technical matters, either. Government becomes more professional and moves, in stages, towards votes for all. Legal and financial structures develop, education becomes more widespread, compassion becomes institutionalised, arts revolutionise. Perhaps, all that was needed to get the ball rolling was a very little shove in the right place and right time, and development, starting slowly, gathered momentum and took off?

It seems, though, that this interlinked improvement

only works if most of the economy is taking part in this self-sustaining change at the same time. One or two rapidly developing industries will quickly grind to a halt on their own. We can see this because we have a remarkable example of one industry that sought to change all on its own, long before the Birth of Now.

Before 1500 ocean sailing – that is, sailing far from land – more or less did not happen (apart from Zheng He's famous, but one-off, Chinese voyages). Sailors were understandably unwilling to leave the sight of land if it were avoidable. On their normal business, European sailors had little need to go far out of the sight of land before 1500.

After Christopher Columbus (1492), Vasco da Gama (1498) and Ferdinand Magellan (1521) and others, ocean sailing was not only the most exciting venture open to a Western European man of courage; it was also fantastically profitable. Asian spices, American gold and West Indies sugar fuelled new and lucrative industries for European countries. For the next 300 years building, sailing and managing ocean-going ships became the hi-tech industry of the age, attracting free enterprise and official talent alike to its improvement. It was the obsession of the two most advanced economies before the Birth of Now, the Netherlands and Britain – both for trade and for their navies. Detailed improvements were made in almost every aspect of ship construction and management. New materials were sourced and new techniques adopted. For example, the new material, hemp, was taken up and used to make much improved rope, gimbals were devised to hold compasses flat, keel designs were modified, sail configurations improved and so on. There were side effects of this new business, such as the improvement in charting, the development of accurate time-measurement, the start of the joint-stock company (with the East India Companies of the Netherlands and England), much improved geometric tables (for navigation), better optics for telescopes and much more. The British Navy Office broke new managerial ground by organising the supply for hundreds of ships and thousands of men away at sea for months at a time, keeping them alive and dangerous with food, water, equipment and munitions.

Yet, despite all this, the startling observation is how little changed. Columbus' ship of 1492, the *Santa Maria*, and Nelson's flagship of 1805, the *Victory*, are recognisably the same basic thing, despite being three hundred years apart. Yes, *Victory*'s sailing quality was better and it was much larger (about thirty-five times the displacement of the *Santa Maria*[35]), but the *Victory*, like the *Santa Maria*, is still a three-masted wooden sailing ship, armed with muzzle-loading, iron cannons down its sides. Naval experts may huff and puff about all the other differences that there were between them but have to be silent when the 300 years between these two is contrasted with the 101 years that separate *HMS Victory* at Trafalgar from *HMS Dreadnought* of 1906. This was an all-iron/steel battleship, powered by steam turbines, equipped with torpedoes and breach-loading, twelve-inch guns with effective distances measured in miles, housed in hydraulically-

---

35 But only about 50 per cent larger than Zheng He's nine-masted flagship of 1405.

powered, swivelling turrets. Apart from being pointed at the front end, it had absolutely no resemblance to the *Santa Maria* or the *Victory*. So, in the 300 years before the Birth of Now, despite the huge pressure, interest, profitability and strategic benefit of improved ocean sailing, far, far less progress was achieved than the improvement of the hundred or so years after the Birth of Now.

It was the continuing cross-fertilisation of change between different industries and their links to and from social and political advances that powered the Birth of Now. The cross-links are everywhere. We have seen how new military cannon-borers made Watt's engine work; we will see later, how the growth in spinning and weaving made the novel a possibility. Advances in materials affect a vast range of machines, advances in accounting make whole new businesses possible and advances in education and science transform industries. The progress of the Birth of Now seemed to depend on everything advancing together. For Now to be born it seems *it must have started more or less simultaneously in every industry and business at the same time*. This fits in with the general perception of the part of the Birth of Now that is referred to as the 'Industrial Revolution'. The start of large-scale production machinery, say, factory looms, was roughly simultaneous with improvements in agriculture, that were roughly simultaneous with developments in transport (canals and rail), improvements in banking, professionalisation of government, abolition of the slave trade, the start of the popular novel, etc. They all happened within the space of one lifetime. There is no direct link between the first British 'summit level' canal in 1761 and the steam engine: the canal was built to carry coal but, at first, only for heating. Nor is there a direct link between the power loom of 1784, powered by water, and the cotton gin[xxxiii] of around 1790. However, once developed, the gin fed lower costs and a greatly increased supply of raw materials into the loom. The Birth of Now, whatever it was, gave them all a simultaneous starting shove across only a short period – and, at a similar period, started social progress, financial innovation and other changes. Once started together, they all fed improvement into each other, generating the development that has continued ever since. What single thing could have had so broad an effect?

MONEY

One of the greatest constraints on the development of any society has been money: specifically, the lack of it. With very few exceptions, money has been uncomfortably scarce in every society in history and it is important to understand why.

The concept of money has confused people for millennia. Money is not gold, although gold has often been used as money. Money, like truth, beauty or the number three, is an abstract concept that we can see examples of in the world. Three apples are a concrete example of the concept of three, but the number three itself is abstract. Gold coins are a concrete example of the concept of money but money itself is abstract. Before we can see the effect of this concept on the Birth of Now, we need to be clear about what money is.

Money tokens, like gold coins, are required for trade because you need them to buy from or sell to people you do not know or that you cannot trust. Within a traditional village or tribe, money is rarely used or necessary. Gifts are exchanged when appropriate and help is given when needed. Everyone expects that equal gifts will be given back when they are appropriate and help will be returned when needed. This is not because village people are simple and generous, but because everyone knows everyone and a fair give-and-take is socially enforced – although the system is often imperfect and arguments about whether someone or other has given fair repayment for someone else's favours are the fuel of much village gossip and dispute. But, if you are selling to someone outside the community, say to a passing trader, you will ask to be paid immediately, since the outsider may not return to pay you later. Similarly, if you are buying something from an outsider, you will have to pay for it there and then, as they cannot rely on you to pay later. So some form of self-evidently valuable, readily exchangeable, easily transported and split-up item is needed to make either buying from or selling to an outsider work efficiently. This is money, in whatever form it takes, and it is essential for trading beyond the self-supporting village.

This is important because simple trading increases the real wealth of the individuals and communities doing the trading. Trading takes place because you swap something of lower value to you for something of higher value to you. The person you are dealing with sees the values the other way round, or they would not do the deal. You both gain something more valuable than you give. Money is simply the intermediary, making the swaps work more efficiently and allowing three-way and four-plus-way swaps to take place. Money is the oil in the engine of commerce, making trade work efficiently, with an output of real wealth.

'Real wealth' here and elsewhere in this book, means having more access to the world's materials, being able to use more stuff for your benefit. A person is 'wealthier' if they can get more of the things they want, not simply by having access to more money. We, regrettably, also use the units of exchange, money, as the units to measure real wealth as well (units of account). This is simply because we have no other 'measuring rod' that we can use to put a number on wealth, so we use money for lack of a better one. Unfortunately, the resulting measurement figures are always wrong and often totally misleading, bearing minimal connection to real wealth. Why this is so will become apparent.

Trade allows people with easy access to something to swap it with people who have easy access to something else: people who live by the sea can swap fish for wood with people who live in the forest, making both better off. Trade also allows specialisation, which hugely increases the output of individuals and groups. A professional boat-builder can build a boat many times better and faster than a farmer trying to build one for the first time. A community of specialist boat-builders, passing skills, knowledge and tools down the generations, again multiplies how efficiently materials are turned into useful boats. But this huge gain in real wealth is possible only with trade, trade that enables the boat-builders to get their food and other necessities from other people. In turn, this out-of-village trade is possible only with money (because there is no security of trust between people who may never see each other again) and money comes in different qualities: Perfect Money, Good Money and Near Money.

Perfect Money has a transparent, unquestionable and universally agreed value. With Perfect Money no trust is required: the person accepting Perfect Money in return for handing over an item knows that they will certainly be able to get an equivalent, or better, item for themselves, from any supplier and get it without extra costs, risk or loss. Perfect Money *replaces* trust because you do not have to trust the person who gives it to you; it is worth what it claims to be worth, regardless of who has it or who gives it to you. When a debtor pays their debts with money, a period of trust is brought to an end. Perfect Money costs nothing to use, it is universally acceptable at a known value that remains constant, it is divisible into small portions to allow payment of the exact sum, it is simple to transport and it is impossible to fake.

Perfect Money does not yet exist – it is a concept, like a perfect circle, that cannot be fully achieved in the real world, but that is useful, nonetheless. Even the electronic dollars we use today, purely numbers in a computer, bring frictional costs to transactions. Banks normally change a couple of per cent for transactions, even for the simple electronic transfer of funds from your account to a retailer's account (the retailer normally pays). Also, for many transactions, say shopping in China, dollars need to be changed into other currency, which has a cost. Dollars also slowly decrease in value, albeit too slowly to affect most transactions. The closer real money gets to Perfect Money, the better it works to make transactions possible and to make real wealth.

What we currently regard as money, electronic dollars, is only a couple of per cent away from Perfect Money. We can call money like this 'Good Money', a form of money that gets quite close to Perfect Money.

Before the Birth of Now, the closest thing to Perfect Money was almost always precious metal, especially in the form of coins of standard size and purity. These were 'Good Money'. The metal in the coins had real uses, so their value was universally recognised. Because the metal's supply was physically limited by the difficulties of mining, it kept its value. Ideally, coins made the weight and purity of the metal content clear and, hence, the value of the coin transparent, but in reality coins were often trimmed, shaken to get metal dust off them, or debased – that is, reissued made from diluted gold or silver. Good Money is not an absolute term but one that goes from close to Perfect Money to close to Near Money. During the 1700s, gold and silver coins of many different countries were used together in places like the Caribbean. Because each type of coin had slightly different purities and sizes, there were hundreds of exchange rate differences between them.[36] They were all 'Good Money' but some were slightly better money than others. Equally, there were fakes, sometimes the currency was debased, etc., etc. but the principle is clear: Good Money is the format of money that gets as close to Perfect Money as the circumstances of the time allow, that requires virtually no trust and, so, retains its value even in the most difficult of circumstances; war, for example. It trades at a premium to all other forms of money.

---

36 The 'Thaler', from the Austrian silver mines of Joachimsthal (Joachim's valley), was generally agreed to be the purest and highest valued. The Spanish pronounced 'Thaler' as 'Dollar'; the word becoming used for the most trusted form of currency and so was adopted by the USA at its start.

Below Good Money there is 'Near Money', things that resemble money but have a limited use or require more trust compared to Good Money. There are many, many forms of Near Money, some nearer to Good Money, some further away. A familiar current example of Near Money is consumer vouchers or coupons that can only be spent on a limited number of goods or at a limited number of outlets (and which become valueless if the coupon's issuer goes bust or the usage terms of the coupon are too restrictive). More significantly, in commercial transactions through the ages, various forms of 'IOU', written promises to pay, act as Near Money. All Near Money trades at a discount to Good Money: if you want to turn your commercial invoices (what your customers owe you, a form of Near Money) into cash (Good Money), you can sell them to a company called a 'debt factor' or 'discount house'. They will pay you Good Money for them, but less than their face value, because Near Money has costs and risks that do not apply to Good Money. Near Money is important because it adds to the amount of money available – and it can add a lot, multiplying the amount of money available by several times. A commercial IOU from a reputable merchant can be very close to Good Money. These, guaranteed by the government in China, became the first paper currency.

A particularly important form of Near Money is certificates of deposit (receipts) given by a bank when you give them Good Money to hold for you. (This was often done to keep the money safe from theft. Because gold merchants had elaborate safes for their stock, they often became the first bankers.) When all is well, certificates of deposit from a reputable, large bank become very close to Good Money: that is, you can give them to other people as payment on much the same terms as if they were the gold coins you have deposited – the first European bank notes were certificates of deposit. But when people get nervous about the bank's ability to return their Good Money (the gold and silver coins they deposited earlier), they can all rush to the bank to extract their Good Money, generally in the form of gold coins. This often precipitates a bank failure, as a lot of the coinage may be lent out and not immediately accessible to the bank if everyone seeks to remove his or her Good Money at the same time.

So the amount of Near Money available is highly variable. When times are peaceful and prosperous, the amount of Near Money increases because trade is strong, merchants extend credit to customers, and various forms of IOU are accepted in payment and passed on to others as payment in turn. The Near Money is also of good quality, because most companies and people are likely to honour their promises and pay their obligations (that is, they will exchange them for Good Money at the appointed time). In times of war and recession, such paper promises become less valuable as people worry that they might not be honoured. Sometimes such notes become completely worthless. In these circumstances, the supply of Near Money dries up.

To recap: anything that makes trade possible without the parties needing to trust each other is money of some sort. Money can only work if it has a trusted value itself – trust in the value of the money replaces trust between the people making the trade. The more confident people are in the value of the items (weights of precious metal, coins, etc.) used as money, the closer they are to Perfect Money. Before the Birth of Now, the value of gold had a high degree of trust, now the value of electronic dollars commands a similar degree of trust. Both were, in their period, Good Money. Many other items are Near Money, mostly paper promises whose value depends on the trust held in the person or organisation issuing the paper. Because it is less trusted, Near Money is less efficient in enabling trade but it is still an important additional source of money, greatly helping trade, because, as we shall see, there is never enough Good Money. (For a discussion of the use of money as a unit of account see endnote[xxxiv].)

So Good Money is, by definition, a universally trusted, easily accessed and traded (liquid) store of value. Because of this, having a store of Good Money is by far the most reliable, the most certain, barrier between your family and starvation. If and when trust breaks down in society, perhaps completely, Good Money will still save you; it will still enable you to get what you need. So people want to keep it for emergencies: they want to have their 'savings' in the form of Good Money, so that they are there even when all else has become worthless. Property and animals, the other traditional stores of wealth, have a much less certain value and are less liquid, less available to 'spend' in times of trouble. As a result of this unlooked-for use of Good Money, it is always being withdrawn from circulation because people want to hold it as savings; people want to hoard their gold coins in case they need them in an emergency. The consequences of this are dire.

Firstly, if money is taken out of circulation, it is not spent; so fewer goods and services are bought (for economics wonks, this is the 'fiscal effect'). If enough people do this, an economic recession starts. Because less is bought, less is sold, so there is less trade, less work and fewer jobs. This reduces people's income, so they have to buy less, which reduces someone's sales, which reduces someone's income and so on. Unless something intervenes, the nervous will clutch onto their savings and seek to increase them. The economy spirals down until the depth of the problem (close to starvation?) forces the savers to disgorge some of the saved Good Money. Without their knowing it, their collective planning to escape the possible problem has made the problem happen. By the time the problem – the recession – gets bad enough to force them to spend the money they were trying to save, much damage will have been done to the economy as a whole.

Secondly, withdrawing Good Money from circulation simply freezes the economy. An engine will lock solid if the lubrication of oil is removed from it: most trade cannot take place without the lubrication of money. Say Mr X wants to buy wheat to make bread but has no money to buy it. Mrs Y has plenty of wheat to sell but, because Mr X has no money, she cannot sell it. Mr X actually has desirable goods for sale himself, say, firewood, but he has not been able to sell it. This is because the potential firewood buyers, the Z brothers, have no money because they cannot sell their spare eggs to Mrs Y, who would like to buy them. But she has no money because she cannot sell her wheat to Mr X. The lack of the money lubricant has impoverished everyone; a three-way exchange has become impossible because the money catalyst is missing. Mr X has no wheat, Mrs Y has no eggs and the Z brothers have no firewood. Had any one of them been able to borrow a gold coin (Good Money), they could all have traded, been better off and then returned the gold coin. Instead, they are all stuck with products they do not want themselves and cannot sell to others. The recession now turns into a depression. (This is the 'Monetary effect' in the jargon.)

Thirdly, withdrawal of Good Money into savings leads to the destruction of the reputation system essential to a Supplier society. Normally, traders bend over backwards to avoid breach of promise or default in payment, as the consequent loss of credibility can destroy their business as effectively as a fire. But when money runs short, some will find themselves simply unable to meet their obligations. Suddenly lots of Near Money, depending on trust, vanishes. If this becomes at all widespread, all the efficiencies that arise from dealing with trusted parties disappear. What trading remains becomes much more complicated, costly and slower – counting and checking every item bought, swapping coin money at exactly the same moment as the goods change hands and so on.

You might think that, if there is less currency going around, a shortage of the gold coins (for example) would simply increase the value of each coin. In practice, this never seems to happen, although it is unclear why it does not. The opposite effect certainly happens. If the supply of coins increases beyond the goods available to buy, the coins do decrease in value. We call this process 'inflation'[37]. Dr Johnson, the great English commentator, noted this odd effect in 1773, during a great growth in the availability of money, and was also baffled by it: "*In speculation* (imagination)," he said, "*it seems that a smaller quantity of money, equal in value to a larger quantity, if equally divided, should produce the same effect. But it is not so in reality. Many more conveniences and elegancies are enjoyed where money is plentiful, than where it is scarce. Perhaps a great familiarity with it, which arises from plenty, makes us more easily part with it.*[xxxv]"

So the tendency for money to disappear from circulation has appalling effects on people's material well-being and on society as a whole. Misery is created and, often, with it comes political unrest. But it is a tendency that was almost always impossible to overcome before the Birth of Now. One of the criteria of Good Money is that it cannot be created at will, so its value can be trusted. But this means that there is no mechanism to replace the money lost to the system when it vanishes into individual savings[38]. Good Money simply becomes very scarce. Even if more Good Money could be found, as sometimes it was through luck in mining, trading or war, it can fail to solve the problem. If individuals simply

---

37 The term 'deflation' is normally used with a slightly different meaning to the opposite of inflation. Real deflation, an increase in the value of money, has occurred rarely and slowly – 1-2 per cent per year – for example, in Japan since 1990.

38 This no longer applies – since 2007/8 Western central banks have done exactly this.

take the opportunity to extract more funds from the system by saving more, a little extra Good Money going into the system achieves nothing. Hence, the perennial squeals across recorded history that there is not enough money in the system[xxxvi].

Before the Birth of Now, trade and its ability to allow specialisation was the only way for communities to become wealthier – other than the temporary luck of good weather or stealing from another community. So having available money was essential to a community's material well-being. Yet, because Good Money was always being withdrawn from the system to act as emergency savings, it was always in short supply.

However, in good times, Near Money filled part of the gap left by the endemic shortage of Good Money. Near Money often starts as a purely practical device. A tailor in Rome around 1450 who wanted to buy 100 gold ducats-worth of silk in Venice (where it had come off ships after the last stage in its long journey from China) had a number of theoretical options. The simplest option is also a practical impossibility: to send a trusted employee or relative with a 100 gold ducat coins on the long and dangerous journey to Venice. This plan is just too likely to fail with the loss of the precious capital to bandits or the person carrying it. The alternative works better: deposit 100 gold ducats with the local branch of the Medici business. They will provide a receipt and communicate with their Venice branch that have gold in reserve, to make the money available to the tailor's nominated buyer in Venice – but only for conventional exchange with a known supplier of silk – all for a small charge. As it happens, the Medici Venice branch is unlikely to be required to produce any gold. When a deal is struck to buy the silk, let us say the whole 100 ducats in one deal; both buyer and seller go to the Venice branch. There the money is transferred from the buyer's Medici account to the seller's Medici account at a stroke of a Medici pen (we still have the, very carefully maintained, books in which this was done). In the meantime, the Medici Bank has loaned most of the gold deposited, say, sixty ducats of it, to the Duke of Urbino, who is paying his soldiers with it. This, crudely, is how banks create money – the Roman tailor has spent the 100 ducats on cloth, while most of the same money, sixty ducats, is being spent by the Duke of Urbino. This works because all the parties trust the Medici Bank and the Medici Bank trusts the Duke of Urbino to repay. This kind of growth in the amount of money available was partially responsible for the wealth of Italy in this period.

Sadly, however, bank-created money can be destroyed as quickly as it can be created. If it looks as though the Duke of Urbino may have problems in repaying his loan, people may start to have doubts about the Medici Bank and rush in to get back the golden ducats they have deposited with it. All the extra Near Money created by the Medici Bank immediately vanishes and the gold ducats are hoarded back under the bed as the economy dies down to a low glow.

So, to recap: money is, itself, a most critical real-wealth-creating tool, because it allows trading and specialisation. Good Money is almost always in short supply because it is constantly being withdrawn from circulation to be held as savings. Sometimes Near Money can partially fill the gap but Near Money can vanish catastrophically, with virtually no warning. The consequences of such a sudden withdrawal of money are disastrous for trade and employment – it is what we call a financial 'crash'. The effect of financial crashes was worse for simple economies, before the Birth of Now, than the effect of financial crashes nowadays. In developed societies there are automatic, as well as discretionary, mechanisms that help recovery from a slump. For example, today, as unemployment rises, government spending on benefits automatically increases. Governments can also actively 'dis-save', borrowing to spend more money than they collect in tax, to compensate for the money being withdrawn by individuals saving. Nowadays central banks also (carefully) create new money and push it into the system by lending it to the government to spend without losing trust in the value of the money. Even so, recessions can be long and tedious. In earlier societies, there were no such mechanisms. There was no reason why they should ever recover from a slump. Bad trade means lower incomes, means bad trade means lower incomes, possibly forever…

We have enormous problems in following the actual workings out of money in history because, until the last 300 years – and then only in one or two places – we have no direct information about the supply of money or statistics about levels of economic activity in any society. Someone writing 700 years ago about the decline in trade may be looking back with rose-tinted glasses at the past or they may be genuinely reporting an economic depression. But when writers bemoan the decline of the times, compared with their recent experience without being able to put a finger on the reason – other than the universal moan of the aging; the moral flabbiness of the current generation – an economic recession must be suspected. This sort of despairing writing can be found in tenth-century Baghdad, which was inexplicably in ruins, yet was still under the, previously very successful, Abbasid Dynasty – and this was centuries before the Mongols captured and destroyed the city. We see something similar towards the end of each of the (Southern) Song, Yuan and Ming dynasties in China. Power and wealth appear to have simply fallen to bits for no clear reason. Maybe incompetence in government was at fault, but there is no reason not to see a full-blown economic depression as the most fundamental cause of their downfall. Once you start looking for economic recessions in history there seem to be overwhelming numbers of suspicious cases: the decline and fall of classical Rome in several phases, the dismal state of seventeenth-century Spain, possibly both the central American Maya collapses of *c.*200 and 850CE, etc. In all these cases, and more as we shall see, such evidence as exists supports the possibility (probability?) of each being the result of an economic crash or several such crashes caused by money being taken out of circulation and into savings. Given how frequently we have had similar slumps in the well-recorded history of the last 200 years, these may be only the tip of an iceberg and many historical declines may be explained by economic recessions.

The opposite of recession, periods of economic growth, must also have arisen from time to time, as locked-up money was released into the system. This could be caused by finding a new supply of precious metal, by a wave of optimism or by the powers-that-be extracting saved money from individuals or organisations and spending it. In Stealer societies, extra money was most often extracted for wars but it was sometimes done simply when the king had the power to do so. For example, the 'Forfeiture' of Chinese Buddhism in 845CE, the French destruction of the Templars in 1307 and the English Dissolution of the Monasteries around 1540 were all primarily caused by the monarch's desire to get the assets of the religious houses to spend for themselves, combined with their military ability to turn their wish into reality.

If we want to understand what effect having more or less money has, in the absence of any reliable figures, we need to look at the few places and periods before the Birth of Now when there were definitely major changes in the money supply. Can we identify evidence of bursts of economic growth or the unexplained misery of an economic depression linked to these events?

The first increase in a money supply we can definitely identify was the effect of the silver mines at Laurion. These lay in the Greek region of Attica, dominated by its capital, Athens, and were at a peak of production between 500 and 300BCE[xxxvii]. The mines were enormous – there were about 350 individual mines, worked by more than 10,000 slaves. We do not know their output at all accurately, but it was talked of at the time in terms of legend, especially after a huge new seam was discovered in 482BCE. Even today, Athenian 'Owl' silver coins of the period are dug up widely over the eastern Mediterranean. After the huge new vein of silver was discovered, Athens rose to dominance in the region, both politically and culturally. One hundred and fifty years later, when the silver had largely run dry, Athens' power and influence subsided and it was absorbed into the Macedonian Empire and never achieved anything like the same independent status again. It was during this 'silver period' – not before or after – that Athenians were able to trial the form of government they called 'democracy', build a small empire and write the histories, plays, observations and philosophies that so impressed later generations. It seems a reasonable suggestion that the silver led to a sustained economic boom. After it ran out, Athens was never again independent or important until it became the capital of a new country called Greece (*Ellas*), more than 2,000 years later.

This seems to be a good example of the effect of a steady and sustained increase in the amount of money available. It created continuous financial growth with little apparent inflation for around 100 years. Sadly, however, it ran out, but not before Athens had created a reputation for learning that was to keep it in business as a university town for another 700 years. (This period was also extraordinary because the Athenians chose to write down so much – history, plays, philosophy, speculation, and mathematics. They, and the Jews, but for very different reasons, were the first people to bother with writing as anything more than a legal, religious and accounting tool. Whatever the reasons, the first two peoples to use writing became, jointly, the founders of Western culture.)

The story of money in China is complicated and uncertain, but there was a significant economic boom in China from around the year 1000CE, during the (Southern) Song Dynasty. In this boom, iron and coal production were raised to levels they were not to see again until the mid nineteenth-century in Europe. This was the first period that a paper currency was introduced. Trade flowed, the population doubled, many books were printed and gunpowder was used in war as well as for fireworks. This and the Yuan boom that followed it are the periods people think of when they talk about China being so far ahead of medieval Europe.

It seems reasonable to suggest that the more plentiful supply of money that the (trusted) paper currency made possible under the Song was a significant contributor to the strength of the Chinese economy. Unfortunately, the dynasty never understood the need to maintain the trust in paper currency and, after a period of success, they developed the idea of increasing their wealth by printing money. This undermined confidence in the paper money and, because most people stopped accepting it, the economy had to return to using the inadequate supplies of precious metals. Maybe this was what caused the recession that, in turn, led to the fall of the dynasty.

The Mongol Khans defeated the last Song emperor[39]

---

39   Their troops and officers were almost entirely Chinese with some Turkic forces and very few actual Mongols.

and reunited the country as the Yuan Dynasty (1271-1368). The underlying economic strength of China then recovered under Mongol rule – they had already ruled the northern part of China for several decades. They reintroduced paper currency in a much more thorough way and supported it strongly. They seem to be the first rulers to really understand money, actually banning the use of silver and gold as currency, allowing people to buy silver and gold but strictly and only for ornamental purposes. At the same time, they brought a period of near-complete peace to the country. This was the time when the wealth and business of China was, according to Marco Polo of Venice, so much more than Europe's[40]. But then, towards the end of the Yuan Dynasty, they faced military challenges and the temptation to print money grew too great. The currency was destroyed by hyperinflation. Around the same time there was a collapse in trade and wealth. There is no clear reason why the collapse happened and the very lack of a clear cause – no plague, war, mass slaughter or unusual levels of anarchy are recorded – suggests the hidden hand of an economic depression may be to blame, probably itself caused by the collapse of the currency. Indeed, it would be remarkable if the destruction of the currency by hyperinflation did not destroy trade and bring a drastic recession with its knock-on effects on civil society and military effectiveness.

The absence of Good Money led the Chinese

---

40   The origins of the stories ascribed to Marco Polo are dubious and many
      of them may be exaggerated but there is no doubt that they were based
      on one or more European's real experience of China at the time: much
      of the information they give – on geography, for example – is accurate.

Government to devise novel forms of Near-Money. They paid some suppliers with 'Monk Licences'. These entitled the holder to become a Buddhist monk. In practice, this simply meant freedom from both taxes and compulsory labour with no real religious requirement at all. But, despite these measures, the economic collapse, if it was that, led to the collapse of the Yuan Dynasty fairly quickly. Their replacement, the Ming Dynasty, arose from an internal Chinese revolt. The history of the Ming may also fit to a pattern of economic growth, money failure and subsequent economic and political collapse. Unfortunately their financial and economic records are too muddled for us to be confident what is cause and what is effect.

When we get to the Qing Dynasty (1644-1912), who succeeded the Ming, we have better records, as well as more written comments, so trends are clearer. There was a persistent, severe money shortage. Attempts under the previous Ming Dynasty to reintroduce paper money had failed because of the lack of government commitment and the concept was discredited. The dearth of Good Money, principally silver in China's case, was gradually alleviated by mining and by exporting tea and porcelain to Europe, getting silver in return. By the middle of the dynasty, the economy was looking steady. But then currency just started to disappear. Some, presumably, was just being squirrelled away but some was also being spent on illegal imported opium. This was being exported into China by agents of the British East India Company, specifically to balance the previously one-way drain of silver into China to pay for silk, tea and porcelain. It became much commented on in China that silver was, again, in short supply. Although there were multiple reasons for the collapse of government power in China during the 1800s, the continuing lack of money and consequent poor trade seems likely to have been an important ingredient.

Empires like the Chinese, Egyptian, Roman-Byzantine-Ottoman or the Iranian, seem to have periods of strength and periods of weakness. Sometimes an unstable political system or a succession of ineffective rulers can be identified as a principle cause of the weakness. Perhaps good or bad luck with harvests can be blamed. But it does seem reasonable to suspect that a frequent cause of weakness was Good Money being withdrawn from the system as people saved it causing recession and Near-Money to fail, freezing trade as money vanished from the system. This may even be behind some of the mysterious fluctuations in the power of pre-Colombian American empires. To put it another way, there is no credibility in the idea that these societies *never* had an economic bust. Political problems are much easier to see and record – say, civil war between rival claimants to the throne – but there is no reason to doubt that relatively unrecorded financial problems also happened.

Returning to specific examples, the various states of Italy developed a reputation for being outstandingly wealthier than other countries from about 1400 onwards. Although there were successful trading republics dotted around the Italian coast generating cash, the great money-mine was the papacy. Money flowed directly into the papal coffers in Rome from its traditional revenues and rents from all over Europe. More money came in from favours granted to kings (favours such as 'annulling' or cancelling inconvenient marriages), selling offices and 'indulgences', certificates that enabled the soul to get to heaven faster. Even more money came from the land and other revenues of the bishops and cardinals who lived in Rome. There was also substantial revenue from those making the pilgrimage to Rome from all over Europe. From Rome, this money flowed out to the Italian peninsula, enriching it all, despite its chronic political instability, frequent wars and occasional invasions. The money spout got under way when the 'Great Schism' ended in 1418. This had been a period with two competing popes, one in Rome and one in Avignon, France, that had drastically reduced papal revenue into Rome. Moreover, as soon as the Great Schism ended, alum, a material vital for dying cloth, was discovered on papal land. The popes ensured they kept a tight monopoly on this and gained huge extra revenues for many decades. Total papal revenues peaked around 1520, when the then pope (a member of the Medici family, incidentally), sold huge numbers of indulgences, raising money to build the new St Peter's Cathedral in Rome. This was the period when people like Leonardo da Vinci (1452-1519), Michelangelo (Buonarrotti) (1475-1564) and Galileo (Galilei) (1564-1642) flourished. It was the glittering heyday of Florence, Venice and Milan. This may be coincidence, but it seems more likely to be cause and effect. Papal revenue started to decline after the Reformation which started in 1517, as many countries changed away from the Catholic Church to become Protestant, and those countries that remained Catholic ran a much tighter church fiscal policy, with less for remittance to Rome. The steep decline of the papal money supply, particularly after 1550, seems to be linked to the decline in the power and influence of the Italian cities at the same time. By 1600 they had only a fraction of their former international importance, while the Netherlands was taking over as the dominant commercial (and artistic) power.

The decline in papal revenues that affected the whole of Italy, coincided, for Venice, with the arrival of competition in the spice trade, causing an economic depression that seems to have lasted for decades or centuries. Venice's decline after 1600 was not helped by international problems, but in its heyday, Venice overcame serious problems of many kinds with ease. Now it slumped before them and largely fell out of history as a force.

The value, or even the weight, of the New World gold and silver pumped into Europe's money supply after Columbus 'discovered' America is impossible to guess at with any accuracy, but it was a lot. People talked of it as huge sums coming in annually. Stealing even a small fraction of it made men unimaginably wealthy. Francis Drake stole some of it in 1577-80 and Queen Elizabeth's half-share in the venture exceeded all her other annual revenue[41]. By 1600 or so it may have more than doubled the amount of gold and silver in circulation in Europe. This brought a noticeable inflation, which is

41   Some say it was equal to half her other annual revenue; a lot, anyway.

estimated at something like a doubling of prices between 1530 and 1580. This implies that Good Money was in plentiful supply over this period across much of Europe. This may explain why, despite the rapid decline in papal revenues after 1520, the Italian economy carried on flourishing until the end of the century. The treasure galleons continued feeding money to the King of Spain but in lessening amounts after 1600. With this huge and long-lasting supply of Good Money, why did Spain not become another Athens or Venice?

One reason is that Spain, actually the Kingdom of Castile, was still essentially a Stealer state (Aragon, the King's other main realm in Spain, had a much larger trading economy but had little to do with America at the time). No amount of money will make a Stealer state more productive. But, even more importantly, the money did not belong to the government of Castile; it belonged to the King, personally. Starting in 1566 and continuing until 1650, the kings of Spain (who were also Dukes of Burgundy, feudal 'owners' of the Netherlands) fought a more or less continuous series of wars in the Netherlands to suppress the independence of the Netherlands' states and their demands for religious freedom. The way the war was fought on the King's side was highly unusual, in that he employed and paid an army. Previously, European armies had been unpaid feudal levies, only paid with the loot of their victories – if they had any – and freelance robbery if not. There had been small-scale mercenary armies before, but the Spanish Army of the Netherlands was the first large-scale, long-standing army to be paid in Good Money in Western Europe since the Roman Empire 1,200 years earlier[42]. So much was the war dominated by the availability of American money, that the arrival of a good treasure fleet in Cadiz was the signal for a new offensive in the Netherlands. Where the King's strategy sprang a leak was in what happened to that money. Some of it went into buying military supplies: guns, powder, clothing, ships' supplies, etc. Fortunately, the Netherlands was the biggest market and manufacturing base in Europe at the time, so these supplies were easy to obtain locally. The remainder of the money went in soldiers' pay and rations. This money was also mostly spent in the area itself – the Netherlands. In short, a great deal of the gold and silver from America went straight into the Netherlands economy, barely stopping in Cadiz on its journey from the Americas. This was the era of Rembrandt, of Vermeer, of great Dutch advances in every kind of technology, of the foundation of the rampant VOC – the Dutch East India Company – of the Netherlands becoming by far and away the richest society in Europe. The Dutch flowering was, to a great extent, powered by regular deliveries of Good Money from the Spanish King's New World silver and gold.

Peace was agreed between the Netherlands and the King of Spain in 1650 after eighty years of war and a slump in the Netherlands economy might have

---

42 Some say that the army Charles VIII of France used to invade the Italian peninsula in 1494 was the first example of a paid army. Without going into details, this matters very little for the argument – that army, which was, indeed, largely mercenary, acted to transfer cash out of France and into Italy, maintaining Italy's financial heyday for a few more years, at the same time as adding to its physical destruction.

been expected to follow. This did not happen because, despite the peace with Spain, the Netherlands continued to be involved in wars on or close to its territory. These wars continued the flow of cash into the region. The most substantial threat (and expenditure) was from Louis XIV of France, who fought a war in the Netherlands that went on, with short pauses, until 1714. In order to fund the ongoing war some of the state governments of the Netherlands developed a crucial breakthrough in money history: the bond market.

This idea is both very simple and very powerful. The government wants money, so it prints certificates which promise to pay the owner of the certificate, say, $5 a year and, after ten years, to pay them $100, ending the transaction. It then sells these certificates, known as 'bonds', for whatever price it can get, hoping to get around $100. If it gets $100, it has, in effect, borrowed the money at 5 per cent interest for ten years. A critical part of the deal is that the bond can be sold at any time by its original purchaser to anyone willing to buy it at whatever price they can get for it.

There is one absolute precondition before bonds can be freely sold (compulsory lending to government is another matter): people must trust that the government will do its utmost to honour its promises. Buyers must believe that the annual $5 will be paid on the due date and that the painful $100 refunding will also be paid at the end of ten years on the day promised. No king can credibly promise this. One day he can get up and decide that not paying the $5 interest and not giving back the

$100 on the due date will make his day feel so much better. Kings frequently did exactly this, so lending to them was a difficult process, only justified by fantastic interest rates, nailed-down pledges of security against some specific revenue stream and titles of nobility for the lender.

There is only one way that people can feel secure that the government will try its utmost to honour the bonds: that is, if the members of the government and their families personally hold their own wealth in the form of the bonds. It is essential that the people making the decisions that affect the value of the bonds will be among the biggest losers if the debt goes bad. If the chief minister, his mother-in-law and most of his government are all going to be ruined if their bondholding becomes valueless, you can feel moderately secure in investing your own money in bonds – they are going to try their hardest to ensure the obligations are paid. In such circumstances, five per cent a year is very alluring when opposed to the zero per cent you get if you keep your savings as gold coins. The ability to sell the bond at any time makes it almost as good as cash, compared to the other safe-ish money earner, buying property, which can be very difficult to turn back into cash at short notice.

So bonds can only be issued effectively by oligarchies, where the government is run by a collective group of rich families, and by some democracies[43]. But,

---

43 Not all democracies. The temptation is to seek electoral success by generous promises met through borrowing until the debt burden cannot be sustained and the economy crashes. Posturing by political parties can also threaten the debt, for example, in the USA.

when this bond-selling scheme works, it has astounding effects:

- The government gets to achieve what it wants, because selling bonds gives it the money to pay for what it needs.
- Savings, which otherwise would have removed Good Money from the system to be hidden 'under the bed', are now used to buy bonds.
- The money saved is, thus, put back into the system by government spending it, rather than being hidden away and lost to the system. This keeps up the level of trade and the amount of Good Money in circulation.
- Wealthy individuals have a new source of income from the bond interest they are getting and so can spend more.
- Because there is a regular market to sell bonds they can be readily sold and turned into Good Money. Since they now hold liquid savings, wealthy people feel more secure and less inclined to panic-save Good Money.
- Because most bonds have the name of their holder registered with the issuer, a lost or stolen certificate can be replaced, adding another level of security for the well-off.
- Investors can now raise the money to put into a new project, say a factory or canal, by selling bonds, not struggling to sell land or the embarrassment of selling the family silver.

All this Good Money, spent and invested, instead of mouldering under the bed, means that the economy flourishes, tax revenues rise and confidence in the government's financial soundness increases, so people are even more willing to buy bonds and may even pay a premium for them – that is pay $101 or more for a bond that will only pay out $100 in ten years to get the 5 per cent interest. This lowers the government's cost of borrowing.

Ten years later, when it comes to repaying the original bonds, having seen ten years of sound lending and interest payments, people are keen to buy more bonds. The government now has no problem selling a new issue onto a busy bond market, enabling the original bondholders to be repaid painlessly with the funds from new bond sales; there is no need to raise taxes or cut government spending. (In practice, most of the money paid by the government to redeem the old bonds will be used to buy new bonds anyway.) So long as the government does not borrow so much that people seriously worry about their ability to repay, they never actually have to repay, they can simply roll over loans. They can also pay the interest on the bonds from the proceeds of further bond sales.

In the long term, issues of over-borrowing can arise but, starting from a base of near-zero government debt, there is a long, long free ride before the government becomes financially constrained by the overall level of debt. In practice, the economy is fertilised by recycled bond money and can grow so fast that tax revenues grow faster than bond interest. If this happens (and sometimes it did) the burden of interest, relative to the size of the economy and government revenue, keeps on decreasing[44].

It is worth re-emphasising the point that this magical system can only work if the people most worried about the continuing value of the bonds are running the government. Until the Supplier state reached its full flowering with rule dominated by a large number of Suppliers who could not be overruled by Stealers, bonds could not work, as people would not buy them.

These, then, were the magic tools invented by in the Netherlands: bonds that enabled them to continue to grow economically and fight the French after the withdrawal of the Spanish King's money supply. So wealthy were the Dutch that, during the French attack in 1688, the leader of the Netherlands, Willem of Orange[45], was able to take time out to invade England and, together with his wife Mary, become King of England and Scotland, subsequently conquering Ireland.

But this was the peak for the Netherlands and they were economically devastated by their victories that soon followed. First, the (largely) Anglo-Dutch army fighting the French moved away from the Netherlands to pursue their retreating enemies, taking their money away from the area. Then, in 1714, peace broke out and the Netherlands' governments stopped borrowing and

---

44 While we know the level of government borrowings accurately – they are probably the first really reliable statistic in history – the size of the economies of both the Netherlands and Britain, their GDP, is only known very approximately, although there can be no doubt, in the case of Britain after 1750, that it was growing very rapidly.

45 Willem's status as leader, 'Stadtholder', of the Netherlands, had varied dramatically over the years but, at this time, he was in control.

spending. The resultant recession, as usual, also saw a lot of Near Money vanish, worsening things. The slump seems to have broken not only the Dutch boom but, to a significant extent, their pride. They never understood how or why they had fallen so far below the achievements of their parents and grandparents and reverted to being a conventional, small country, albeit still with a significant trading empire. They no longer 'punched above their weight', nor did they continue to lead the world in technology or art as they had done. The Birth of Now did not happen first in the Netherlands.

The British had learned a great deal from the Dutch over the years of Netherlands' dominance and the process was completed with several leading Dutch citizens coming to England with Willem and Mary to support their rule with Dutch ideas. Starting the Bank of England was an early attempt by them to provide a trustworthy borrower so they could borrow to finance their wars. It was a kind of arms-length organisation that was run by businessmen, not the untrustworthy government, that would borrow money from individuals and then lend it on to the government. This did enable some essential funds to be raised at the time but the transforming belief that money lent to government was completely safe was only built up slowly over the years. Initially, memories of Charles II's default, the so-called 'Stop of the Exchequer' in 1672, was a raw memory to savers and the first bonds could only be sold at interest rates quite close to those asked of a full king – around 11 per cent. With the accession of George I, who spoke no English and largely let Britain run itself, it became clear that the oligarchy in the form of the Prime Minister, Robert Walpole, and his cronies were in charge and had committed their own money to bonds, so interest rates started to drop. The British bond market still had a number of scares to overcome and nearly failed with the financial hysteria and crash of 1720 (the 'South Sea Bubble') and a bad wobble at the time of 'Bonnie Prince Charlie's' revolt in 1745. The story of the early bond markets in the Netherlands and Britain had many other complications, ignored here, and many different types of bond were tried out, some with better results than others, before the trust built up enough and the British finally hit on the simplicity and scale of the 'consol' bond in 1752. This was a simple £100 bond paying $3\frac{1}{2}$ per cent with no fixed redemption date that you could cash-in at any time for its face value with the Bank of England. It had segments round the edge of the certificate that you cut off and took in on the due date to claim your interest each year (the original 'coupons', from the French *couper*, to cut). Consols were very popular and had a large, liquid market, based on the previous fifty-plus years with no bond defaults and the perception that members of the government were totally financially committed to them. A significant proportion of the consols sold over the next fifty years were bought by foreigners, mainly the Dutch, who owned around 14 per cent of them, pushing more Good Money into Britain (and out of the Netherlands).

After George I took the throne in 1714, Britain became involved in a century of wars, all of which demanded funding, none of which caused any destruction in Britain. The principle ones were: the War of Austrian Succession (1739-1748), the Seven Years' War (1756-63), the War of American Independence (1775-1783) and twenty-two years of war following the French Revolution (1793-1815). Fortunately, we are now getting into an era where a few reliable numbers become available. British Government debt rose from £14 million in 1700, peaking at £843 million after the end of the Napoleonic Wars in 1818[xxxviii]. This peak debt was over 250 per cent of GNP: that is, more than two and a half times everyone in the country's pay and wages for a year, a higher level, relative to national wealth, than has ever been achieved anywhere since then[46]. This vast sum was borrowed relatively easily and cheaply. Even when the British Government was forced by the difficulties in war to suspend the convertibility of the (paper) pound in 1797 – that is, they would no longer swap paper pounds for gold pounds – and there was a sharp drop in the bond market, it still soon recovered. Almost all this sum, the equivalent of something like £70 billion or $100 billion in today's money, had been spent in Britain and Ireland, most of it over the years between the start of the Seven Years' War in 1756 and the end of the Napoleonic Wars in 1815, creating a powerful and long-sustained economic boom.

The contrast between the history of British government finance and French government finance during the 1700s is startling. Through much of the same century, France had, in Louis XV (king as a minor from 1710, reigned

---

46 And three times its current forecast peak; more than the peak debt of the Greek Government after the financial meltdown of 2007 (175 per cent of GDP), the Irish (117 per cent of GDP), etc. The Japanese Government is, however, getting close to matching this level at the time of writing.

1723-1774), one of the best of kings: moderate, intelligent, caring and, in consequence, all but forgotten. France had a catastrophic financial 'Bubble' and crash in 1720 with the 'Mississippi Company Bubble', matching Britain's 'South Sea Bubble' the same year. But thereafter the financial paths divide. The French Government's shortage of money was continuous, causing endless internal disputes as new taxes were proposed and resisted, hampering foreign policy and military operations. As the century wore on, increasingly desperate measures were tried. The national debt was repudiated and such bonds as could be sold were dishonoured. Future tax exemptions and annuities were sold for lump sums, collecting immediate cash in return for future costs. Borrowing at ruinous rates was tried, often at over 18 per cent per year; but few would lend, even at these rates, such was the lack of trust. It is said that the last straw was the cost of supporting the United States in their War of Independence. Finally, French government finances were so bad that the Estates General (Parliament) had to be called for the first time in 175 years in the hope that it would raise new taxes. When it met in May 1789 it set off the French Revolution instead. The contrast with Britain's surging money supply could hardly have been greater. (If you are confused as to how money can multiply while the amount of currency is fixed by a finite amount of gold, see endnote [xxxix]).

The money borrowed so easily and cheaply in Britain was, as we have seen, mostly spent within the country, largely on naval supplies. Most of the money would naturally have been spent in Britain and Ireland but frequent wars and blockades exaggerated this habit of buying at home wherever possible, both by the government and by the general public. This sustained economic growth for the best part of a century, moving to up to a boom towards its end. Businesses were selling more every year to the government alone, sometimes a lot more, year after year, cumulatively. This meant they were also buying more of the ingredients of production, including labour, every year. Government borrowing as a proportion of national wealth reached a peak in 1818, just after the Napoleonic and second American war ended. This is why there were multiplying numbers of water-powered machines looking for extra power from steam engines in 1800; this is why the mines were flourishing; this is why canals were paying huge returns; this is why cotton, linen and wool were being demanded, spun and woven as never before; why ironworks and brickworks were in place to make the railways when the war demand stopped[xxxx].

It would also appear that much of the gold Britain gave to its allies, mainly Prussia and Austria, during the French Revolution and Napoleonic Wars, was returned to Britain to buy goods. There is no good data on this but, with enemy manufactures excluded from them, that is French, Dutch and Italian goods, Britain's supplies must have been attractive. Anecdotally, all the armies involved marched on British-made boots (including the French army when it could, via capture and smuggling). Like the post-World War II American Marshall aid, much of the British money donated to allies may well have fed back to industry at home.

Throughout this whole process the value of the

British currency was carefully maintained, although some price rises were impossible to resist at the height of the Napoleonic Wars. So concerned was the government with keeping the value of the currency constant, that the Bank of England and Royal Mint felt obliged to have gold physically in their possession, ready to redeem for gold every single paper currency note, silver and copper coin issued if they were presented to them. This requirement to have the gold to back its coins meant that the Mint simply ceased production of copper coins in 1773. There were constant complaints – ironically, with the booming money supply overall – about the shortage of copper coins. This made small transactions difficult, including paying employees. Leading employers were forced to pay their employees with their own 'copper tokens' – effectively their own coins. Many of these 'coins' were struck by Matthew Boulton (Watts' partner in steam engines) at his own mint in Birmingham. This continued until 1797, when the need to provide gold for the allies became too urgent to keep up convertibility to gold (it was restored at the war's end). When the hard link between currency and gold reserves had to be suspended Boulton was commissioned to produce proper, national coinage (not backed by official convertibility into gold but, being made of copper and silver, with a metallic value anyway) and the small coins crisis was over.

While this policy had caused a shortage of small coinage, the reassurance of a reliable currency it represented was a great help to trade and investment. The reputation of the Bank of England, who had stubbornly resisted any erosion of the currency, was so great that when the right to exchange paper money for gold was suspended in 1897, it had less effect on confidence than might have been expected – there was a wobble but no crash.

At the start of the Birth of Now, moving large sums of money to make a payment was a serious problem – it still mostly involved the physical transport of gold coins. But, as commerce developed, the supply of Near Money started to expand. Some provincial merchants started to accept 'bills' (deposit certificates) drawn on reputable London banks for payment (at a discount). By the middle of the century some of these merchants had become 'Country Banks', accepting deposits and lending on interest. In 1784 there were 119 such Country Banks and by 1808 there were around 800, a growth to match even the cotton industry.[xli]

The growth in the number and size of banks creates Near Money and can also act to recycle more savings back into the economy (remembering the example of the Medici Bank and the Duke of Urbino). This adds to the demand for goods and services and, while the effect was probably still small in comparison to the input of government spending before 1820, it came on top of a boom time anyway. (Long-term bank lending was only possible to the few people or institutions with good property titles as security. It was not until much later that the mass market in mortgages added substantially to the supply of money.)

But people of the time did not understand that the government's bond-funded spending stimulated the economy. The growth of trade, towns, manufacturing and even leisure is often mentioned by contemporary writers, but as if it was a natural phenomenon. Indeed, the idea that there was such thing as 'an economy' and that it could grow was unknown. Most contemporary financial commentators could see the burgeoning figures for the (British) national debt and saw it as a terrible 'millstone of debt' hung around the neck of future governments and generations. This is understandable: at the end of the Napoleonic Wars, 60-70 per cent of all British government income went into paying interest on the debt and there seemed no conceivable way in which the principle could ever be repaid. But the effect on the real economy was transformative and the financial drag of the debt on the next generation turned out, by a lucky turn of events (see below) to be minimal. From time to time after 1820, there were attempts to repay some of the debt, but relatively little of it was paid off in cash terms. A century largely of peace and prosperity later, the UK national debt was still £652 million in 1913, down in cash terms only a little from its peak of £853 million in 1818. But the economy had grown so much by then that this sum was less than 50 per cent of GNP; relative to national wealth it was only one-fifth of what it was at the time of its peak and, as such, effortlessly affordable.

Britain had, quite unintentionally, found a way to stimulate growth and tip oil into the machinery of the Supplier society with the successful sales of bonds, the resulting boom in government purchases and the steady supply of Good Money. The business of business became meeting the ever-growing demand. Initially demand from government was largely for naval supplies of guns, cordage, canvas, uniforms, gunpowder, preserved pork, barrels, ships, etc. But soon the demand spread wider. Increasing quantities of coal needed to be transported from mines to markets, leading to a canal-building boom. Demand for clothes was such that new machinery was developed to speed production. The persistent underemployment of all societies before the Birth of Now was soaked up as the navy and army ballooned and industry expanded to meet demand – so much so that new and better opportunities opened up for women in work. Newly wealthy individuals and speculative builders started to build new houses, developing the idea of terraces, squares and 'estates'. Cities started to grow wildly, factories and markets to spread out from their original locations.

The long, long economic boom was having a startling effect…

.5.

THE BIRTH

In any historical situation there are a million particularities that precede an individual event. Before the Birth of Now, Britain, north Ireland and Wallonia combined several relatively rare circumstances: a settled Supplier society, lengthy wars fought without the land being scorched, low levels of belief politics (religion, Nationalism, etc.) and the presence of large and easily accessible supplies of coal and iron ore. But we are not looking for a list of the conditions at the Birth; we are looking to determine what *caused* the Birth of Now and what the Birth of Now *was* that it caused. What unique thing or things happened? What *one* change means that we are not today still a society dominated by a fluctuating agriculture and the fear of famine and war, as all societies were before the Birth of Now?

The Birth of Now was a century-long economic boom in demand due to the surge in availability of Good Money. It lasted from around 1750 until 1846 in Britain and north Ireland, together with a similar economic boom for related, but slightly different reasons in Wallonia.

The boom in Britain had two phases. As we have seen, the first phase grew from the development of 'consols' in 1751 until around 1815. The success of these bonds and the demands of war enabled a vast expansion of military demand and a strong money supply. This brought the knock-on economic effects of a consumer boom, a property boom, a transport boom, a banking boom and an agricultural boom. These booms encouraged capital investment in production machinery and transport, which reduced costs and prices and improved the quality of both finished and input materials. The growth of wealth allowed more people to educate their children for longer, it improved the standard of living of the poor and so made slavery look very different to ordinary poverty and made it possible to do something more than the minimum to help the needy. The bonds enabled the government to spend a billion pounds a year more than they raised in tax, every year for over fifty years (on average, at modern values). This they spent mostly on the Navy and other arms. The revenue from this demand was then multiplied by increased consumer confidence and demand, a great growth in good quality Near Money, investor confidence and capital investment.

Hundreds of figures are available to illustrate the dramatic rate of growth. Let's look at just a few for illustration; in the eight years from 1775 to 1783, British production of cotton cloth rose from 57,000 yards to 3,500,000 yards. Or we can look at the imports of raw cotton over the longer period: these rose from £2.8 million per year in the 1750s to £173 million in the 1820s. The first canal built in Britain was completed in 1761. Forty years later and 165 canals were completed or being built, connecting every major industrial centre and mining area. Railway passengers increased from zero in

1824 to 5.5 million in 1838, 30 million in 1845 and 111 million in 1855 – that is in thirty years from zero. But there are hundreds of such figures and, looking around at the Georgian stately homes in the British countryside and the terraces and squares of the townscape, there is an equally impressive physical reminder of how this period multiplied everything over only a few decades – including population.

This startling and rapid economic growth and social change has become almost typical of 'catch-up' economies, as the Birth of Now spread around the world. At the time of writing, the average person in China is fifteen times as wealthy as they were twenty-five years ago. This kind of growth transforms not only individuals but also society, enabling it to provide work, leisure, entertainment and care in a way not open when many are struggling to survive. However, such booms normally end in a bust. The one in Britain did not because, as borrowing and war spending ended the injection of Good Money into the economy after the peace of 1815, another vast source of Good Money opened up.

The second phase of the Birth of Now in Britain, discussed in detail below, was an export-led boom, caused by the increase in manufacturing and commercial efficiency that the earlier boom had brought about. Because the first boom had maintained demand for so long, capital investment, production scale and machinery development had moved forward hugely. There was new transport efficiency through canals and improved roads with 'macadam' surfaces and new financial efficiency through the burgeoning banks. But the biggest effect of investment was in machinery. Production soared and prices dropped spectacularly. Clothing dropped to less than one quarter of its original cost over the period 1770-1815. This extraordinary new efficient and cheap production system was largely built in isolation from other countries, isolation brought about by twenty-two years of war after 1793. Then, after the end of the Napoleonic Wars in 1815, other European countries were suddenly exposed to it. British export sales took off and the boom continued, again with wobbles, until the slump of 1841-6. But, by that time the virtuous circle of continuing improvement was set: 'Now' had been born.

Everything that we see as the Birth of Now, all its effects, followed from the sustained growth in demand caused by government spending, funded from borrowing made possible by trust in a stable Supplier state. The sudden export boom at the end of the Napoleonic Wars prevented an economic crash, a crash that might have stopped the Birth of Now in its tracks.

Cotton textiles boomed in Lancashire, yes, but so did wool in Yorkshire and linen in Belfast; and ceramics in Stoke-on-Trent, and bootmaking in Leicester, and lace in Nottingham, and silk in Macclesfield, and carpets in Kidderminster, and hats in Luton, and coal in Northumbria, Lanarkshire and South Wales; and non-ferrous metal mining in Cornwall and Ireland – including a little-remembered gold rush in County Wicklow, 1795-1830; and ports in Liverpool, Bristol and

London, and metalworking, engineering and jewellery in Birmingham, and shipbuilding in Glasgow, Newcastle, Sunderland and Belfast; and banking and insurance in London; and agriculture and construction boomed mostly everywhere[47].

Alongside the manufacturing and services boom came its inevitable handmaiden: a property and construction boom. Thousands of miles of canal were built, followed by thousands of miles of railway. Posh new estates were developed in London, with the Bedford, Grosvenor and Regent's Park developments most noticeable, as well as the New Town of Edinburgh and much of the centre of Dublin. Complete resort towns like Bath and Harrogate sprang up from very little. But, above all, huge new commercial cities appeared; Glasgow, Liverpool, Manchester, Birmingham, Leeds, Belfast, any one of which would have been among the world's largest cities only a century earlier, accompanied by the explosive growth of London and the creation of new, large towns too numerous to mention.

These booms are also the reason why the price of agricultural products shot up in Britain; the price of wheat was 45 shillings a 'quarter' in 1789 but, between 1810 and 1814, it averaged 102 shillings[xlii]. As a result land rentals approximately doubled over the period 1790-1820, adding greatly to the prosperity of landowners and clergymen, who were largely paid from land rents. Because of the general

---

47 But note very little from the south and west of Ireland, which remained in a pre-Now state, along with some parts of Britain e.g. mid-Wales, for many more decades.

boom, however, there were fewer cries of desperation among the poor that would normally accompany such food price rises – there was full employment for all men in the armed forces and in industry, and many jobs that had been exclusively male previously became available to women. Meanwhile, the rise in prices prompted a surge in agricultural output that confined famine in Britain to just one brief period of natural disaster in 1816 and after that to history. Yet, at the same time, the dramatic increase in industrial efficiency was lowering the costs of other products, especially clothing, while lowered transport costs were reducing prices across a wide range of goods, notably coal for heating.

The flow of money and the confidence it brought with it did not only affect industry. This is why there are so many stately homes in the Georgian style; why Wedgwood's London showroom (opened 1768) was packed with eager customers interested in the latest designs; why the furniture makers Sheraton (1751-1806), Chippendale (1718-79) and Hepplewhite (1727-86) and the painters Constable (1776-1837) and Turner (1775-1851) flourished.

This extended period of economic growth in Britain, Wallonia and north Ireland was the cause and the means of change from 5,000 years of near-universal grinding poverty, everyday pain and cruelty, *Then*, to a period of continuous change that has brought large portions of humanity to health, material prosperity and compassion, *Now*. Summarising, Britain's Birth of Now came as the consequences of two events:

Event 1

The change from a Stealer society to a Supplier society, leading to the creation of an oligarchical government that enabled...

Event 2

- The development of a system of trusted, government borrowing, enabling...
- The government to borrow and spend, mostly at home, over two and a half times the whole annual national income, creating...
- An extended, decades-long economic boom, leading to...
- Major improvements in manufacturing, transport and commercial methods, lower costs and improved product quality, generating...
- A second, export-led boom of twenty to thirty years, as well as...
- Victory in an extended war and domination of world trade, resulting in...
- Confidence, a sense of political responsibility and the financial power to make a change in basic social structures, which...
- Combined with the technical change to create a virtuous circle of constant material, financial, social and political improvement, which is...
- The Birth of Now.

But Britain was not unique. Wallonia also experienced a long economic boom. Unlike Britain's double-boom, one from government spending and one from exports, Wallonia's was export-based throughout – and so more like the booms of the countries that later came to join the Birth of Now, as we shall see. In Wallonia, as in Britain, they had developed a Supplier-society structure. This was largely copied, like Britain's, from the Netherlands. Wallonia's Supplier character and mineral wealth and excellent transport links made it the leading iron and arms manufacturing area of Europe, selling especially to France. As Britain found a gold mine in bonds, so Wallonia found one in being the armourer to Europe, for a similarly long period. The repeated wars of the 1700s, climaxing in the long Napoleonic Wars, fed money into Wallonia from all across Europe[xlii]. Then, when the wars ended after 1815, the demand for tools, machinery and the structural use of iron in rebuilding Europe, rose to fill the gap caused by the (small) decrease in arms sales. By 1820 at the latest, the Walloon iron industry was as far advanced as the British iron industry.

The fact that the Walloon 'Industrial Revolution' was in parallel with the British – although, some say, ten years behind – shows that it was not peculiarly British institutions that created the Birth of Now. Wallonia and Britain are different in so many ways: continental/island, Catholic/Protestant, constantly disrupted by armies/untouched by armies, no waterpower/ample waterpower, etc. They shared only a few characteristics at this period, two of them being a flood of good money and participation in the Birth of Now (although both areas at the start of the Birth of Now also had coal). We can speculate that, without the much larger and broader-based British Birth of Now, the Walloon economic boom might well have followed the more typical path of the earlier Netherlands' economic boom and ended in a bust; but we cannot know.

There are plenty of factors that helped the process but were not vital to the Birth of Now. Yes, Britain is an island: but Wallonia is not. Yes, Britain had coal: but it could have imported it, as it did with cotton from America or, earlier, iron from Sweden. Yes, if the wars had been shorter, the government might have borrowed less and development might have been slower. Yes, Britain was politically stable, but that was as much the effect of wealth as the cause. It was not charm or intelligence that kept mad King George III as king. It was not skilled power play that kept his son, the debauched and idiotic George IV, on the throne. It was that Britain – less so Ireland – was largely contented by prosperity.

It also helped the Birth of Now that much of the British government spending was on relatively hi-tech naval supplies in the British economy, rather than on the pay of armies in foreign parts. There was also a great deal of simple commercial optimism and excitement around – as there always is during a boom. Fortunes had been made, commerce was widely successful – and had been for decades – the slave trade had been abolished without the threatened collapse of the cotton or sugar industries and a great war had been finally won. Because leading investors had plentiful, very liquid bonds that could be sold to provide cash for investment, commercial capital was easy to find in this optimistic atmosphere and added to the flow of Good Money. But all these factors came only after and because of the original prolonged flood of Good Money from government spending into a Supplier society. That was the fundamental cause of the Birth of Now.

Surprisingly, joint stock or limited liability companies of the type we take for granted now, were illegal. They were seen as enabling incompetent or villainous business owners to avoid the responsibility for their own decisions. In consequence, every investor in the new and expanding businesses was potentially risking every penny of his or her wealth should the investment fail and debtors need to be paid. In the circumstances, the widespread willingness of individuals to invest in risky businesses was astonishing and a tribute to the confidence sustained economic growth can generate (although many investors kept a careful eye on the liabilities that might be taken on by the companies they had shares in). Apart from the development of bonds, sophisticated financial or commercial borrowing and funding systems did not exist until after 1820, when, almost as soon as they were invented, they fuelled a financial bubble-and-bust, which broke in 1825 (but affected only the financial sector and investors, such as the novelist Sir Walter Scott, badly, not the 'real economy'). But without some luck, the British Birth of Now might have crashed sooner and much harder, as the earlier (Song/Yuan) Chinese, Netherlands and Venetian economic booms had and as later booms were to do again.

The first issue that should have prevented the British

Birth of Now is that the level of debt the government took on was clearly unsustainable. The rule (for countries and corporate bodies) is that some debt is good, more is better, too much is catastrophic. Yet catastrophe was avoided. At its peak of more than two and a half times the national income, the interest on the debt alone took most of the revenue of the government – and that was with most war taxes still in place. Normally, interest rates rise higher as the level of debt becomes troublingly high and people seek to put their money elsewhere, sometimes getting nervous enough to panic-sell, causing a collapse in bond value and disaster. But not this time. Furthermore, attempts to reduce the debt level could only have been paid from tax increases, killing demand and triggering a recession, making the position far worse. This seems to be largely what happened earlier in the Netherlands.

So what went right? There was the form of the debt: consols. These had no expiry date, so did not need to be paid off and refinanced by new borrowing, as fixed-term debt is today. They were refundable, on request, at face value, making a run on the bonds a possibility – but one that never happened. A mixture of reasons prevented a run on consols. There were very few other places to put the money; the commercial debt, foreign bond and equity markets did not exist until after 1820. The government suspended the convertibility of the currency at the crucial moment – the idea of selling bonds and getting gold might have had considerable appeal to the nervous as the French wars went on but from 1798 until 1821, just as it was becoming most attractive, that opportunity was withdrawn. The idea of selling one type of government-backed assets, 'bonds', paying 4 per cent, for another type of government-backed assets, paper money paying 0 per cent, is much less alluring than it would have been if the bonds could have been sold for money made of gold.

Then there was a simple lack of economic knowledge and information – there were no 'Business Pages' to start an alarm. What people did know was that the British Government had maintained a solid currency and paid its debt interest without the slightest wobble since the 'South Sea Bubble', eighty or so years earlier. Despite many crises, it had, apparently, been a model of fiscal regularity. The financial serious-mindedness of the government was repeatedly emphasised as the idiotic heir to the throne, later King George IV, and his brothers continually overspent and had, reluctantly, to be bailed out by the government with stern lectures on the topic of fiscal rectitude.

The second apparently likely disaster, economic collapse after the peace with France and the end of war spending, was also avoided. The government did start to reduce spending in 1814 after the Napoleonic Wars appeared to have ended but had to suddenly raise it again to meet the return of Napoleon in the campaign that ended at Waterloo in 1815, as well as funding the ongoing second American war. Even this small reduction caused huge hardship that coincided with a very serious failure of the harvest the next year, 1816. Although the slump of 1816 led to several years of hardship as the army and navy were returned to a peacetime footing, a full-blown recession was avoided with exports beginning to pick up as the disruption of the war faded. So quick was the recovery that the period 1820-25 saw the growth of a financial bubble.

But the debt was still too large to be paid off or even for the interest to be paid from taxation in the long term. It was only the continued dramatic growth of the economy over the next fifty years that sorted out this problem, reducing the cost of debt interest in relation to the taxes paid to an affordable level.

The dramatic increase in efficiency and lowering of costs was key. First, it acted to reduce the rising price inflation that the excess of money and demand was generating. Around the year 1800, the British economy was becoming overheated and, normally, the continued injection of money would have started inflation as growth in demand exceeded growth in output. But not this time. Food did increase in price substantially, as we have seen, but this was somewhat offset by the huge increase in output and lowering of prices in other areas, especially the lower prices of the other essential of the poor: clothing.

It is characteristic of new technologies that the first developments offer huge gains or advances, the next improvements provide substantial but smaller gains, the next fewer and so on. When the field is mature, further improvements are small and improvements have to be squeezed out with great effort (we will have much to say about this pattern later). To give just one example: before this period, half of those employed in silversmithing had been engaged solely in the process of hammering ingots of silver into flat sheets. Introducing power-hammers reduced, by nearly half, the labour used in producing a finished silver object. This large early-technology gain in efficiency was profoundly true of the textile business. Producing, picking and cleaning the raw material, spinning, carding, weaving and finishing cloth by hand are intensively laborious and often skilled manual processes, requiring many man-days to produce enough material for even a few garments. The innovations from around 1770 to 1820 improved the efficiency of labour by factors of five, six and seven times, while making the cloth more consistent and, where desirable, finer than handmade cloth could be. When European and other markets opened up after the peace in 1815 it was almost as though UK textiles were from another planet – a planet with much cheaper and better textiles. Moreover, textiles are easily transported and form a very large market – everybody needs them.

While textile exports catch the eye, there were many other markets where the British had similar, if less well-documented, advances and cost reductions. In each one, the development of the technology and of mass-production systems had been nurtured by booming demand, created by the UK war spending. Each, after the peace of 1815, found huge and comparatively backward markets opening up to them. The only substantial area where the UK did not have an immediate advantage was in iron and iron products, where Wallonia was equal to the UK challenge. The UK never became as big an exporter of machinery or iron products as it did in other areas.

What is initially surprising is that, once the process

had been started, it continued, so that, unlike any previous period of growth, it has never stopped. Recessions, wars and destructive beliefs have failed to halt the process of change. Change became self-catalysing, continuous and broadened as it deepened. We can't put a precise point when, like a car being push-started, change became self-propelled and the point of no return was reached. Most observers would say that change had become self-propelled before 1800, but an economic crash might have stopped it, nonetheless. It seems to have done so before in some of the other places we have looked at. If this had happened, people of the future might have looked at Europe and commented, as we now do of Song/Yuan China, "How extraordinary that, having invented so much, they just stopped and went backwards!"

We can look at the Birth of Now another way. The Birth of Now was the result of taking away the two great blockages in human development: first the Stealer society that destroys development and initiative and then the shortage of Good Money that prevents trade and stops economic growth. Once these constraints are removed, humankind strives to better itself, both individually and as a society. In a Stealer society, you get ahead by taking from others (or crawling to the Stealers) and the dominant ethic is violence. In a Supplier society, you get ahead by selling to others and the dominant ethic is trust – the more you are trusted, the easier it is to progress. Before the Birth of Now, little could be done to reduce mass misery and squalor; after the Birth of Now, it became possible to relieve large-scale suffering. The development of altruistic political parties and philanthropic individuals and groups shows the desire to help fellow humans, a desire frustrated before the Birth of Now both by lack of funds and the apparent inevitability of gross poverty. After the Birth of Now, people could hope that 'the poor are always with us' would one day become untrue.

It seems appropriate at this point to explore why the Birth of Now and its causes have been comparatively neglected. Why has there been so little comment on the British financial boom after 1750, the demand it caused and the transformative effect it had on the world? Only a few writers, notably Matt Ridley and Joel Mokyr[xliv], get close to identifying increasing demand as the key initiator of what we have called the Birth of Now.

One reason why demand is so little studied is that it falls between social history, industrial history, political history and financial history. Each of these is individually well covered, but none covers the process all the way from finance to demand to commerce, to agriculture and industry and then to society.

We were also, until recently, very close to the towering events of the First and Second World Wars and the Cold War and these huge events dominated the view. Now that they have receded a little behind us, we can put the hills of twentieth-century war into perspective and see the mountainous scale of the Birth of Now behind them.

Then there is the 'Industrial Revolution', a name which begs its own answer: if you write about the 'Industrial Revolution', you are more or less obliged to talk about industry, whereas the cause of the Birth of Now was outside industry. Industrial output is also relatively easy to quantify, which makes it a more concrete and satisfactory area of study for many than the softer and less tangible issues of the time.

The Birth of Now was also simultaneous with the political earthquakes of American Independence and the French Revolution. The US War of Independence is a most satisfactory source of legends and characters, but the system that resulted from it differs only in detail and style from the systems in the smaller (population) states of Canada and Australia with a similar colonial background but no founding war. The French Revolution was dramatic indeed, but the result, after all the noise, was a wobbly restoration of the previous monarchy and modernisation had to start all over again later. The next time there were major political changes in France, it was after the Birth of Now had affected the country. Although these two dramatic political events dominate writing about the period, the less dramatic Birth of Now has had an incomparably larger impact on humanity.

Finally, to understand the forces that made the Birth of Now requires an appreciation of the role of money. But the term 'money' in the Western mind implies greed or an excessively materialistic view of life. We have mental contrasts of pure love, opposed to filthy lucre; 'things of the spirit' versus 'things of the flesh'; 'God' against 'Mammon'; charity not commerce. Even the study of economics is defined without using the word 'money', preferring less compromised terms, for example: *a science concerned with the process or system by which goods and services are produced, sold, and bought*' (Merriam-Webster).

Yet advances in using and understanding money have, throughout history, advanced the human condition and bettered the lot of humankind. Trade was the key to elevating humankind above the level of subsistence and money is central to trade. It is money that makes trust a virtue instead of violence – and that makes it possible to live by the word, not by the sword. It was an accidental by-product of the Dutch/British system of government finance that multiplied the number of these units of trust, without diminishing the trust they embodied, hugely increasing the real wealth available to the community.

It was this ready availability of money that caused the Birth of Now and transformed our world from persistent poverty, misery and violence to frequent wealth, health and peace.

.6.

LIFE AFTER BIRTH

The Birth of Now, the 100-year economic double-boom in the UK and Wallonia, was a period of economic growth that started a loop of development and improvement continually feeding back into itself. The boom started with a financial revolution, went on with a property boom, industrial and agricultural revolutions, aided by a transport revolution, involved an education and communication revolution, created a social and political revolution and continued with other 'revolutions'. Focussing on the 'Industrial Revolution' alone in the Birth of Now is similar to focussing only on the Pacific campaign in the Second World War: it is important, but only a small part of the whole picture.

One change led into another and back into the original change, continuously, in industrial, agricultural, commercial and transport technologies and in financial, political, economic and social development. New ideas and improved inputs that were developed for one use went on to make improvements across all industries and across society. Some improved inputs were material, such as better quality iron or steel, improved transport and precision tools but just as many were intangible inputs, such as better education, professional retailing and marketing, uncorrupt government, better banking and insurance, accurate accounting, improved legal structures, etc., etc.

In this section we will look at how the Birth of Now generated its many effects and how it went on to spread to other countries, bringing us up to today with the world still split between part in the 'Now' phase and part still left in 'Then' conditions. The effects of the Birth were so comprehensive and affected every aspect of society and economy that it is too complex to do more than illustrate how the changes of 'Now' developed with a few examples. Firstly, a relatively obscure area as an example of the way that the changes of the Birth of Now interlocked.

The increase in British government expenditure caused by the Seven Years' War in the 1750s led to more and better-paid employment. This created a huge rise in the demand for clothing, because more clothing is one of the first things people buy when they have money left over after basic food and housing costs are paid, especially in chilly north-west Europe. The increased demand multiplied the supply of clothing made and worn (leading to factories and everything that stemmed from them, but we are not following this particular story here). So great was the growth in the sale of clothing and household fabrics such as sheets and curtains that it had the side effect of rapidly increasing the supply of rags (worn-out fabrics) and lowering their cost. Rags are the basic raw material needed to make paper[48] and this led, together with improved manufacturing machinery,

---

48   The use of wood pulp to make inferior quality paper came only after 1851.

to the cost of paper dropping by more than half. This led to cheaper books that increased sales, so print runs became longer, bringing considerable additional cost reductions. On top of these, there were improvements in printing and binding machinery – these were often copied from innovations in mechanised weaving and cloth-handling. Lower book prices, combined with the general prosperity, allowed middle-class people to buy books just for pleasure, talk about them to each other and again multiply the size of the book market. This greater availability and affordability of paper itself also contributed to improved education, with more access to textbooks creating more readers and writers. All these factors – cheaper paper, better literacy, more prosperity – led to a growth in letter writing and, as the rising volume of post lowered the cost of delivering each individual letter, fixed-price postage became a possibility. Having just one price for letters created huge efficiencies; it is said that just not having to look up the cost for each letter's destination in itself lowered postal costs per letter by half, enabling the price to be kept at one penny per letter for many years. So, as one minor consequence of the increased clothing demand after 1750 both the best-selling novelist, Sir Walter Scott, and the man who developed the 'Penny Post', Sir Rowland Hill, received knighthoods.

Simpler linkages can be made between, say, the improvement in iron quality demanded by the Navy for better cannons and the development of the pressure steam engine. But many, many interlinked factors were involved in holding back development before the

Birth of Now and it was by gradually removing them all together that the virtuous spiral of development was achieved, not by a simple cause and effect. We can follow the effect of cheaper books further to illustrate the point.

The Birth of Now made book reading, book borrowing and book buying a leisure activity. There was a sufficiently wealthy, sufficiently educated class of people who could read well enough to read for pleasure, a concept virtually unknown before the Birth of Now[49]. The growth in the book trades, publishing, bookselling and commercial subscription lending libraries was typical of many industries in that it was demand-led. This demand increased investment in production equipment, which resulted in lowered costs and then onto more demand, leading up to the Public Libraries Act (1850). Many of these readers were women. This was the first period in history when a significant proportion of women were educated for long enough to read for pleasure. Before 1750 novels effectively did not exist. What little written fiction there was tended to be political or social morality tales (although verbal story-*telling* is as old as mankind). The Birth of Now made the novel a viable commercial proposition for the first time and allowed authorship to become a profession so, by the 1790s, novels were available in numbers. This new profession, together with the broadening of education, empowered women: the novel – and popular writing generally – was the first art form where women and men competed equally from the outset. Women did not only

---

49   Such evidence as exists suggests that almost everyone literate before the Birth of Now read word by word and, normally, out loud.

lead in fiction either; the first million-selling author was Hannah More, writing ethical and religious guidance. From this period, fiction becomes an important influence on attitudes, heavily influenced by the female readership. We are so habituated to the idea that we no longer see how startling was the concept of a novel, like *Vanity Fair*, with a female leading character, written by a male author. It may be impossible to quantify, but is just as impossible not to feel the increasing role of a female approach over the period, until we get to female exemplars such as Florence Nightingale (1820-1910), while still without a formal, political role, having a direct and profound effect on her area of interest[50]. A good measure of the increasing influence of women is the rise in male fulminations in this period against the insidious effects of educated women and the invention of the term 'Bluestocking' for them.

The Birth of Now produced a dramatic improvement in real wealth. Meaningful figures for the growth in real wealth over the Birth of Now are difficult to provide but indications can be given[51]. In 1870, British milk output was nearly four times what it had been in 1750 and pork output was up by much the same[xlv]. These are fairly typical of agricultural output figures for the period. Coal output increased by around ten times in the same period and we have seen the vast growth in fabric production. Whatever figures for material output are chosen, they

---

50 Women, even in Europe, have always had access to roles of power as wives, widows, heiresses and mistresses. This new power was beyond and different to these traditional roles.

51 Figures for the rise in GDP are poor indicators of real wealth in this period, as much of the gain was in lowered prices, which shrink recorded GDP, as much as in increased volume.

show a vast increase in the amount produced and so in the amount people were able to consume; a huge growth in real wealth per head, even taking into account the growing population. As the wealthy were not able to consume much more milk and pork at the end of the period than they did at the beginning of the period, so much of this additional output must have added to the diet of the not-so-well-off.

It was during the Birth of Now that the concept of the 'shop' first developed. Previously, the needs of everyday folk were met through occasional markets, where travelling tradesmen would set up temporary stalls in the centre of towns on regular dates. Grandees had goods displayed to them at their own houses by the merchant. Perhaps the closest thing to a shop in most towns and villages was the blacksmith's forge or the inn. The first conventional shops as we understand them started in this period and dealt mainly in tea, sugar and coffee, probably the first imported goods anywhere sold to a mass market since the height of the Roman Empire. At the time, many marvelled that even common folk were able to buy a product as exotic as tea. Between 1700 and 1800 the world's first shopping street with large glass windows was developed around the Strand in London, a move taken to its retail peak by Josiah Wedgwood's spectacular china showrooms, opened in 1768[52].

The first improvements to meet demand during

---

52 It is said that one Strand retailer was so successful at selling special starched collars known as 'Piccadils', that he built himself a grand home amongst the London houses of the aristocracy. This was regarded as getting above himself and, to remind him of his common origins, the house and later, the road it was on became commonly known as 'Piccadilly'.

the Birth of Now were achieved by practical and straightforward methods, sometimes by people with limited education and almost invariably by people with little book expertise. But one of the key effects of the Birth of Now as it developed was professionalisation. There were few professions at the start of the period, but, with the Birth of Now, jobs that had previously been done by generalised managers became professions. This is signalled by the development of professional associations such as Civil Engineers, 1818, the British Medical Association, 1832 and the Chartered Accountants, 1854 in Scotland, (1880 in England and Wales). Sometimes, the move to professionalism was less structured, such as the transformation of the UK government service following the Northcote-Trevelyan Report of 1854.

It was towards the middle of the 1800s that intellectual and scholarly thinking started to have practical effects on the Birth of Now. By this time, the extent of the change, and the UK's leading role in it, was becoming obvious. The Free Market economic thinking of Adam Smith and David Ricardo started to be applied in practice, with widespread support for the free markets' they recommended leading to the near-disappearance of UK tariffs. At the same time, academic science started to make its first contributions to industry and social theories started to build into political socialism (prioritising society as a whole over individuals) and the communist belief.

The Birth of Now went far beyond the economic sphere in every way. It led to parallel developments across society: enlarging the voting franchise, providing an ever wider and deeper spread of free primary education and developing a professional approach to secondary education. Voting and education are linked, as it is difficult to make the case that illiterate voters can make reasoned choices on abstract issues, such as the make-up of Parliament.

The period after the Birth of Now in Britain saw the rise of social and political philanthropy. Before the Birth of Now, provision for the utterly destitute was often no more than enough food to get them to the next district, so that the costs of their burial would not fall on this district. Charity provision for poor children in many areas ceased at age seven because they were, from that age, expected to earn their own living. But, after the Birth of Now, charitable giving and political campaigns for better provision for the needy developed wide support. This led to the provision of workhouses, places where the needy were guaranteed food and a place to sleep in return for work. These were often (deliberately) grim places but, even so, they were generally seen by the poor as better than no workhouses. Model towns and workers' estates started and grew, as did charitable housing associations to provide low cost accommodation. Benign urges towards other people could now come out, no longer held in by either Stealer conventions or plain lack of resources. Once you have access to far more food than you need, you can spare a thought for, and feel guilty about, those who do not have enough.

Both Enlightenment thinking and Western religions have a theoretical belief in fundamental equality, but any form of equality was only practiced, at best, for the first few years of the beliefs. The widespread concern for the needy that came after the Birth of Now, although not new in principle, was new in practice. Stealer societies are characterised by the indifference of Stealers to the suffering of the poor. The move to a Supplier society softens the degree to which society is split into radically different 'classes' and begins to generate among the better off some sense of fellow-feeling with the needy. But the rather academic Enlightenment idea of equality was made more realistic by the wealth provided by the Birth of Now. The visible developments of the Birth of Now showed people that the world was changing and that old certainties were being reforged by the power of the human mind. The speed of change and the growth of wealth meant that many people felt that they could do something to change even age-old wickedness – and that they ought to.

Before the Birth of Now, 'doing the right thing' had never been considered as a possible role of government; ruthless self-interest was the rule, except in the enforcement of religious conformity. Now the British observed that they were, in practice, leading the world and many felt they should take the lead positively. We have already encountered the first major example of morality in the role of government: the UK abolition of the slave trade in 1807. This was despite the slave trade being as old as humanity, despite it being completely endorsed by Christian scripture and despite it being highly profitable right up to its abolition. But this rise in concern for the poor was not limited to official slaves. Imperceptible, small steps saw social responsibility become part of the government's role at home and the UK's role abroad. There were Factory Acts to improve the conditions of workers in 1802, 1819, 1831, 1833, 1844, 1847, 1850, 1856, 1878, 1891, 1901, 1937, 1959 and 1961. The most overt illustration of the new sense of equality that emerged after the Birth of Now was the extension of the vote. The right to vote was extended to owners of smaller properties and constituencies were adjusted to reflect population in the Reform Act of 1842. Then the vote was extended to all men over twenty-one, then to older women (1918), then to all women over twenty-one (1928) then to all those over 18 (1970). In parallel, trade unions were decriminalised and political parties specifically dedicated to representing labourers arose.

There has been a long and arduous debate as to whether, immediately after the Birth of Now, the life of the poorest was rendered worse. There have been a number of historians who found that statistics, child deaths, average lengths of life, etc., indicated an improvement in the living standards of the poorest, albeit from a starting point of the basest misery. But the louder voice over the past 150 years has been of those who claim that the life of the poorest was degraded by industrialisation. Most notable of this group were: Karl Marx, whose theories required that the living standards of the labourer got worse with industrialisation; his friend and colleague Friedrich Engels, who wrote *The Condition of the Working Class in England*[53]; Arnold Toynbee, who

---

53 Engels published this in German only in 1845 and it had very little influence in Britain until the first English edition forty years later in 1885. In his 1885 preface to the English edition he says 'the most crying abuses described in this book have either disappeared or have been made less conspicuous...' Marx never visited an industrial establishment, despite Engels urging him to, and personally avoided working-class areas and contact.

first popularised the term 'Industrial Revolution' in the 1890s, and, most popularly, E.P. Thompson, in his book, *The Making of the English Working Class* (1963). Some believe the poor in the UK remained worse off than they had been before the Birth of Now until after 1945.

After the Birth of Now, people did crowd into cities and become more exposed to pollution and infectious diseases, which explains some of the perception of worsening conditions of the poor. But, before the Birth of Now, few wrote about the miseries of the poor. The poor were there and their lives were hideous and miserable. But that was the nature of existence before the Birth of Now and few earlier writers thought there was any point in commenting on it. But every grotesque social horror that later writers talked about was at least as prevalent in Georgian London – before the Birth of Now – as it was in Victorian London after it, generally more so. Grim urban lives long pre-date the Victorians, as does the use of small boys to clean chimneys, which those same Victorians banned[54]. Engels was not wrong about the appalling conditions of the working class in 1845, although he exaggerated them by quoting horror stories from old reports (abuses that had been long remedied as a result of the reports), but he was wrong to suggest that these poor conditions were new. Charles Dickens and other powerful writers campaigning on poverty made no claim that the appalling conditions they described were worse than they had previously been, but often said that that they were more shocking, because it

---

54   In Britain child chimney sweeping was first, ineffectually, banned in 1788, a bit more effectively in 1840 and completely in 1875.

was now possible to do something about them. Emma Griffin has studied the lives of 350 'common folk' who both lived through the change of the Birth of Now and described their own experiences. She calls her book *Liberty's Dawn*[xlvi]. Again and again, the lives of people that started in the deepest misery escaped it through the new jobs that became available in the economic boom.

Although city crowding exposed more people to pollution and death from contagious diseases, the population of Britain expanded as never before. The population of Britain had already started to grow as the Birth of Now started. But, although it approximately doubled between 1700 and 1800, a similar rate of population growth had occurred during the relatively prosperous and peaceful period of the Southern Song Dynasty in China, so it was not unprecedented. But this was nothing like the growth in British population after the Birth of Now: it grew six times faster between 1800 and 1900 then between 1700 and 1800[xlvii]. This is much faster than any previous population growth-rate recorded anywhere[55]. It seems unlikely that this was a symptom of worsening misery.

We can also look at similar processes of industrialisation going on today in pre-Now areas, such as Bangladesh and parts of Africa. The conditions of the poor today in these countries, at home and at work in the garment sweatshops strongly resemble those described by the Victorian critics. But this work, often arduous, sometimes dangerous and always badly paid, is not

---

55   There was mass emigration from the UK in both centuries as well, largely to the US, Canada and Australia.

as bad for the poor – in their eyes – as not having the income. They take the available employment, despite its grim aspects. When asked, they say that it is very much better to be working than the alternative of complete and utter destitution of unemployment in those societies[xlviii].

The Birth of Now would be unique amongst economic booms if it made many worse off. Booms normally have the effect of improving people's material lives, at least for as long as the boom lasts. Undoubtedly life for the Victorian poor was often hideous but life for the poor before the Birth of Now was even worse. In the whole period of settled agriculture before the Birth of Now, life was worse for the landless poor than we can easily comprehend from our comfortable chairs today.

In parallel with the increasing numbers who were lifted out of poverty, levels of sickness dropped and lifespans extended. Sometimes it is difficult to pin a reason on why illness became less prevalent, especially when crowding seemed to make it worse early on after the Birth of Now, but better hygiene is normally given credit for much of the improvement. Careful antisepsis and preventative action started to achieve a great deal, even before modern medicine arrived after 1945. Average life expectancy has risen, generally by more than a year every decade, since accurate figures began around 1850.

The other reason for the improvement in health was the improvement in diet. After the Birth of Now there was enough food, for more people, for more of the time. Slowly, the choice available became better, especially in winter, and the effects of periodic harvest failures became less and less significant. The last year in which there was large-scale starvation in Britain was 1816, with the crop failure caused by very bad summer weather, said to be a consequence of the volcanic explosion of Mount Tambora in 1815[xlix] Probably the best definition of a 'Now' society, compared to a 'Then' society, is that mass malnutrition is inconceivable in a 'Now' society, while it is a regular visitor in a 'Then' society. But, while mass (peacetime) starvation had indeed become inconceivable in Western Europe by 1900, poor children in some parts of the UK were still recorded as markedly shorter than middle-class children as late as the 1930s, presumably because of diet. Today, the main dietary problem of developed society is obesity, due to the plentiful supply of attractive food available at a price that makes it effectively unlimited. This improvement in food supply continues – the output of a typical English wheat field is said to have increased by a tonne per hectare every decade even since 1940.

Another contribution to the increase in longevity is the collapse in the amount of serious crime. Before the Birth of Now, the period we are calling 'Then', murder was comparatively common: the figures suggest between fifty and a hundred in every million people per year in England in the 1700s but, given the nature of reporting and recording crime at the period, it was almost certainly higher. Murder and war were the biggest causes of death among young men. Violence was almost an everyday experience. Since then, there has been a dramatic drop in crime: murder (in the UK) is now less than ten in every million per year[xl], perhaps one tenth of the level 'Then'. There are reasons to believe other violent crimes have decreased more, although figures are much more difficult to compare than murder statistics. Since the Birth of Now, serious crime levels have varied a great deal, rising from time to time but, overall, have dropped to fractions of the levels typical before the Birth of Now[xli].

The new attitude of concern for the poor, while admirable in many ways, was often hugely arrogant, an arrogance that led to growing resentment among those so patronised, most importantly abroad. The change in the attitude of the British in India was the principle cause of the 'Indian Mutiny'. The individuals who acquired power under the flag of the British East India Company in the 1700s may have been greedy but they were not racist. As the 1800s – and the Birth of Now – progressed in the UK, the British in India moved to an assumption of racial and cultural superiority. The 'Indian Mutiny' rebellion of 1857 started among some of the soldiers of the British-officered Indian army because they thought the British were attempting to impose British culture onto their beliefs. When new rifle cartridges arrived in packaging that needed to be bitten open, the (probably correct) rumour arose that these were greased with pig and cow fats, forbidden to Muslims and Hindus respectively. The mutiny was put down by other Indian soldiers, also commanded by British officers, but only after a great deal of slaughter.

British post-Birth of Now paternalism was tainted by frequent hypocrisy. The same period that saw the UK ban the slave trade saw it promote the sale of opium in China and fight to keep it there. But the hypocrisy of the Opium War was at least acknowledged by some in Britain: "*a war more unjust in its origin, a war more calculated in its progress to cover this country with permanent disgrace, I do not know and have not read of,*" said a young MP, William Gladstone, presciently.

There is no question that the confidence and arrogance of the UK was extremely high by the 1830s and 1840s. Missions of every sort to improve the world were in hand, from the care of children to the protection of animals, from '*bringing Christianity to the benighted Hindoo*' to encouraging Nationalism in Europe – Nationalism was seen by many as clearing the path for liberal improvement, with few anticipating the slaughter it would later cause.

Another effect of the gradual but universal acceptance of human equality in 'Now' societies was the growing acceptance of human diversity. This started in the UK with the slow progress towards religious equality after the Birth of Now. Political disabilities were removed in UK law in 1829 for Catholics, amid some violent protests, and from other, non-Christian religions in 1846, although social prejudice often continued well into the twentieth century. Next, discriminatory laws, rules and attitudes, distinguishing people by their gender were gradually removed, a process largely completed by the end of the twentieth century in those countries that went through the Birth of Now first. It also took until the late twentieth century for 'nationalist' and 'racist' prejudices to subside, although they reappear from time to time when political events give nationalist beliefs a boost. Diversity of sexual orientation, notably homosexuality, was illegal and still, after legalisation, regarded with distaste by some as late as the 1990s. Varied sexual orientation became socially accepted by the start of the twenty-first century, as did the desire to accept equally the disabled and disfigured in all aspects of life as far as possible.

Leisure time and leisure activities are concepts that arrived with the Birth of Now. A feature of Stealer societies is that, except for brief periods of unremitting activity, such as planting and harvest, there is often nothing much to do and people just hang around. (An easy way to diagnose how much 'Stealing' there is in a society is to see how many of the adult male population are simply hanging around on the streets in the mid-morning. Add to them those who are waiting for customers in semi-jobs, such as portering or taxi driving. The more there are, and the less they are doing, the greater the power that the Stealers have in that society.) They don't do much while they hang around; certainly they don't engage in sports or other formalised 'leisure activities'. We do not know what prevents these idlers from developing or playing the games that later became popular, unless it is just that Stealer societies teach the lesson that the poor must act miserable or they will be reduced to greater misery. So popular sports and most other hobbies do not exist in Stealer societies, either for people to play or spectate. The exception is fighting: cockfighting, dogfighting, hare coursing, bear-baiting, human 'prize' fighting, sword fighting and jousting, etc. were all popular diversions before the Birth of Now. Stealers do have horse racing and hunting but even these are not practised as often as post-Birth of Now leisure activities.

After the Birth of Now, long hours at work filled many ordinary people's time almost completely. But almost everyone had one day a week off and now, it seems, people wanted to fill even this relatively brief period with activity. To fill the gap, both participating and spectator sports were developed. Because Britain was the first 'Now' country, most sports were developed there. Football [56](soccer), rugby football (the Americans adapted their variety of football from rugby), golf, tennis, badminton, curling, bowls and bowling, field hockey, from which ice hockey was developed, baseball and cricket were all games that started in Britain. Leisure activities that had previously been limited to the aristocracy had to be restructured for a mass market: horse racing and music halls all became available to the masses and popular during this period, while the home piano became the prime symbol of middle-class culture.

Tourism started, predominantly but not exclusively, among the better off. Previously leisure travel in Europe had been largely limited to a once-in-a-lifetime pilgrimage but, as the Birth of Now developed, so did a desire for travel. Initially, the excuse for this was to visit a 'spa', a town that had mineral-water springs that were claimed to improve health. It is telling that the first of these was in Wallonia, at the town of Spa itself, the town that gave its name to the concept. As the Birth of Now got under way, Britain rapidly filled with 'spa towns'

---

56 Some form of sport were played earlier – Oliver Cromwell was said to have wasted his time playing football as a student – but it was never organised as it was after the Birth.

as local businesses saw the money-making potential: Bath, Leamington, Harrogate, Tunbridge, Droitwich and forty-three others all claimed to have waters with spa qualities. At the same time, in the late 1700s, 'sea bathing' started, again with the initial excuse of health. The idea of leisure travel for the broad middle-class was well established by the time railways started to promote it in the 1840s.

So, very quickly after the Birth of Now, the skeleton of the current world was in place. It has taken a couple of hundred years to put the flesh on the bones of the modern lifestyle fully, to get universal education to eighteen, ample food, clean air and water, the vote for every adult, central heating and air conditioning, women's rights, the principle of universal social security, extended annual holidays, etc., etc. But, although completion has taken time, every aspect of the change that has created the modern world was in place before the end of the Birth of Now, which we can date to around 1850, when many neighbouring countries had roughly 'caught up' with the UK in wealth. A more symbolic marker ending the original Birth is the London Great Exhibition of 1851, the Crystal Palace Exhibition in Hyde Park, London. This is a perfect symbolic event to define the point when all the strands that shape the modern world were in place, just needing time to complete. Millions of train-borne 'common folk' came as tourists to visit a technology exhibition in a system-produced glass building. In that building a significant proportion of the leading technology came from outside the UK. Even before the first Birth of Now had ended, it had moved on and new Births had started and already matured beyond the UK and Wallonia.

Since the original Birth of Now, country after country has undergone a 'catch-up' Birth of Now. Neighbouring countries in Western Europe (France, Belgium, the Netherlands, Scandinavia, Germany, northern Italy) rapidly caught up with the United Kingdom, so that, after 1850, the differences between their levels of wealth, social progress and productivity were matters of detail, although the United Kingdom retained its lead in textiles, shipping and finance for considerably longer. They can all be considered equally 'Now' countries, changing and developing in rough synchronisation. (Variations in figures for wealth and output-per-head between the European developed countries after 1850 depend, not on their urban level of development, but on how big their traditional agricultural sector was. So, for example, the figures for Belgium indicate a country richer than France, but that is only because France has more agricultural regions: the urban hubs of the two countries were at effectively identical stages.) The USA, Canada, Australia, Argentina and New Zealand were at least as wealthy as the UK in 1850, but their wealth mainly came from their rich agricultural sectors. Each had developed a society at least as liberal as the UK, with the exception of attitudes to people with dark skin[57]. In the second half of the 1800s, their immigration rose and they rapidly caught up in industry too, overtaking the UK in overall wealth. The USA, Canada, Australia,

---

57 In Britain, which did not have much variation in complexion, bigotry was reserved for Catholics in general and the Irish specifically.

Argentina and New Zealand were the first countries to achieve the stage when all citizens, apart from some of those suffering mental or physical disability, have practical access to sufficient food, protective housing and medical services, the stage of 'minimal material want' (MMW).

The concept of MMW is important to qualify. Even with rich 'Now' societies there are those who suffer deprivation. Around fifteen per cent of the population of these societies suffer from want by various definitions, some for reasons of mental or other illness and others for reasons that seem to defy easy categorisation. MMW is the point where the overall wealth and available benevolence of society ceases to affect the numbers who live in deprivation: people are poor not, as previously, because there is not enough money for them, nor because society does not care, but for some other reason. There are people who are living in straightened circumstances in Canada and Sweden, to name two rich and generally well-managed societies that have long sought to make well-being universal. But the number in want has not been diminished over many years by their society's increasing wealth nor by carefully constructed policies seeking to lessen deprivation in either country. People who are worst off in these societies are still drastically better off than they were before the Birth of Now, but the continued existence of such, apparently unnecessary, suffering is sad indeed. However, its causes and solutions are as impenetrable to this analysis as they have been to all the others to date.

The disastrous effects of extreme Nationalism and Communism delayed the roll-out of the Birth of Now during the first half of the twentieth century. However, as soon as they had recovered from the Second World War, development restarted in Germany and Japan, followed by (South) Korea, South-East Asia and Taiwan. Since then, country after country has suppressed Stealing and gone through a catch-up Birth of Now. The belief of Communism, as practised in the USSR from 1917 and its puppet states from 1945 had held Russia and many European countries with their development suspended part way through the Birth of Now. After the collapse of the USSR in 1989-91, these countries were able to join the developing crowd.

Since the Second World War we can use the presence of democracy as a very approximate marker of the number of countries that have moved into the 'Now' phase of development. In 1970 there were, by a generous count, only forty-five democratic countries; by 2010 there were 115 democratic countries out of 194 countries in total. We can question the detail of such a count and the degree of linkage between democratic government and development, but the trend over only forty years is so strong that it cannot be seriously questioned.

Now, in the early twenty-first century and in very approximate terms, one third of the population of the world has MMW societies, one third is catching up and one third is still in bone-poor Stealer states or regions. Within some large countries, such as China and India, there is a mixture of areas and industries: some 'Now', law-abiding, wealthy and productive, others of crude, impoverished Stealerdom.

The process of 'catching up' is straightforward and faster than the original Birth of Now. The individuals and businesses in an undeveloped country, once freed from the threat of arbitrary confiscation by Stealers, simply copy every aspect of developed country business. This enables them to produce adequate products at much lower prices than those made in 'Now' countries, resulting in an export boom and a flood of Good Money into the country catching up. This imitates the effect first observed in Britain after 1815: export revenue feeds into investment and growth, continuing until the country 'catches up' with the first post-Birth countries.

Initially, manufactured products in markets such as textiles, toys and hardware dominate exports[58]. Existing product models from developed countries are simply copied, made on production lines bought from developed countries, often very similar lines to those the originals are made on. These products are shipped out to markets where they sell easily because they are recognisably similar to, and cheaper than, the originals they are copied from. The products are cheaper, not only because they are made by low-wage labour but, even more importantly, because all their other costs, bar transport, are also lower or non-existent. Companies in catch-up economies do not need to bother much with provision of employee comforts or benefits such as heat, light, air-conditioning, safety measures, sick pay,

---

58 Except in India, where continuing Stealerdom prevents manufacturing doing well but has been slow to find ways to Steal from software and computer services that, as a result, lead exports.

pensions and training. All their other costs are lower as well: negligible development costs and few 'externality costs', such as compliance with safety, planning, accounting, reporting, licensing, product liability or pollution regulations. Marketing costs for products that sell on the basis of 'nearly-the-same-but-cheaper' are not onerous either.

The help provided to catch-ups by the example of the already-developed countries is more extensive than that, however. Governments and services follow the same path. Areas such as immigration law, pensions' regulation, traffic rules and so on and on, are also simply copied. If the European Union has spent twelve years working out a set of pension regulations satisfactory to its twenty-eight member countries, you are unlikely to devise a better set than you will get by simply copying what they come up with[59].

Services and cultural items, too, are imitated as far as possible. If you want to sell a motoring magazine, produce a successful family TV show, write insurance for bus companies or sell popular songs, why would you vary from the successful examples in other markets? You simply translate them into your language, with only the minimal modification needed to fit particular local market issues.

The many intermediate stages the first developing countries had to go through are skipped by the catch-ups. In plumbing, only plastic pipes are used, the earlier, transitional use of lead, cast iron and copper being mostly unheard of in this role; the use of film to take

---

59   China did this in 2011.

photos, with all its costs and paraphernalia of processing, negatives, etc. is unknown; desktop computers and cheques can be passed-by in societies that move straight to mobile IT and funds transfer.

Having caught up the wealth of the existing developed countries, the catching-up country will start to experience the same costs as its developed competition – pay increases as the market grows and the population will no longer tolerate social costs such as pollution, arbitrary eviction for purposes of construction and dangerous food. At this time the newly wealthy catch-up may start to notice a lack of some elements of development, such as a culture of independent innovation or the know-how to create and manage originality, and this may begin to show. Sometimes these skills, or knowledge of how to export them, have not been built up or there is too little flexibility and the country suffers a period of adjustment, such as the UK experienced after 1960, Japan and France at the time of writing. However, with the exception of Argentina, which has returned to a semi-Stealer (or 'Rentier' economy), each catch-up that has joined the 'Now' countries has stayed there, each keeping up a similar level to each other (once the effects of war are removed). Today, catching up, at different rates in different countries, is almost universal. Few countries and regions are completely unaffected, although Stealer elements fight back, keeping some countries poor or developing only slowly. Nevertheless, at current rates, the whole world will have achieved minimum material want (MMW) before the year 2100.

Within the group of fully developed, 'Now'

countries, progress and growth in real wealth also continues. Their economic growth is slow compared to catch-up countries, typically averaging 1 or 2 per cent a year, perhaps doubling constant-value money wealth every forty years. This means that each generation is twice as wealthy as the previous one. That is, an average person of the current generation has access to the same economic assets as a person of double average wealth in the previous generation. The exception is in areas of life where there is a 'crowding effect', where supply is difficult to increase. Examples of such areas are: property in desirable locations, road-space downtown and tickets to watch top games and shows live. Technological advance probably adds as much or more than economic growth to the increase in real wealth of individuals in developed nations. The cost savings provided by computerisation, the Internet and mobile telephony are rarely mentioned and they are not recorded as economic or any other sort of growth. Although we have no official measure, information technology advances have transformed the efficiency of developed economies over the last decades as well as the entertainment and choices available. Calculation, written communication, typing/typesetting, stock control, record-keeping, navigation, technical drawing and many other routine activities that were done manually as late as the 1980s and 1990s, are done now automatically with huge cost-saving efficiencies. The increase in efficiency enabled by e-mail, Internet searches and mobile access is not directly measured but is large. A product or service can be found without laborious telephoning around, using agencies or making physical visits. The ability to access people anywhere and at any time prevents many wasted trips and meetings while communication is immediate and recorded. But beyond just gains in efficiency, computer games, social media and video streaming have opened up opportunities for enjoyment that did not previously exist.

So 'Now' countries are enjoying ever increasing real wealth, greater provision for the needy, more freedom, better health, longer lives, more access to entertainment, greater comfort and less crime and fear. Although there are still pockets of Stealer stasis and poverty, much of the rest of the world is somewhere in the catch-up process and, barring a complete change of direction (see next chapter), will be at the same place within fifty or so years.

But, at the time of writing, a substantial part of the world is still living in 'Then' societies, where the typical quality of life is reduced (by the Stealers) to close to the minimum required for continuing existence – or, with war, below that level. At the same time the 'Now' benefits have spread to most healthy residents of developed countries, and to developed regions of countries like China. This means that people's desire to move from one to the other becomes great. Because of their size and isolation, this had much less effect on the US, Canada, Australia and New Zealand, probably the first countries to achieve MMW, than it has had on the more recently prosperous countries. Over the last twenty years, China has experienced the greatest movement of people in human history, as over 200 million people have moved from the still-undeveloped parts of the interior to cities that have already gone through the Birth of Now. The issue of immigration into Europe, which has 'Then' areas very close to it, is one that will persist. It will probably become more severe, until the vast disparity between Then and Now societies is reduced – presumably as the remaining Then societies catch-up as they, too, get to Now.

This place, 'Now', is so much better than 'Then', that it seems beyond belief. The more you look in detail, the more extraordinary is the transformation triggered by the economic boom in Britain, 1750-1850, the Birth of Now. This is especially true when contrasted to the stasis of the previous 5,000 years.

But we should turn the observation around. The Birth of Now resulted from taking away two great blockages in human development: the Stealer society, which destroys development and initiative, and the recurrent shortages of Good Money, which strangled trade and economic growth. Once people are allowed to improve their world, it turns out that, on average, they do. There have been false trails and hideous errors in the continuing step-by-step search for better lives, but humanity is succeeding overall. Certainly there is incomparable improvement in every materially measurable sense, if not necessarily in the spiritual and emotional sense.

Previously, historians have looked for reasons why development started. In this analysis we asked the reasons why there was so little progress until the Birth of Now and found the reasons why change and development did not start much earlier. Without ever saying it or even quite thinking it, we had assumed that what made progress so slow was that people in the past were stupid; grown-ups at a childish stage of intelligence. This unwitting assumption explained why so many obvious devices, from the horse collar to the plough mouldboard, took so long to develop or spread. In this picture, humanity is seen as slowly growing up like a child, grasping new ideas as it does so – it is such a powerful and obvious analogy it is almost irrestible. The Victorians explicitly thought this, and thought that non-Europeans were less grown-up than they were themselves. Africa was at a low level of economic development because the Africans were too childlike to come up with the spinning jenny: *'Your new-born sullen peoples, half devil and half child',* according to Kipling. This vision of an idiotic population ties neatly into other legends; like that of Gutenberg inventing printing (or moveable type}, and the pre-Colombian Americans who did not 'invent the wheel'. It wasn't the steepness of the mountains but the lowness of the foreheads that prevented this 'breakthrough' in the Andes.

Enough cheap mockery. We all believed something like this without realising it. It is implicit in the way we were all taught about our world. The story here is very different: before the Birth of Now, people could do nothing to make things better; now that they can, they do. Mankind has not stopped looking for money for nothing – 'Rent-seeking' economists call it – for monopolies, for licence fees and biased terms of trade but, in a Supplier society, we do not often get away with it. Generally we can only make money by supplying what others want better then someone else can. As soon as the brakes were taken off, humankind cumulatively improved everything tangible. In some areas we have had more than two hundred years during which individuals could get up every morning and not be prevented from improving some aspect of life, however minute. There were mistakes: the modern beliefs, Communism and Nationalism, created wars and repression, and there were unanticipated side effects of economic improvements, such as pollution. There is the continued persistence of 'Then' countries, where Stealers still rule, but their numbers are falling and will continue to fall. These problems have been addressed and will be solved. Today, the progress of Now has a regular forward march, advances far outweighing the odd slip-up. Where will the dynamic of Now take us in future?

.7.

NOW AND FOREVER

Forecasters of doom have always been around, at least since the Birth of Now. They are generally regarded with respect, even when their doomsdays lack conviction and sometimes even after their disasters have failed to materialise at the predicted date. It seems we use them as a talisman of protection; we gain comfort from their gloom.

While we, the large majority in the developed world, view our own personal futures and those of our family with a balanced optimism, opinion research also shows that we expect serious future national and global problems to arrive, possibly even disasters. Our personal future and that of our family will be OK, we expect, but we fear that the world faces increasingly acute difficulties. There are good reasons for these opinions.

If we expect the worst, we will be happily surprised when reality turns out better then our forecast, which it probably will. If we expect good things in future, we feel that we are likely to be disappointed. This disappointment might be much worse than our present gloomy opinion of the future, which we know we can handle without too much pain. Adopting a pessimistic view about the future of the world is like saving money; it causes a controlled amount of distress or suffering now, in order to make the future more pleasant. Building a buffer-stock of gloomy anticipation means that a turn for the worse is only what we expected. We are ready for it. A pessimistic view of the future is the provident, sensible stance.

We are all taught from the youngest age, by legend, fairy tale and film that pride not only 'cometh before the fall' but, mystically, it causes the fall. So we must avoid being complacent or self-satisfied or we will bring on our own downfall. Equally to be avoided is a half-witted, happy-go-lucky approach, as this also brings on its own doom in popular legends. The repeated lesson is that sensible, relatively small precautions, taken in advance, prevent catastrophic disasters later. Looking for problems in advance allows you to avoid them happening. Gloomy forecasts in the popular culture are like engineering safety factors: with luck they will not be required, but it would be madness not to have them.

Finally, many of us believe – and at a visceral level we cannot control – that a spiteful prankster controls our destiny. We cannot help but feel that, the moment you let your guard down and say something complacent, you will be proved wrong. After any remark such as, *"At least the family have been healthy,"* we say *"Touch wood,"* to prevent life from grabbing this unreasonable smugness and provide immediate disproof by making a family member sick. This, pure voodoo, is very powerful and affects almost any statement or decision we make about the future.

As a result of all this, optimistic forecasts make us profoundly uncomfortable, quite regardless of any evidence supporting them or lack of it. We cringe if someone starts predicting universal happiness, wishing that, even if they believe it, they would avoid voicing it. But, on the other hand, we dislike as much the person who predicts unavoidable doom. A person who tells us that we will all die soon and horribly will be ignored and despised. It is one of the strengths of the global warming scare that, while it predicts grave problems, we can see that *our* families are likely to survive them in relative comfort. Indeed, having a defined future problem that we can see and that we can handle, removes the uncertainty. For the reasons above, we have to perceive that some disaster is coming and it is much better to know what the disaster will be, especially if we can see ourselves, maybe after a struggle, surviving it quite well. Much better than the unknown, at any rate.

Because it is such an emotionally charged area, it is difficult to read predictions without preparing mental defences in advance, without arming ourselves with scepticism and indifference, preparing cynical rejoinders to counter both risky over-optimism and dispiriting doom. But readers can be reassured. For a few pages, you may fear that the future predicted is too flip and rosy but you should not worry. We will, in the end, suggest that humanity will face some serious problems, but problems that you, your family and descendants will, nonetheless, be able to cope with. With that assurance, let us start the analysis.

The new perspective we get from focussing on the Birth of Now, is an understanding of how quickly and how thoroughly human life has been changed. No longer do we see prosperity, social equality and freedom in the post-Now countries as the product of thousands of years of slow development: it is the result of less than 250 years of rapid development. Across all the previous millennia, few advances of importance happened. In contrast, each of the past twenty-five decades has produced historically significant advances, advances so influential that cities and lives have become unrecognisably changed several times in that short period. The first airplane, flown by Wilbur Wright, took off in 1903. It flew one person 260 metres in fifty-nine seconds. One hundred years later and, at any moment in the day, 39,000 commercial passenger aircraft were flying more than half a million people. Remember the rough figures mentioned in Chapter 1, that from 1800 to today population increased by sevenfold, total output of goods increased by 120 times, energy consumption by sixty times. Change has been very fast and very great since the Birth.

When we saw our current lifestyle as a product of thousands of years of development, it looked as though we were on a long, slow path of improvement at a gentle pace. This became built into our picture of the world without our realising it and in Chapter 1 we gently mocked it as the unspoken theory of CSP, Constant Slow Progress. But we now recognise that very little fundamentally changed from the start of history in Sumer until around 1750 and that, since then, there has been rapid and accelerating change. That means that we are 'going into the future' much faster than we thought. We are, by analogy, in a rocket, not a train and we must expect change in the future to have a substantial impact in our lifetime, just as changes in the recent past have done since the Birth of Now. We must also expect that current trends will move so fast that they will come to their end or completion in a few decades: after all, the trend of an ever-expanding railway network, the trend to extend the vote to a larger proportion of the population and the trend to socialistic governance have already long since reached their end.

If there is a gigantic volcanic explosion or a comet strike in the next few years all forecasts are irrelevant. These have happened infrequently in the past and, hopefully, we will find ways to prevent or handle such problems over the next 100 years or so, after which we can expect that we will be able to deal with these things. But, apart from this unlikely possibility, we can now try to track to see where this fast rate of change will go and, possibly where it will end.

Before we turn to what the future would look like if our current rate of progress continues, we need to check to see if there are things humanity could do to itself to break the pattern of economic improvement that has characterised the world since the Birth of Now. After all, we have seen that it was humans themselves that held humanity back in poverty and misery for thousands of years because of the Stealer society. Are there ways we ourselves could bring about the return to such a state again?

Over the whole period since the Birth, output has risen much faster than population – although our expectations have risen as fast, so that we still struggle to keep up. The first problem this suggests is that the resources needed to continue growth will become exhausted; we will simply use them up.

Looking in more detail at the resources we will need, we do not need to worry about the many resources that cannot be 'used up'. Copper is an example. Unless it is flung into space, it remains here on earth. So, unless we find a way to make used copper inaccessible to recycling, it will not be 'used up'. Fossil energy, on the other hand (coal, oil, fuel gas), *is* used up and must run out over time and, although, today, we seem to find as much as we use every year, this cannot go on forever. But fossil fuels are only one form of energy and many other forms of energy are available, although at the moment they cost more. But that cost will come down – since the Birth of Now technology costs have a track record of getting lower over time – and we cannot use up the total resource of accessible 'energy' – there is much too much available from the sun alone.

Since the Birth of Now we have run out of important resources several times. Sperm whale oil, for example, was a critical and valuable resource, an incomparable lubricant. Its use, along with all the other 'vital' whale products, was banned to prevent whale hunting and extinction. But the complete loss of this resource has not had any appreciable effect on human development.

We must face the fact that if output has increased by 120 times over the last 250 years and such resources as have run out have been substituted without problem, then that process is likely to continue. There is no reason – other than the desire not to be complacent – to think that so long-established a trend will suddenly change direction. We cannot duck the issue of our future so easily by assuming that resource availability will prevent it happening. Even the problem of the population explosion is shrinking as population growth slows down. Numbers are forecast to peak later this century at about 50 per cent more than today's population level.

If we negatively affect the natural habitat through pollution so as to make large areas of it useless, it would cause problems in the supply of agricultural products. But for the foreseeable future, this is a possibility thousands of times beyond our small powers, even if we meant to do so deliberately – after all, we can only use reshaped natural products to make the mess anyway. Making as much mess and pollution as even a small volcanic eruption would be costly and difficult. The idea that we can do something to nature that is either larger than natural disasters already achieve or of a different character to them seems arrogant and lacking perspective. We are not nearly powerful enough, yet. But we do not seek to make messes deliberately and we cut pollution as soon as we have the money to do so: London, Los Angeles, Athens and now Beijing, have all been through the process of getting richer and dirtier before they got still richer and cleaner. Notorious concentrations of human-generated filth from the recent past such as Manchester, Pittsburgh and Essen are now clean and healthy.

War, on the other hand, may be different. War has been a constant companion of humanity. So it is a reasonable assumption that war will be as inevitable in the future as it has proved unavoidable in the past.

It is easy enough to explain war in a Stealer society: it is simply regular Stealing, ramped up to a larger scale. The gains of victory in war are simple: taking from the defeated the animals and the portable items of value, raping and enslaving them and, longer-term, the opportunity of taking over another Stealer's MYOBers and territory. Because Stealer societies dominate history before the Birth of Now, this explains most wars. It also explains current wars in areas that remain Stealer-dominated.

Supplier societies are inherently non-belligerent: trade is badly affected by war. This was expressed light-heartedly by Thomas Friedman as the 'Golden Arches Theory'. This states that 'no two countries that both have McDonald's have fought a war against each other since each got its McDonald's.' While not strictly true, exceptions appear to be due to McDonald's boldness in entering countries that are still dominated by a Stealer ethos, rather than some Supplier societies being warlike[li]. There is little profit in one Supplier society conquering another, as the ethos of Supply prevents it stealing – if Denmark 'conquered' or 'was given' Sweden, what use would it be to Denmark or the Danes? What change would it make? The largest Supplier 'Empire', the British Empire of *c.*1900-1950, more or less 'broke even'. It provided Britain with occasional benefits and occasional dis-benefits, fairly equally. The Empire's impact on the British economy can be judged by the stock market value put on the company that ruled India, the East India Company. At its peak, before the Indian mutiny, it was valued at less than the London and North Western Railway Company[liii]. Although the Empire provided additional troops to Britain during the First World War, it required defending by British troops during the Second World War. Meanwhile profit was being made from British trade outside the British Empire, say, with Latin America, at least as much as from trade inside the Empire. The dictator of the Soviet Union, Stalin, demonstrated the confusion of Stealer and Supplier war aims. At the end of the Second World War, he stole the industrial equipment of the countries he took over – whole factories – notably in the eastern part of Germany and took them back to Russia. He believed that the equipment was what made their wealth. It was not, and the equipment scarcely worked at all in his Stealer society. As soon as the acute phase of war recovery was over, the Soviet Union managed to stay poorer than East Germany, which still retained some Supplier qualities, despite being under Soviet domination.

War between two or more Supplier societies must, win or lose, lead all involved to drastic impoverishment of their economy as well as mass death in its population, so you might think that war would never happen between Supplier states. But beliefs[60] can and have still led them to war. The nationalist belief rose to mass popularity shortly after the Birth of Now and the communist Belief shortly after that. Nationalism caused many of conflicts,

---

60 A Belief is a system of behavior dominated by conviction in an unproven fact. Traditionally beliefs are divided into either a religion if it started before the Birth of Now (Christianity, Islam, etc.) or an ideology if it started since (Communism, Nationalism, Environmentalism)

notably the First and Second World Wars, based on the need to attack other countries because other countries were likely to attack them. Besides killing millions and leading to deprivation and hardship for all involved, both wars set back development by something like a decade each. When extreme believers in Communism took power, initially in Russia, they acted to freeze all improvement in the life of their population once the economy had recovered from the war, until the system collapsed. Last century, these two Beliefs were, by far, the most significant drags on improvement since the Birth of Now.

It seems likely that at least a few governments will be taken over by extreme Beliefs sometime in the near future. At the time of writing, movements to turn back the clock are building in several Muslim states and sectarian wars at different scales are in progress across much of the Islamic world. Environmentalism, the newest Belief, is an ideology directly opposed to development. Its faith is that side effects of development will bring humanity's doom so development must stop and be reversed as far as possible. Because they believe that the whole future of humanity is under threat, some Environmentalists do not consider the consequences of the programmes they propose to matter, even when they have caused mass death[liv]. Communism, a similar belief in many ways, started as a group of idealists in 1848 and took sixty-nine years to gain power in one country, Russia, in 1917. If we start the clock for Environmentalism in 1970, when Friends of the Earth and Greenpeace started, and use the same timetable as Communism, we will get an Environmentalist government somewhere, dedicated to reversing development, by 2039.

Whatever the Belief, it is likely that, once it gets power in one country, it will use that power to seek to convert the rest of the world. In the end, the non-believers will probably prevail as they did in both the violent destruction of Nationalism in Germany and the peaceful end of Soviet Communism in Russia. The strategy of non-believers can be purely practical while the strategy of Believing states is distracted by the requirements of the Belief. The disruption caused by past Beliefs did no more than to delay development by a decade or two and it seems unlikely that any future beliefs will do more. But if Beliefs can only delay development, can money stop it altogether?

The trigger for the Birth of Now was a change in the availability of Good Money in an already existing Supplier society. This, on the face of it, is odd. Money, like the number three, is a mental artefact of our human culture and there is a feeling that we ought to be able to control the things we create. But we cannot fiddle with the concept of the number three without destroying its usefulness. If we do not take the inviolability of numbers seriously, the whole of mathematics fails. In the same way, the idea that money can be created, destroyed or ignored at will has been tested many times and found to be both mistaken and hideously destructive when attempted.

For all our sophistication, the behaviour of money is still out of control. The apparently endless succession of booms and busts continues. Even during periods of economic calm, our incompetence with money generates huge waste. There is, today, always a large number of people with the capacity and desire to work, and others with the desire to benefit from their work, but the money link between them is missing. These are not just the idle, the incompetent or those held in a benefit trap, but intelligent, well-educated, healthy, mostly young people, suffering unemployment. Nowadays, as economies 'hot-up', the number of people sitting around unproductively decreases but it never reduces to minimal levels.

By contrast, in Western Europe between 1955 and 1970, effectively zero unemployment was achieved. In this period unemployment figures rarely rose above the 2.5 per cent seen due to frictional effects. Equally, during the major wars of the twentieth century, unemployment was eliminated in the combatant countries. But, since 1970, we have not found a way to organise money so that there is always full employment. We seem to be less able to control money then we than we used to.

Unemployment is nothing to do with advancing technology destroying jobs – technology has been doing so, relentlessly, since the Birth of Now. Just as relentlessly, it has created new ones. When people spend money, someone must receive it. So, if an increase in efficiency means that an individual loses their job, the money that was used for their pay must go elsewhere (other things being equal). If the efficiency results in a lower product price, the money goes to consumers; if the product is still sold at the same price, the money increases the product profit, etc. Whether this money, formerly used as pay for someone, goes to consumers or into profit, when it is spent it must provide someone else with work[61].

The study of economics is like the study of dreams; despite the attention of many intelligent individuals, supported by funding and popular interest, it appears impossible to make progress. Engineering methods have been developed to ensure that any concern is addressed objectively, so the collapse of modern bridges is vanishingly rare. Not so with the study of economics: there is no certainty that the economic system will not fall down. Famously, it did partially collapse in the USA in 1929 and again in 2007, with plenty of collapses in different parts of the world in between. The response of government and central bankers to the crash of 2007 was more effective than their response in 1929 – although those involved in the clear up all stress how close run it was. It is remarkable that in the sixty-plus years between the two we forgot how to stop crashes happening in the first place.

There is every reason to believe that further economic collapses will occur. The record of repeating 'boom and bust' since the Birth of Now suggests that it is a certainty, unless a completely new type of advance is made in economics. Could the future 'bust' be much worse than previously, so bad that it breaks the whole economic system of 'Now'? Could the world's economy follow the dismal, permanent economic collapse of Venice after 1600 or the Netherlands after 1700? Perhaps: there seems to be no law against it.

---

61   There are lots of 'ifs' and 'buts' that can be added to any specific example – buying imports puts the job abroad, the money could be saved not spent, the money could go in rent, etc. But these effects will, on average, be matched by opposing effects, making the statement correct in general.

Following the 2007 'bust', several governments and central bankers invented additional money and mostly gave it to their government to spend (a process drolly named 'quantitative easing'). This made up for some of the money people were withdrawing into savings. They did this with caution and got away with it – confidence in money did not much diminish. But this may not always be the case and it may not be so next time, leading to a complete financial bust. Nobody knows, but it seems unlikely. Good will, a desire to support the system in general and the availability of emergency tools, such as temporary rule by regulation, suggest that we could, over the medium term, 'muddle through' any economic crash. The bailout of 2007 was a seat-of-the-pants escape, but it worked. We can hope that the next bailout will be as successful but it could still be that money will finish 'Now' just as it began it.

So we are left, face to face, with the likelihood that the development and changes of Now will continue. The traditional disasters of exhausted natural resources, burgeoning population and pollution seem to be getting less, not more, likely. A takeover somewhere by a pathological Belief seems probable and regular economic crashes inevitable, but it is likely that these will only slow the process of development by a decade or two, as they have done for the last 200 years. If we want to get a vision of the future we cannot use these dodges to avoid the issue. Realistically, we must expect our current development and progress to continue: our fate awaits us.

To see where we will go in future let us first look at

where the Birth of Now has led us recently. Although our forebears of 100 years ago would barely recognise much in the developed world today, it is worth considering what, specifically, they would find astonishing. They would not find the freedoms we enjoy astonishing; they were possibilities contemplated for their future. But the ease and normality of travel, sex, holidays and communication is completely unexpected. They would also not be amazed by technological products of today; they were all thought of and expected to happen, but what they did not expect was how universal the gadgets are; how easy to use they have become.

Taking technology first: one hundred years ago, in 1910-20, they had telephones, cars, movies (silent until 1927), electric lights and airplanes. Radio communication (using Morse code) was long established and radio broadcasting was just starting. Even then, photography was nearly 100 years old and mail order from catalogues had been popular for decades, especially in the wide expanses of the USA. In this decade they also had various forms of automation, from the programmable Jacquard loom to the 'player piano', recorded sound (phonogram), washing machines, vacuum cleaners and refrigeration. However, all these were rare, expensive and difficult to operate. The US census bureau was using punch-card machinery to sort its data. The television was talked of in this period and first demonstrated in Britain, Hungary and Japan in 1926, and first commercially broadcast in the USA in 1928. Atomic power was also anticipated and first demonstrated in the USA in 1934.

So it is not the *idea* of a car that would have surprised

our forebears of 100 years ago, but the idea that every family would have one, and many two, cars and that these cars would be easy to drive, fast, comfortable, safe and reliable. The same pattern applies with the telephone, telegrams/text messages, radio communications and airplanes. People knew of the principles of all of these, they had seen examples in newspapers and sometimes shop windows and shows. They had heard that the rich and powerful had access to these and could sometimes (with difficulty and some discomfort) use them. But they never anticipated that such devices could be as universal, cheap and easy to use as they have become.

Near-instantaneous sound and vision communication between distant locations was anticipated, even before 1920 and, together with other aspects of what we now call the Internet, were staples of sci-fi comics and stories. The telegraph, a form of near-instantaneous electric communication, had been in existence and transmitting across continents for over fifty years by then, the telephone was well-established and people were working on television, so it did not take much to envisage a mixture of the two as a possibility. But that such communication would become fully accessible every day to ordinary folk for a trivial sum or free would not have been considered. How people saw the technological future is shown by Alexander Graham Bell saying of the telephone, "I do not think I overstate the possibilities for this machine when I say that, one day, every large town in America will have one."[lv] It is not the idea that you can holiday from England to Thailand that would have astonished – a few people had already made such long trips at the time – but that tens of thousands would do so every year, just for a week or two, would have been outside the possibilities considered.

Looking at the social development of this period, 1910-1920, there were already recently introduced universal old-age pensions and votes for adults in many 'Now' countries, as well as laws controlling workplace conditions and forbidding the adulteration of food. Very few people, virtually none of them women, yet went to universities. Toleration was gently expanding the acceptability of people who were not entirely mainstream; people of different religions and foreign birth, for example. People saw that toleration would go further and the 'class system' would gradually die away. Even so, the idea that married women would want a professional career and that gay and divorced people should be not only openly tolerated but also socially respected would have been truly a surprise. The idea that society would be rich enough and technology ubiquitous enough to lead to the virtual extinction of household servants would be less surprising, but still unexpected. There was a long-standing direction to social developments toward greater equality and greater inclusion.

So, 100 years ago, the future came about by working through the technologies and trends already established, not by the development of new concepts. Perhaps, then, our future will follow the same pattern. So if we want to see what will happen we should follow the same rule: innovations that are difficult, rare and expensive today will become easy, familiar and cheap in future. Less dramatically, social inclusion will continue to extend, smoothing out the remaining inequalities. So our programme for future prediction is decided and clear: follow today's novelties and the consequences of their becoming simpler, cheaper and universal. But, before we move onto that programme, are there reasons why it might not apply? Are there areas where progress will be held up? We need to consider the constraints before we look at the progress. There are three main limitations to progress over the next century: technological limitations, the limits of possible improvements and the limits to creative space.

Technologies have a slowing rate of advance. When a new area opens up, discoveries or developments are quick and substantial. As time goes on, they become less so, in an approximately hyperbolic curve of decreasing gains: each improvement getting smaller and smaller. We saw in the steam engine the first stage of improvement was a fourfold improvement in efficiency by using a separate condenser, followed by a more than doubling of efficiency with a pressure system, another increase in efficiency with complex compound engines, then yet another with the switch to steam turbines at the end of the nineteenth century. It seems likely, though, that all the improvements of the last 100 years in large (turbine) steam engines, put together, has improved their efficiency by less than 10 per cent[62]. At some point in every technology, further improvements can only be trivial. These areas, such

---

62 In power stations and the like there have been substantial improvements in boiler efficiency in this period. Also the wide abandonment of combined heat and power has decreased efficiency but these are distractions from the main point.

as steam-power generation, have reached, or very nearly reached, a technical limit. But this is by no means a limiting factor; a new technology may restart the improvements. In many roles the steam engine was replaced by the internal combustion engine. This improved dramatically in its efficiency but is now being overtaken by electric and battery technologies in key roles. Nevertheless, we need to keep an eye on the decline in the rate of technological advance as we go forward.

Sometimes purely mathematical factors constrain the amount each successive development can improve the end result. If the time taken to go from London to New York is six weeks, then going twice as fast saves twenty-one days. Once the time taken for the same journey gets down to seven hours, a further doubling of speed saves a much less game-changing three and a half hours. This benefit is also tempered by the hours still needed to get to the airport, to get through the airports at both ends and to get from the airport to your specific destination at the other end. In 1873, the idea you could go round the world in eighty days was astonishing and required much heroism, hardship and luck to achieve. Now it can be done in twenty-four flying hours of comfortable tedium. While cutting this further to, say, six hours will make a difference, it won't be a big difference. The airport time at each end will take some years to reduce – the electronic improvements in the speed of immigration control seem likely to be offset by ever-larger crowds going through. World centre-to-centre travel is approaching the point where future increases in speed will have minimal impact. The cost reduction that has gone on in parallel now makes a much bigger difference – and has much more scope for worthwhile further reduction – than the small further decreases in travel time available.

But, most importantly we need to deal with the surprising fact that there are many areas we are already at the point where, for a typical person in an advanced economy, things cannot improve, simply because they are as good as they can get. This is not that technology cannot advance but that the *end result cannot significantly improve*. Interior air conditioning/climate control may well get simpler, cheaper, more fuel efficient, less noisy, more widely available and so on. But, once a room is maintained with a gentle airflow at the right temperature and humidity – as it often is today – it cannot get more 'climate-comfortable'. The *end result* cannot be significantly improved.

This is an important concept, the point where the delivery of a benefit cannot be improved. The technology may vary, it may become more efficient, it may change in style, but the net result cannot be better or can only be better in ways that are vanishingly small. We will call this point the End Result Achieved point, the ERA point. Climate control in modern buildings in developed societies has reached its ERA point. It can be spread more widely, it can be achieved by different technologies, but it cannot deliver a better end result.

There is a simple test of whether development in an area is getting close to its ERA point: do very wealthy individuals currently have access to a significantly different or better version of whatever it is. For example, the significant difference between an expensive new Ferrari and a second-hand Toyota – as a method of transport – is normally nil. Obviously their symbolic qualities are quite different and their price and running-cost differences are huge. But they get from place to place in the modern world on ordinary roads at exactly the same speed, providing their passengers with the same comforts and entertainment. In practice, the Toyota is likely to be more comfortable, more spacious, quieter, easier to get in and get out of, easier to see out of, simpler to drive and more reliable as well as cheaper. The Ferrari's advantages are all in style and image, its theoretical advantage in speed unusable in all but the most unusual situations. This confirms that individual human-driven local transport, the car, is at or close to its ERA point[lvi]. With electronics the rich have no advantage over the middle class at all, although that is probably more because of the structure the technology imposes, rather than just because much of it is getting close to an ERA point.

If you are exceedingly rich, private airplanes are a faster way to travel then public planes. But this is not because of their advanced technology – business jets generally fly more slowly than commercial jets – but to their exclusivity, which is not extendable to the population generally with advancing technology[63]. Their main advantage is that you skip airport delays by using small airfields (or special terminals at larger airports) and, sometimes, when you go to an outlying area, you

---

63 Air transport is remarkable in that journey times are generally more than they were fifty years ago. Planes fly more slowly (to save fuel) and ground delays are much longer.

can go direct to an airfield closer to your destination, rather than the larger commercial airports. The main disadvantage of private planes is that they crash many times more often than commercial jets.

If we look at the homes of the very wealthy we observe that, apart from ostentatious scale and desirable locations, they resemble very much the homes of the median household with more expensive knick-knacks. They are Ferraris to the everyday Toyota: desirable, luxurious, capable in theory of doing more (speed for the Ferrari, parties and swimming for the mansion) but, in practice, merely different in style – book a hotel for your party, swim at a local pool, rent a holiday cottage or stay at a resort; it's often easier anyway.

A self-closing door is great; but, unless you are disabled, it makes no real difference compared to one you close yourself. Decor that changes colour according to mood is a gizmo. Thermostatic clothing simply enables you to have a smaller wardrobe and put your coat on or off less. Hyper-sound drying showers avoid you having to use a towel. These are not significant; the 'Now' countries have already made the advances in median lifestyle, taking it close to the ERA point. Houses are temperature controlled, pleasantly decorated, pleasant smelling, comfortable and full of personal cleaning devices, waste removal, communication systems and entertainment equipment. Not all houses are like this, but the new and renovated houses, such as those occupied by the average family in the developed world are. This 'Median Now' humankind is getting close to being as well-fed, as comfortable, as well-entertained and as surrounded by communication, as it is possible for humans to achieve. Further advances can only have a small impact on our well-being. Our discontents are largely to do with our relative position in society and crowding effects. We cannot all of us avoid these. There is logically no way to make everyone feel above average all the time. We can lessen the differences by reducing the scale of financial, educational and physiological differences between people. We can multiply the measurements, so that being below average in one way is offset by being above average elsewhere. But we cannot eliminate entirely the overall differences people perceive between each other, a difference that leaves some feeling disadvantaged. Nor can we make front row seats available to everyone.

It is a similar picture with food moving towards its ERA point in the 'Now' world. For anyone in the developed world there is enough food, with enough choice. Maybe the future will have a more extensive choice of mulberry varieties and Tahitian cuisine will be added to the extensive range currently available and so on and on. But these will not make any practical difference. Countries in the 'Now' phase have moved far from the precarious subsistence of life 'Then', through a stage of adequate-if-limited-diet, to current lifestyles with, for some, excessive and damaging availability and choice of food. As with interior climate control, the job is done: we have the ERA point in food supply. Home entertainment is also getting close but probably needs another decade before any film, programme, book, game or whatever is immediately available to all. Adding three dimensions will be nice but, as several relaunches of the concept show, it adds very little beyond a brief novelty or, in the case of full-immersion goggles, nausea. Touchability will probably also be seen as a gimmick but we will have to await developments.

So when we talk about 'advances will continue until they can go no further' we have to recognise that, in our daily life, our home and our transport we, the Median Now people, are already getting close to the point where further possible advances are largely trivial – in terms of impact on life, not in terms of technology or lower costs. In these everyday areas we are approaching the point where advancing technology cannot advance our comfort, pleasure or work further, where they have all got closer to their ERA point. The cities will focus on the young and the very wealthy, the suburbs for families, all in apartments and houses that will not differ very greatly from those we see today. We will soon get to a point where effective 'lifestyle' change stops. We will call this period 'Forever', fitting the pattern of the three different periods of human development: 'Then', before the Birth of Now; 'Now', our current period of rapid change and dramatic improvement in material life; and 'Forever', after the changes are completed and all the relevant aspects of life are close to or at their ERA point for most people. Then, Now and Forever: the three great eras of human history.

Is it good or bad that this Forever lifestyle is already similar to the lifestyle of many Median Now people today in the cities, the shopping malls and the suburbs of the developed world? Good – it is a comfortable and fun lifestyle. Bad, because we are still left with ourselves, not always as content and fulfilled as we would like to be. We lose the prospect – the illusion – that somehow we would be happier, more contented people in a futuristic world; the fond belief that the elimination of something by a technological or social advance would make us into the happy, admirable people we believe we naturally are. How attractive and contented we would be if only we were not frustrated by something or other that holds us back. This thought, alas, trickles away if we think that it is impossible to be significantly freer or materially more comfortable. But the flatness of the 'Forever' world is heightened by another side effect of technology and its ability to race to an ERA point where it cannot be functionally improved: the arts and sciences.

Since the Birth, technical advances have opened up one new area after another for creative development. The start given to the novel by the developments in paper has been described. Technical advances opening new creative fields have transformed almost every artistic endeavour since the Birth of Now. Take the great burst of classical music composition, led by Mozart (1756-1791), Beethoven (1770-1827), and many others. It was made possible by technical developments that allowed a large group of musical instruments, an orchestra, to stay in tune long enough to play a symphony. This possibility was not open to the only slightly earlier genius of J.S. Bach (1685-1750). Rock'n'roll could not have happened without sound amplification: you just can't make a loud enough noise without it. In painting, the new ideas of the French Impressionists c.1870-1900 were also made

Waterstones

United Reformed Building

89a Broad Street

Reading

RG1 2AP

0118 958 1270

SALE TRANSACTION

BIRTH OF NOW, THE	£9.99
31785891229	
lance to pay	**£9.99**
sh	£10.00
ANGE	£0.01

VAT Reg No. GB 108 2770 24

TORE	TILL	OP NO.	TRANS.	DATE	TIME
011	2	775875	245794	12/12/2016	15:26

9990200110022457949

Waterstones

Refunds & exchanges

We will happily refund or exchange goods within 30 days or at the manager's discretion. Please bring them back with this receipt and in resalable condition. There are some exclusions such as Book Tokens and specially ordered items, so please ask a bookseller for details.

If your Kindle is faulty we will replace it when returned within 30 days. For those returned after 30 days but within the manufacturer's warranty period, we will gladly arrange a replacement from the manufacturer.

This does not affect your statutory rights.

Waterstones Booksellers,
203/206 Piccadilly, London, W1J 9HD.

Get in touch with us:
customerservice@waterstones.com
or 0808 118 8787.

Buy online at Waterstones.com or Click & Collect. Reserve online. Collect at your local bookshop.

Did you love the last book you read? Share your thoughts by reviewing on Waterstones.com

Waterstones

possible by technical innovation. New types of pre-made paints could be carried and used outside. For the first time, the artist's full equipment could be taken on the (new) trains to a location and the (dry) paintings taken back. For the first time in the history of art, the Impressionists could actually see the scenes they were painting. New, rectangular-head brushes enabled the brush-stroke to become more visible, more part of the painting.

With each technical advance, artists of all kinds rush in to fill the new 'creative space' that becomes available. Once the early arrivals have explored that space, tried the variations and marked the edges, the space starts to become used up. The next generation has less space and has to work in the less well-lit corners. John, Paul, George and Ringo could not recreate the Beatles' astonishing originality without the advantage of being in at the early days of high-quality sound-mixing. With time, additional artistic efforts are simply variations, perhaps even copies or pastiches, of the masters who first worked in the area. Orchestral music illustrates this: simplistically, starting from the period of Haydn, Mozart, Schubert and Beethoven, we go onto Brahms, Tchaikovsky, Verdi, Wagner, Strauss, Mahler, Liszt and Bartok. Further on in time and the masters are getting fewer and less titanic: the creative space provided by the existence of orchestras is becoming used up. By the time we get to the middle of the twentieth century, the age of orchestral giants is over. Not because human creativity has died in this area, nor have orchestras ceased to exist. It has just 'been done'. We have to look to music using newer technologies, technologies that gave rock and pop their heyday. So, although there are thousands of trained musicians in the world today who could write a superb symphony, no one cares. Any they compose now would be simply a variation of a form whose highlights and limits have already been fully explored.

The effect of using up the creative space is strengthened because nothing is nowadays lost to be rediscovered later. Everything can be reproduced and, if a new creative development is original and high quality, it will gain near-instant worldwide awareness. It was this possibility of reproduction that killed graphic 'fine art'. Everyone can now see the work of Botticelli, Rembrandt, Monet, Matisse and all the great masters at will. To avoid immediate comparison, a painting has to be totally different to theirs and the other greats, or it becomes merely a less good version of their work. Graphic art became a relentless search for novelty until it moved off flat surfaces altogether and became a search for conceptual innovation and shock-factor.

Reproduction also fundamentally changed the rules of music and drama. Until the twentieth century music and drama were, effectively, one-offs. Each time a piece was played or performed it had to be recreated and so was remade with inevitable variations. There is no 'original' performance of *Hamlet* or Beethoven's *Symphony No. 9* in existence. This means that each performance of these classics, each with its particular variations, can be an equally valid and worthwhile interpretation. There is, however, an original *Citizen Kane* (film) and *Sgt. Pepper's Lonely Hearts Club Band* (music album) and remakes and cover versions have to compete with an 'original', a task that proves, with very few exceptions, to be impossible. The greater the original, the more it is embedded in people's heads, and the more difficult it is for them not to see covers as flawed copies of the original.

This would not matter if technical advance could continue endlessly but much of it cannot. Once you can make any noise you want, there can be no further advance in music technology and technology can take music to no further point; the ERA point of music technology has been achieved. A few brilliant innovators find new approaches within existing formats, each filling some remaining crevice of creativity and making it more difficult for the next. Eventually almost everything becomes just a variation on an old theme presented with a new face.

Popular TV started in the 1950s, in the USA. Since then there have been several major 'rule-changing' technical advances. We can track the programme formats that each technical advance made possible, showing the speed that creative space gets used up. The original TV camera technology was extremely limited in the way it could be used, with large and heavy cameras requiring strong light to work. However, this did enable the development of the sitcom genre, with *I Love Lucy* standing out as the first classic TV sitcom, starting in 1951[64]. Because it was the first, it was able to use the most familiar setting available as its location: a middle-class, mid-life family of husband and wife with

---

64 There was an earlier, brief TV sitcom on the BBC TV but it had virtually no audience.

children. In the nearly seventy years since *I Love Lucy*, the format has been worked on again and again and it is fair to say that the scope for novelty is getting close to being exhausted and the genre has only a fraction of its old audience appeal. With variations, the same can be said of the other leading genres such as 'cop shows' and hospital dramas; the possible plots have been used, the situations explored and the characters varied to the point of incredulity. That said, the scope for individual human drama is infinite: in a soap opera one person's marriage, divorce or loss, is not the same as another person's, just as it is not in humanity at large.

Natural history programmes became more attractive after the introduction of colour into TV. But increasingly the space is being mined out. New series are commissioned on more extreme and remote and minute natural history topics. These new series shy away from broad topics of previous series, say, onto the world of ice or the deep sea, in an attempt to be original. But all the time they are filling in ever-smaller gaps of the remaining creative space of natural history programmes. Fortunately, miniaturisation of cameras, remote automatic triggering and other electronic advances in the early twenty-first century have opened up another new world of natural history programme possibilities, a new world that is, in turn, rapidly being mined. There is only one biosphere; and it is being comprehensively filmed far faster than the geosphere was mapped out and its exploration completed.

The same miniaturisation of cameras made 'reality TV' possible as a genre. The many ideas this opened up were quickly exploited, notably for real-life filming of the public. But the novelty soon wore off and many of the formats lost audiences quickly. Then there was the advent of anarchic people's TV, made possible by the combination of cheap, high-quality cameras and internet access (the most famous being YouTube). There may be more technical advances to keep TV fresh but, sooner or later, the last truly original creative space will become mined out and everything will be a 'cover version' of a previous format.

In future all areas of the arts will be far more restricted. Never again will writers enjoy the freedom with detective/mystery fiction that Conan Doyle (Sherlock Holmes), Agatha Christie (Hercule Poirot and Miss Marple), Georges Simenon (Maigret) and Raymond Chandler (Philip Marlowe) had. No one in future can write sci-fi without knowing that something close to their idea was covered by Isaac Asimov, Arthur C. Clark, Robert Heinlein, Ursula Le Guin or one of the other mid twentieth-century masters of the genre, nor can they film it without some reference to the many, many plot devices of *Star Trek* or *Dr Who*.

The same seems to be happening with fundamental science and mathematics. The discovery of the basic rules has limited the space available for major new discoveries. You cannot repeat the importance of Newton's or Euler's or Darwin's or Pasteur's discoveries. All these giants lived over 100 years ago. Areas such as fundamental chemistry reached a limit with the completion, first, of the periodic table of elements around 1890 and then the theoretical understanding of chemical bonding given by quantum mechanics around 1940. Fundamental particle physics shows a similar pattern, with dramatic and astonishing developments from 1905 slowing down gradually until around 1974, followed by little more than experimental confirmation of the remaining theoretical particles – despite much expenditure[65]. Obviously, there are vast areas that are at their dawn. Biochemistry and genetics is the most exciting area, while other sciences are still rich in problems awaiting technology and ingenuity to solve – astronomy/cosmology springs to mind. (The exhilarating advances in IT and electronic gadgets are not science, new knowledge, but technology, new applications of knowledge, specifically information and communications technology (ICT).) But we should be aware that, like global exploration, there will come a point in all fundamental sciences when they are effectively 'done': there will be much subsequent technical development, as chemistry and IT show. But, just as there is only one world to discover, there is only one universe to discover and when its basic structures are completed, you can no longer explore, you can only fill in the gaps between.

Now that we have looked at the things that may prevent the future developing along the same lines as the past we can, at last, follow our earlier analysis. This, you will recall, suggested that the best way to see where we are going is by following the rule of taking things that are scarce or difficult or just starting now and considering

---

65 There is a hope among particle physicists, that the 'next layer down', the ingredients of the current unsatisfactory mess of 'fundamental particles', will provide another burst of activity once we have the technology to open up this 'creative space'.

the effect of making them universal, cheap and easy to use.

Starting with the most prominent modern development, ICT and its software. Currently, we are building various online identities, via *Facebook* and other 'social media'. Their usefulness and importance is forcing even those who want to avoid them to become involved. They are a bit clunky and still very optional, much as a motor vehicle was in 1920. In future, every person will have one or more data 'personas': the representation of you in the data world (not all always available for others to see). These will, either separately or together, be fully detailed and associated with every aspect of your worldly identity past and present: name, where you have ever been and are now, education and employment history, possessions, all your relationships and every encounter with others – lovers, family, friends, colleagues, juniors, bosses – as well as your beliefs and taste preferences for leisure time, food, sex, art, music, etc. In his famous *His Dark Materials* trilogy, Philip Pullman creates the idea of individuals linked in a fundamental way with a 'daemon', a semi-autonomous, animal-like entity embodying their personality and character. This is probably the best portrait of the future electronic persona. Its portrayal of individuals who, when they are separated from their daemon, become zombie-like shells, may also be ahead of its time. In a refinement that Pullman did not consider, it is difficult to see how we can avoid being followed by an electronic identity that has the opinions and comments of others on aspects of our personality. Currently every book, game, software package, consumer durable, tourist attraction, etc. has sites where they are rated and reviewed, whether they like it or not. There seems no way that individual people will not go the same way. At least you will be able to confirm that you are a terrific lover...

As these personas are developed for everyone, it will become impossible to get away with any crime, as your location and activity at any moment will be traceable. To a large extent they already are in the Now world, with the mobile phone, car number recognition, credit card, travel ticket, CCTV, etc. all providing location tracking records. Indeed, lying of almost any sort will become very likely to be exposed. The money individuals receive will be completely traceable, putting paid to corruption and any sort of tax avoidance. By the same token, paperwork will largely cease – even electronic paperwork will be heavily automated. There will be little role for passports, tax returns, application forms, etc. The legal framework for this development will need to be built to allow a reasonable feeling of freedom while, at the same time, using the system to abolish bureaucratic tedium and all but the most impulsive of crimes. The near-abolition of crime will provide a huge extra cost saving and make life much more convenient; locks are unnecessary when all your goods are identifiable as yours from a mobile scan and provide a complete trace of their location since manufacture.

Medicine is the other great area of human endeavour nowhere near its limit. It is fair to say that modern medicine started only in the 1940s with the introduction of the first antibiotics and it started slowly. So it has less than a century of development and is accelerating fast: the basic development tools of DNA analysis and replication are essentially twenty-first-century developments. Medicine has moved rapidly to eliminate most serious infectious diseases in the Now world and will complete the removal of all infectious diseases within a few decades at most. Medical developments are moving onto diseases caused by failures of the body's own systems, diseases such as cancer, MS and the autoimmune diseases generally. Crippling bodily illnesses will continue to disappear and our treatment of mental illnesses will improve, resulting in most being effectively cured. Those with life-affecting illnesses will be reduced to a minute number. It has been commented that, in Europe, in the 1930s, the disabled were visible everywhere. Birth disfigurements of hare lip, club foot, squint, etc. and the effects of crippling diseases like polio had been added to by those mutilated during the First World War. Now there are far fewer disabled people, even in the remaining 'Then' countries. Following the rule that this progress will continue until it reaches its ERA point, our grandchildren will probably never know an illness, not even a cold or tooth decay.

It seems that aging will also be eliminated. Lifespan is increasing at a regular pace already and the effects of this on career and marriage patterns are visible. The arrangements of both were developed in the expectation of a limited span of life, marriages in the pre-Now period are said to have averaged around only fifteen years before one or other partner died. The structure of careers was designed for promotion over time until retirement, but extended healthy lifespans and postponed retirement make this pattern impossible to retain. Both structures already have to bend to a norm of five or six decades of healthy adult life and have a lot more bending to go before they fit even with current life-spans. We must expect this trend of ever-lengthening lives to continue, possibly to accelerate. There does not seem a stop point to this process.

Removing aging, and so extending human lifespans to thousands of years, will be a different order of change. There is no reason to believe that ending aging is 'forbidden by nature' any more than human flying is 'forbidden by nature'. Aging appears to be a consequence of natural selection finding that the costs of a long breeding life did not pay off in terms of offspring[66]. Before the Birth of Now, any mutations that led to a longer life would only have succeeded if they had no negative effects on earlier reproductive success. This seems rare; most genes that have the effect of extending life-span seem also to reduce reproductive success. Because so many people in the past died an early death for reasons other than aging – disease, malnutrition, war and childbirth, even if a mutation did arise that extended lifespan with no negative effect on youthful reproduction, it would still not have spread widely.

Currently, around 59 million people die and 136 million are born every year but the figures are converging and are expected to become the same around 2070. The forecast is for a stable or slightly declining population of around 9-10 billion. When (and if) natural death stops, possibly

---

66 The menopause illustrates the neutral or even negative breeding value of extra reproductive lifespan. The menopause enables a woman to help bring up more grandchildren, rather than risk the dangers of attempting more childbirths themselves so the gene for it spreads through the population.

around the same time, world population will continue to grow by around a billion every ten to fifteen years, which will become unsustainable at some point. Perhaps a large number of people will decide to die anyway (given that they are enabled to do so) or not to have children voluntarily[67]. An alternative will be that society as a whole will have to impose restrictions, that some people will be forced to die or stopped from giving birth or some combination of both. The state would have to have coercive powers to kill or sterilise selected individuals. This step is very much counter to the trend of increasing freedom and humanitarian respect, so it is unlikely to happen and another alternative will have to be found. What this 'alternative' may be can, for now, only be guessed at.

It may seem trivial in comparison, but, in future, people will be beautiful. Already people in the Now world feel they require straight teeth and, if these are not naturally achieved, they are straightened as a matter of course. So it is now, with major defects to the face being remedied in the developed world, and increasingly with minor defects being addressed. In future a lack of beauty will increasingly be seen as a defect that can be and should be addressed to 'give a child a fair chance'.

How far are we through the Birth of Now and how much further is there to go before we get to the era of Forever? You cannot sum the factors that have reached close to their ERA point, like interior climate control,

---

67 This is especially unlikely. Ever since the advent of efficient contraception, there has been heavy selection in favour of people who want children, rather than just sex, an attitude that they must, on average, pass on to their offspring. The implication is that people are getting more enthusiastic about breeding, more 'philoprogenative'.

and those that are far from it, like medicine. Nor can you estimate accurately when each undeveloped country will start its catch-up or how long they will each take to join the Now countries. Anyway, the indications are that development never stops completely, its advances just get smaller and smaller: the End Result Achieved point is not a point but a dying fall.

But, on the other hand, perhaps there *is* a symbolic way we can tell how far we have gone since the Birth and how far there is still to go to the end of Now and the start of Forever.

The maximum height a building recognisable as a skyscraper and built with the strongest realistic materials is somewhere between 1,000 to 1,500 metres high[68]. After that, the materials at the bottom will crumble under the weight. The current highest building is 828 metres high. If the symbolism of building height we started with in Chapter 1 has any applicability, the Birth of Now is between 55 and 80 per cent of the way to its limit. So, following this, and depending on which specific date you take as the Birth – many choose 1770 – Now will reach its end sometime between 60 and 200 years' time and Forever will start. This is very soon, if you take the whole of history as your timeframe and, given the improvement of medicine and extending lifespans, probably within your or your children's lifetime.

So, starting sometime soon, beautiful, near-immortal, crime-free, disease-free; what's not to like about Forever?

---

68   There is no theoretical limit to the height of buildings if you allow them to be mountain-shaped, with an enormous base supporting a tiny peak.

.8.

AND TIME YET

So what will the world look like when the changing period of Now that we live in is complete and the period we are calling Forever starts?

The most everyday observations about the way the Birth of Now is developing are that the world is becoming more integrated ('globalised') and that it is becoming less varied. Both trends seem certain to continue: already many townscapes are only distinguishable from each other to the experienced eye. There is no sure way to tell from pictures whether a new apartment or shopping mall is in Oslo, Norway, or Kuala Lumpur, Malaysia, or whether a cityscape is of Urumqi in Western China or Sao Paulo in Brazil, unless you are personally familiar with the city in question. Even today, cities are already fighting to build new and retain old distinctive landmarks and areas of traditional buildings. But their differences are becoming increasingly cosmetic as the same human needs dictate the same set of services and building functions. Santa Fe insists on every building having an adobe finish, Paris rejoices in its Haussmann boulevards, Beijing is polishing its hutongs. But the distinction between these and their theme park copies already gets less everyday. The same cafes, the subway trains, the same cars, the same wash facilities and interior decoration. It is characteristic of tourism that it turns popular destinations into theme parks of themselves; streets are re-cobbled and ill-fitting buildings rebuilt in style. For visitors, semi-compulsory visits must be made to a defined list of sites, each prepared to handle its flood of visitors before they retreat, exhausted to Starbucks for a coffee, having caught the compulsory selfie of themselves in front of Big Ben or the Taj Mahal: different photograph, same experience.

Today there are still shrinking areas where life is almost completely untouched by the effects of Now and areas where its effects are small enough for distinctive local habits – sometimes including the 'Then' specials of war and famine – to remain. But integration has further to go beyond the current homogenisation caused by catching up. In many parts of the world most people are still unable to speak the world language, English (in addition to their local language). This is unlikely to last for more than another two generations.

A long-established trend since the Birth of Now is for machines to replace human work and this will continue. However, it is one of the joys of the economic system that all such 'job losses' automatically open up new jobs (other things being equal). We have seen this again and again since the start of the Birth of Now, as whole industries and professions have vanished and new ones have arisen. It is often said that the new jobs created tend to be at higher skill levels than the old ones that go, creating problems for those who are unable to develop high skills, but there seems little evidence for this – modern computerisation can adapt systems to individual skill-preferences. Caring, a big growth area for future employment, is not a profession that everywhere demands sophisticated skills. There will also be changes as the work patterns that developed before easy communication, such as the eight-hour day and the office building, adapt to the ability of telecommunications to link people – although the office building is proving a very hardy institution, despite its costs and inconveniences.

Developments since the Birth of Now have also already removed much of the 'chiaroscuro', the light and dark, of life in developed countries. This is partially a result of reducing the dark side of life: the personal tragedies of untimely death and crippling illness, group conflicts and wars. These are remote to most people in the developed world. Nowadays people rarely encounter the personal reality of murder and accidental death: once or twice in a typical lifetime, if at all. Very occasionally, a part of the Then world intrudes with a reminder of the cruelty and horrors that preceded the Birth of Now: a child killed for being a witch in London, an outbreak of tuberculosis in New York, a gang attack amongst immigrants in Sydney.

A picture emerges of a society in Forever that is pleasant, but lacking in excitement and novelty. The endless pageant of human relationships will continue. Our personal triumphs and disasters and our interest in the lives of our family, friends and communities will continue to provide a gripping tale – to us at least. The struggle to climb the social and communal ladders that we create for ourselves will continue. But when despair and disaster are reduced, when tragedy and catastrophe are avoided, then some intrigue and interest must be lost as well.

Fashion too will continue to change as it always has. Clothing has been at its ERA point for many years. The main requirement before the Birth of Now was for clothing to function well and for any individual to have enough clothing to keep warm and clean. But, by the mid-1950s, in America at least, these aspects could be taken for granted and the focus for many, not just the wealthy, turned to whether the style was on trend or expressed the wearer's personality. This concept of fashion has spread to other areas – cars, for example – and will continue to produce regular changes, often cycles, in all other arts, foods, music and graphic design. Sports too, will provide a constantly changing and varied picture, as they do now, each season or meeting bringing on new tales of triumph and disaster.

Changes will continue in the Forever era, but they will not have a direction, they will not be 'progress': they will just be change.

But we perhaps should take an even longer perspective. Humankind's forebears started to use stone tools around 2,500,000 years ago and fire at least 400,000 years ago. We currently think they continued to use crude stone tools until around 12,000 years ago when, abruptly – in this kind of timescale – much changed. This is called the Neolithic (New Stone) Revolution. The change was in many areas: animals were domesticated, the quality of the stone tools improved dramatically, pottery started, agriculture started, irrigation started in some areas and probably the nature of clothing and housing improved as well. With agriculture, the Stealer society started as well. We should perhaps see this, 10,000BCE, as the start of the era that has just ended with the Birth of Now.

The importance of this date is increased by our new approach. In the old vision of history as Continuous Slow Progress, the absence of metal artefacts found to date before 5000BCE was seen as supporting the step-by-step picture of early human civilisations: 'Stone Age' to 'Bronze Age' to 'Iron Age'. But it seems equally likely that bronze and iron date back to the Neolithic Revolution and that we have just not yet found the evidence for it. This would not be surprising. The only good evidence would be a recognisable metal artefact, very closely linked to a very early village or a datable artefact in such a way that it could not have been dropped at a later date. Very few such ancient villages have been found – almost all old villages and towns were made of wood and have long since rotted away. But it is even more unlikely to find such an object because bronze and iron corrode and, if buried, would have disappeared in over 5,000 years in all but a minute number of circumstances. One very unusual find, the 'ice man' or Otzi, a 5,000-year-old warrior found fully equipped in an alpine glacier in 1991, had a copper/bronze axe one thousand years older than any previously known to exist in the continent. Metal objects were also extremely valuable for reworking – it is much easier and cheaper to make a new metal object from scrap metal than to start again from metal ores. Any metal object found before the very recent period would have been reused and the original artifact lost. As it is, some claim a metal pendant from Iraq dates to *c.*8,700BCE. Pottery was much more widely used than metals and does not corrode or decay and cannot be remanufactured. We can find pottery objects that go back much earlier, to around 20,000BCE, long before we think the main Neolithic Revolution occurred. It does not take much to suggest that, were metals so durable and un-reusable, they, too, might be found to date this early.

Now that we have disposed of the iron grip of the theory of Constant Slow Progress, we can re-inspect the gaps in the archaeological record in a different way. The theory of CSP required that, if we found no writing before a certain date, then there was none. If we found no copper tools before a certain date, then there were none. There had to be progress, so these innovations had to be invented over time. The theory of Constant Slow Progress said it was more likely they were invented in 5,000BCE then 10,000BCE. Again, we have the hidden picture of the race of morons, taking thousands of years to build the brainpower to smelt copper or write. But, when there are strong reasons why we would not have found certain things from so long ago, the assumption that not finding articles means they did not exist at the period is just that: an assumption. If humankind could smelt copper in 5,000BCE, there is no reason, apart from the theory of Constant Slow Progress, to think it was not smelted in 10,000BCE or earlier. This is also why so many of things claimed as 'inventions' after the Sumerians may well have pre-dated them. Because we have not found examples is not a good reason to assert that they did not exist, unless you are a dedicated follower of the theory of CSP.

But CSP theory is shown to be wrong the other way as well; sometimes peoples did not make 'progress' for thousands of years after an innovation had settled in elsewhere. Many peoples did not use writing until it was introduced from outside relatively recently. For example, the Slavic-speaking peoples of Europe had no writing until it was introduced in the ninth century, 4,000 years after it was used in Sumer. This is not because the Slavs were backward but because their agricultural society had no need for writing. Writing in Slavic lands was only required for religion after Christianity was introduced.

Throughout this book we have started with the 'dawn of civilisation' in Sumer around 3,000BCE, together with the very slightly younger civilisation of Egypt. But we should not run away with the idea that ancient Sumer or Egypt was exceptional 5,000 years ago. What makes Sumer and Egypt stand out is that they largely lacked trees – or rather that, as fertile river plains surrounded by desert, the trees they had were quickly used up. As a result, they had to turn to virtually indestructible stone and pottery as materials to replace the easier-to-work but perishable wood used elsewhere. Because of this we can find their remains, whereas we cannot find the remains of wood-based civilisations. One other place lacked wood at this time – the Orkney Islands, off the north of Scotland. There, a 5,000-year-old civilised village of stone, known as Skara Brae, has been found indicating a good quality of life, with a better quality shelter than a typical hovel of around 1600CE, in part because they had drains. We can believe that the Orkney Islands and the desert valleys of Sumer and Egypt were uniquely civilised places, thousands of miles apart with few and barbaric peoples between them. But it seems much more likely that what was different about these places was the lack of trees and the need to use stone rather than wood. This, simpler, theory supposes that plenty of people lived equally civilised lives between them and elsewhere in the world. They have just not left evidence of their existence because they used wood and organic materials and these, with few exceptions, vanish over millennia in wet climates. What is unusual about Stonehenge is not the scale of coordination or effort required to bring the stones from afar to build it, but that among the many henges we have some remnant evidence of, it is made of stone. The wooden henges may have been vast towering pagodas; but we cannot know now. The scale of the few items that last, like Stonehenge and the vast earthworks such as nearby Silbury Hill, suggests that the buildings made in the easier and more obvious material of wood would have been impressive indeed.

All this implies that civilisation may have been earlier and more widespread than we had previously envisaged. CSP is the only reason to think that there were no early civilisations, rather than that all signs of such civilisations have disappeared.

But now it seems that the Neolithic Revolution, 10,000BCE or thereabouts, when agriculture started, is the relevant date and it may be earlier. We have seen that there is little reason, apart from the theory of CSP, to suggest that the 'dawn of civilisation' could not be tens of thousands of years earlier than Sumer. Because 'the dawn of civilisation' means agriculture and, inevitably, the Stealer society, nothing of any significance would have changed after the 'dawn' until the Birth of Now, whether the 'dawn of civilisation' was 5,000, 12,000 or 50,000 years ago.

So, if we take a long-term perspective we can see that, across all history, humanity will experience only three extended stable phases of existence and two periods of change:

No Change (c.500,000 years)	Old Stone Age
Change c.10,000BCE	Neolithic Revolution
No Change 10,000BCE – 1770	Then
Change 1770 – c.2100	Now
No Change (how long)	Forever

The 12,000 years between the beginning of the Neolithic and the end of the Birth of Now may itself be seen, thousands of years hence, as an insignificantly small period that made the transition from an essentially animal, Palaeolithic lifestyle, to an essentially human one. The few hundred years of revolution we call 'Now' being simply an astonishing moment of transition in history.

There is an instinctive objection to this analysis because it forecasts stasis in future: an indefinite period without directional change: comfortable, clean, healthy, well-fed, rich stasis; but stasis all the same. A society without long-term trends or developments, just cycles of fashion. But individuals will change and develop: people will fall in love; they will triumph and fail, as they always have done. People should not be bored – already consumer electronics bring in entertainment, provide a huge choice of games, connect friends and encourage exploration of interests so that children and young adults are probably less bored than at any time in history. But, even with these comforts, it does sound bland and lacking zest.

That is the other part of the instinctive rejection of such a forecast. Many people long for a change that would mean an end to humanity's absurdities, with its triviality and its failings abolished. We hunger for something to end our petty-mindedness, spite, insecurity, embarrassment and a thousand other undignified facts of life. The prediction that suburban America today is as good as it gets is pretty inglorious. We know how flawed that is, and we long for better. Yet, simultaneously, we are repelled by the banality and boredom implied by the smoothing out of variation and loss of tragedy. We hanker for drama and reject the blandness of an unchanging world, so much so that in sci-fi films set in the far future, the military technology still uses human aiming and other excitingly flawed mechanisms from the Second World War or before. Even the current technology of fully automated, self-aiming weapons, is too dull to make exciting movies, let alone the virtually human-free systems of our near future.

We want the future to turn our descendants into flawless heroes who live in a world of exciting challenges. Instead we are suggesting that they will remain flawed, foolish humans (albeit good-looking), living in a world of banality. That is, putting aside the possibility of contact with extraterrestrial intelligence, the consequences of which are unknown.

There is also one unavoidable difference between us, the prosperous members of the developed world, and our descendants, living the Forever lifestyle in the Forever period. In Forever, they will be aware of the eternity of similarity and the absence of change. Now, for us, we have a huge and continuing change over our lives. Wars are fresh in the collective memory and still occur in pre-Now parts of the world, as do many hideous aspects of the Then life – hunger and disease. Today, music, art and science still ring with titanic changes, although the resonance is fading slightly of late. The changes in our communications technology are working through with lightning-quick effects and our medicine is just at the threshold of its conquests.

All that sense of change goes away in Forever. It probably *does* matter that all the sitcoms will be remakes, that all the music will be hundreds of years old, that the record for the 100-metre' sprint will be, say, 2,000 years old – as well as the record for eating the most jalapenos. It must affect us if we have lived with the same partner for hundreds of years, if we can never lose anything or get lost anywhere, or go anywhere that feels different, or that our child is over 100 years old herself; that fictional adventures have to be set in a world of uncertainty and change we can only dream of; that no one has anything original to say or do; that there is no escape, not even madness, suicide (without permission) or acts of desperation.

We have seen the future and it will be dull.

CONVENTIONS

This book is not intended to uncover new information but to look at existing and well-established facts in a new way, so the vast majority of facts quoted can be checked and expanded on with a quick Internet search. (I refuse to conform to the pretence of many non-fiction books that the Internet, Google and Wikipedia and their ilk do not exist. Nor are they significantly less reliable then other sources: like all sources they need to be checked before they are used). Where a fact is obscure, needing more than three or four Internet clicks to find preliminary confirmation, references are given. These are also given for facts that seem to contradict received wisdom, so you can check them quickly: for example, that printing with moveable type was 'invented' and widely used at least 700 years before Gutenberg[lvi]. References are also given for direct quotes or figures used. Where figures are quoted they are well founded. Where the only figures available are informed guesses, which is everything before 1700 and almost everything before 1850, they have been replaced with qualitative statements such as 'the majority', 'few', etc.

Dates are all from the Current Era (CE or AD),

unless they are identified as before the Common Era with the letters BCE after the date.

Discussion of history depends on the degree to which facts can be established. The use of writing to record events is rare before the Birth of Now. It is biased toward the Middle East and greater Greece in the period before the Common Era. In the Common Era up to the Birth of Now, China and Europe have much the best written sources. During the early period of the Birth of Now, for the first time, there are some reliable statistics from Europe and a few from America. As a consequence, the discussion here tends to reflect these regions at these periods and, regrettably, the mention of areas with little written record – Indian, African and American regions – are necessarily minimal.

NOTES

i.   Meteoric iron was known to the Sumerians. Crude smelted iron is a poor material, shattering easily, so they may simply not have bothered with it. The date of the first smelted iron has gone back a lot in the light of recent discoveries to around 2000BCE but the start of the traditional 'Iron Age' is still set at around 1200BCE to fit the theory of CSP. Maybe the use of iron seems important to us only because it was so symbolic to the Victorians, who saw iron production as a symbol of the progress they had made. Some have suggested that the success of the Assyrian Empire in battle from 1200BCE was connected with their used of iron tipped spears but other factors such as organisation, discipline, etc. seem likely to have been more important.

ii.   Those sleeping in Versailles did have chamber pots which were removed by servants in the morning, but the daytime provision seems to have been more haphazard. Some simply went on the lawn (including some ladies), where their ability to pretend that the gawping gardeners did not exist impressed some commentators.

iii.   There are Assyrian bas-reliefs that show liquid fire being used, probably around the tenth century BCE. In Thucydides' History of the Peloponnesian War, the fourth-century BC war between Athens and Sparta, we find the earliest description of chemical warfare. The Bible has Daniel preparing a bomb and blowing up an idol of a snake (or dragon). Daniel 14:27 in Catholic Bibles, a separate section, Daniel Bel and the Snake, in the Apocrypha in many other Bibles.

iv. *Decline and Fall of the Roman Empire ch. LIII, last pages.*

v. The so-called Baghdad battery seems obviously to be that – a battery that could give a tingle to your tongue. Unfortunately Eric Von Daniken picked it up as a demonstration of his 'ancient astronomer' theory, so the possibility is hotly denied by all respectable people.

vi. There is a great deal of interesting variation in the social structures of different hunter-gatherer societies studied by anthropologists. It does seem, however, that the idea of the MYOB/Stealer split can help in explaining some of these variations: roughly speaking, the more the situation allows Stealing and security for the Stealer, the more the society will tend to look like the split of commoners and chiefs found in settled agricultural societies. The less there is to steal and the less protection there is for Stealers, the more egalitarian the society seems to be.

vii. Entry for 1137.

viii. In England, resentment of this extra level of Stealing has often been anachronistically ascribed to resentment of the Normans' foreignness, a concept that arose much later. William was, if anything, less foreign than the Danish King, Knut (Canute), who had ruled England fifty years earlier. Canute had provoked little popular resentment because peasant-crushing castles had not accompanied his takeover.

ix. Professional vs. feudal or nomadic armies: It can appear that the success of the Mongols and other horse conquerors against Chinese, Iranian and European armies throws this assertion into doubt. But, in fact, the armies led by the Mongols were made up of many troops from many regions and were generally highly professional and competent, the horse component being only a part of the army – and a highly disciplined and supported one as well. The armies they faced were, in the case of the Chinese, disloyal to their leaders who were also incompetent. In the case of Iran, the opposition was fragmented and often disposed to join the Mongols rather than fight them and, in the case of Europe, it was ill-disciplined and disorganised in the extreme. When they faced a competent, professional opponent, such as the Mamluks of Egypt, they were quite capable of being beaten as they were decisively at Ain Jalut in 1260. This is also the first battle in which cannons are recorded being used.

x.   Indulgences: These appear to have been the first large printing contracts in Europe. Gutenberg made his original money from printing indulgences, before going on to print the Bible. The funding indulgences gave to the development of printing is a key factor in the Reformation, probably second only to disgust at the commercial cynicism 'indulgences' themselves symbolised. The money from the indulgence business got printing operations well under way, so they was able to print best-selling leaflets that acted to undermine the authority of the Church. Early printing was a secretive and subversive business that, from the first, made money by distributing illicit material.

xi.   The relationship between towns, Stealers and Suppliers is very varied. Europe can, for example, be divided into three rough areas during the Middle Ages. The south-east, Byzantine Empire, where the old structures of the Roman Empire largely persisted, centered on towns and administrative and trading centres within a centralised empire. The south-west of Europe, where the same heritage of towns as centres of power persisted but without an effective empire. Here the towns became, in many cases, early Supplier towns like Florence and Barcelona. Finally, north-western Europe where, with few exceptions such as London, the castle was built first and the town grew up around it. There were similar variations in China, especially with greater practical independence in the south leading to a stronger Supplier-city tradition.

xii. The French Revolution had strong popular support in the Netherlands. When, in January 1795, a French army invaded, the stadholder, William V, had to flee to England and the Estates General dissolved itself. The new pro-French government enjoyed widespread support and sent soldiers to fight in the French armies. Napoleon replaced the government anyway, making his brother the King of Holland, and when the Price of Orange (son of the stadholder Willem V) returned to the Netherlands, he simply declared himself 'King', a symbolic indication of the fall from being the great Supplier society it had been.

xiii. James's biggest challenges to the established system were in his plundering of the City of London guilds to make them sponsor the development of 'Londonderry' in north Ireland, something they resisted strongly. His obsession with George Villiers, making him Duke of Buckingham, also raised a few eyebrows.

xiv. At the start of the period, 1700, a Land Tax provided a significant proportion of the tax revenue. However the tax was rarely paid in districts far from London and without revaluation of land, became worth less and less as the century wore on, becoming completely insignificant by its end. Although a property tax with extra charges for properties with more than ten windows started in 1696, it was at a very low level until 1778.

xv. It is important to distinguish between promotions through influence and promotions through family. The system was that virtually all promotions were linked to recommendations or influence from senior officers.

But these recommendations were very largely given because of professional respect although friendship and family often counted as well. A senior officer was, himself, partially judged on the performance of those he had recommended.

xvi.   *Cannon, Aristocratic Century,* p33, quoted in *Britons*, Linda Colley (Yale University Press, 1992)

xvii.   The enclosures did not reduce the amount of labour required to farm the land, especially as the food output of the land was rising swiftly. Rather the previous system had divided the land between many underemployed people who were reluctant to leave for fear of losing their rights. Once the land was enclosed, the population was divided into full-time workers and the unemployed, who then moved into the growing towns.

xviii.   The term 'Empire' comes from the title 'Imperator', originally used for the senior Roman general at times of emergency before being adopted by Augustus as a permanent title for himself and his successors. In doing so he became the first official emperor, although the title is often used for previous single rulers, notably the 'First Emperor', Qin Shi Huang, of China, who unified China 170 years before Augustus created the title of emperor.

xix.   The position of the so-called Kings of Spain at this time was almost impossibly complicated and varied over time. However, in the interest of accuracy here is a brief summary. Charles of Hapsburg, the Duke of Burgundy, who was born brought up in and ruled Flanders (but not, of course, Burgundy), inherited the crowns of Castile and Aragon in 1516 (slight simplification here). These kingdoms covered much of the peninsula then called Spain (but now called Iberia), so we call him the King of Spain (although he did not rule Portugal which is also part of the peninsula). The crown of Aragon also included southern Italy and other territories. He inherited Austria and associated territories in central Europe in 1519 and was elected Holy Roman Emperor, the somewhat notional overlordship of much of what later became Germany. In 1556, he abdicated, splitting his empire between his son, Philip, who got Castile, Aragon and the low countries and his brother, Ferdinand, who got Austria and the Holy Roman Empire

xx.   US War of Independence: This was fought with little enthusiasm and even less bloodshed on both sides. The figure for American deaths in battle in eight years appears to have been fewer than 1,000 per year, although there are endless attempts to make this figure larger, so as to make the struggle more heroic. Compare the American Civil War with over half a million killed.

xxi.   After the Birth of Now, there were at times horrific episodes in the history of 'Imperialism'. Perhaps we should especially remember the deliberate extermination of the native inhabitants of Tasmania, Patagonia and Namibia, the appalling treatment of the locals by the early conquistadors, the nightmare rule of Leopold of Belgium in the Congo and the cruel behaviour and careless slaughtering of the Japanese Empire 1900–1945. But many 'imperial' rules were more benign than any likely alternative would have been, a fact often well understood by the people concerned. Much of the later imperial rule, especially in Africa, was almost entirely symbolic. Nigeria, for example, was only 'taken over' by the British from the private company that was there previously to avoid the Germans getting it. This vast area of millions of people was 'ruled' by a couple of thousand British district officers.

xxii.   *'Slaves, in reverent fear of God submit yourselves to your masters, not only to those who are good and considerate, but also to those who are harsh,'* 1 Peter 2:18, *'Slaves, obey your earthly masters with respect and fear, and with sincerity of heart, just as you would obey Christ'*, Ephesians 6:5, *'All who are under the yoke of slavery should consider their masters worthy of full respect.'* 1 Timothy 6.1, New International Version. The King James Version uses the word *'Servants'* rather than slaves. The word used in the original Greek is *'Oiketai'*, which was most commonly used to describe slaves.

xxiii. Any comment that this is in any way an exculpation of the slave trade displays the crass stupidity of the commentator. The trade was a 'very wicked business'.

xxiv. Cited in David Robinson and Douglas Smith, *Sources of the African Past: Case Studies of Five Nineteenth-Century African Societies (New York: Africana, 1979) 189-190*

xxv. *Niall Ferguson, Empire (Allen Lane, 2003)*

xxvi. The ills caused by European empires were very varied. They go from deliberate genocide in Tasmania and southern Argentina, through undeliberate genocide by disease in the whole of the Caribbean and North America, then to the position in the Indian subcontinent where a good argument can be made that British rule was, in general, better for the mass of people than that of the local rulers it replaced – not least because they discouraged wars between rulers – and, finally, to places such as Hong Kong, which benefitted greatly from being a British colony until 1997.

xxvii. *Joel Mokyr, The Enlightened Economy (Yale University Press, 2009) p33.*

xxviii. *Kai-Michael Sprenger, ,"volumus tamen, quod expressio fiat ante finem mensis Mai presentis'. Sollte Gutenberg 1452 im Auftrag Nicolaus von Kues 'Ablaßbriefe drucken', Gutenberg-Jahrbuch 74 (1999), 42-57*

xxix. 'His name is not mentioned in any literary source earlier than Pappus, (300CE), who quotes from his Mechanics. Hero himself quotes Archimedes

(d. 212BCE) which gives us the other time limit. Scholars have given different dates, ranging from 150BCE to 250CE but the question has been settled by O. Neugebauer, who observed that an eclipse of the moon described by Hero in his Dioptra (chapter 35) as taking place on the tenth day before the vernal equinox and beginning at Alexandria in the fifth watch of the night, corresponds to an eclipse in 62CE and to none other during the 500 years in question.' "Hero of Alexandria", Complete Dictionary of Scientific Biography, 2008. Retrieved from Encyclopedia.com: <http://www.encyclopedia.com/doc/1G2-2830901965.html>

xxx.   Hills, Rev. Dr Richard (2006), James Watt Vol. 3: Triumph through Adversity, 1785-1819 (Ashbourne, Derbyshire, England: Landmark Publishing), p. 217,

xxxi.   Watt did invent the 'Watt linkage' which solved a problem in the machines he was building. But many engineers of the time had to solve the new challenges their machinery threw up and the problem the linkage solved, connecting a straight power thrust to an arc at the end of a lever, so that both pull and push are powered, is not a huge challenge. Watt also patented, but did not invent, the 'sun and planet' system of converting reciprocal power into rotary power. This device was needed purely to avoid a patent that had, unbelievably, been granted on the idea of the crank to one James Pickard, despite cranks having been used for thousands of years. This shows, even if all the other ludicrous patents of the time are ignored, the absurdly unselective way patents were granted at the period to anyone who had the money, presumably on the basis that they could be challenged in court later.

xxxii.   To be fair to Edison, he did progress, almost violently, the idea of wiring up houses and providing a district electricity supply for lights and all the domestic machines we now use. However, even this can be criticised as his tireless support for DC electricity meant that there had to be a smelly, noisy power station every few hundred yards and huge cables were needed to conduct the current around. He was sure that AC, which can be transported much more easily, and was supported by his competitors, was too dangerous. To emphasise the dangers of his competitors' product and the safety of his own DC current, Edison promoted the idea of execution by AC electric chair, possibly the sickest promotional stunt ever devised. It has been suggested that he never meant the idea to be taken seriously but that when the idea was taken up he was stuck with supporting it. It did not work well.

xxxiii. 'Gin' is short for engine. It mechanically removes seeds from cotton bolls, providing a huge cost saving over manual removal of the seeds. The story of the cotton 'gin' illustrates the challenge of many invention stories. A businessman of dubious principles called Eli Whitney, who later won a government contract by falsely claiming to be able to make guns with interchangeable parts and used the money largely to pursue his own interests, got a patent for 'an improved cotton gin' in 1794, just ahead of four other patents for similar improved gins. But the gin is a simple device and many people claimed to have been using similar or related machines for years and continued to do so afterwards. It had been impossible to patent ideas in the US before 1793, when the US patent law was passed, so they may well have been telling the truth. According to Wikipedia 'The popular image of Whitney inventing the cotton gin is attributed to an article on the subject written in the early 1870s and later reprinted in 1910 in The Library of Southern Literature'. Whitney's attempts to get individuals using such machines to pay him royalties because of his patent failed. Still, because his name is on the patent, he is credited with its invention but it seems likely that he was simply a chancer. We cannot know now.

xxxiv. If Near Money, good quality IOUs, etc., trade at a discount to Good Money, not-at-all-Near Money, such as property, should be valued at a much larger discount.

xxxv. Boswell, *The Journal of a Tour to the Hebrides*, 'Thursday, 19th August'.

xxxvi. The measurement of assets actually predates fixed coin-type money by more than 2,000 years. Some of the very first writing we have is the records of the assets of the temples of Sumeria as so many oxen, so much land and so on. When money became standardised into fixed units, normally represented by coins, it became easier to record the value of everything by the amount of money it could notionally be exchanged for. So, rather than trying to assess how many oxen were equal to how many chickens, or, even more difficult, how many oxen were equal to how many days' labour, each was given a value as an amount of money. This confuses the understanding of money. Money is a catalyst for transactions, in order to work money has a widely accepted known value or it is not money. Measuring everything in terms of its value in money makes money units look like a measure of assets, which it categorically is not and which generates some very misleading concepts. Valuing assets (like oxen) in the accounts as if they were Perfect Money – instantly exchangeable at a known value for something else, gives a wrong measure of their value. In practice oxen, and most other assets, are very illiquid: they are not even Near Money.

xxxvii. Strabo states that, around 70BCE, the tailings were still being worked but presumably the output was a fraction of the peak production.

xxxviii. <www.ukpublicspending.co.uk> and Lawrence H. Officer and Samuel H. Williamson, "What Was the UK GDP Then?" MeasuringWorth, 2013URL: <http://www.measuringworth.com/ukgdp/>

xxxix. Huge growth in the supply of money with a fixed amount of currency: Annoyingly, we have no way of knowing what proportion of gold coins vanished 'under the bed' as savings at any time in history. There is no reason to think that it had to stop before it reached a very high figure at times – say 80-90 per cent of all coins in existence withdrawn from circulation into savings. In economic jargon the solution to increasing the money supply with a fixed supply of currency is that the velocity of circulation increases. The identity $MV=PY$ can help, where M is the amount of Money, V is the Velocity of circulation, P is the level of Prices and Y is Output. In this period in Britain, the amount of money (M, gold) was more or less constant and prices (P) did not change a lot until right at the end of the century, so any increase in the velocity of circulation (V) will lead directly to an increase in output (Y). The velocity of circulation increasing is another way to say that large quantities of currency were no longer taken out of circulation to be held as savings. In previous slumps, many gold coins held in savings were probably not used for decades which is undeniably low velocity of circulation. If it is clearer, rather than thinking of these saved coins as being part of the money supply but going round with very, very slow velocity, you can think of them as simply being taken out of the supply altogether and buried. When bonds reintroduced them into circulation, they were unburied, like a gold mine being discovered, and the money supply shot up. Both pictures are accurate enough.

xl. A brief economic note may help clarify the claim that government borrowings fuelled an extended economic boom for economists who are aware that, although it is a normal effect, this does not always follow. The main claim is monetary: that a period of normal economic growth was not strangled, as it was in the Netherlands, Venice and other Supplier city-states, when money was withdrawn from the system into savings. Because the savings were put into bonds, rather than under the bed, government spending recycled the money, and specifically the gold. In Britain over the period 1750-1820, there was also undoubtedly a fiscal boost from the deficit spending. While examples exist, such as Japan 1990-2010, of huge government deficits not resulting in a fiscal boost because of compensating private saving, this is unusual. It is worth mentioning that similar, if not so large, British deficit financing during World Wars I and II did not have the same effect as the deficit financing of 1750-1820. The key reason is that the war effort precluded private spending – there was basically nothing for people to buy, beyond their rationed food and so they were forced to save. This drastically reduced the velocity of circulation, much as the Japanese determination to save did after the 1989 crash there. To illustrate the point simply, during the war of 1939-45, a soldier who was paid by the government was often forced, by the lack of anything to spend it on, to buy war bonds with it – to save it. No such constraint applied to the soldier of 1800, who had no restrictions on his purchasing and was likely to spend his pay buying things. This passes the money onto the merchant who buys things in turn. Gradually the money is withdrawn bit by bit by savers as it goes round but not before it has caused sales of a substantial value, sales that could not happen to the equivalent money during WWII. Another way to look at this is to say that in 1800 there was still plenty of room in the economy for growth in wealth whereas during 1939-45 the economy had no capacity left over for growing wealth; it was fully stretched in war production.

xli. Bailey's British Directory, quoted in *Iron, Steam and Money*, Roger Osborne (The Bodley Head, 2013)

xlii. Linda Colley, *Britons* (Yale University Press, 1992)

xliii. Napoleon's economics were to make his defeated enemies pay for their defeat. Large quantities of this money then flowed through his coffers, much of it then into Wallonia to buy more arms. Without constant funds from defeated enemies, his empire was bankrupt. This is the principle reason for his disastrous invasion of Russia in 1812; his empire was facing financial ruin without more contributions from conquest.

xliv. Matt Ridley in *The Rational Optimist* and Joel Mokyr in *The Enlightened Economy*.

xlv. In 1750 British milk output was 134m.gals per year and pork 78m.lb: in 1870 these were 517m.gals and 290m.lb.

xlvi. *Liberty's Dawn*, Emma Griffin (Yale University Press, 2013)

xlvii. Population of Britain was around 7 million in 1700. The census figures were 10.9 million in 1801 and 30.5 million in 1901. Not that the census figures can be taken as anything more than a general indication of population as the methods used were very inadequate.

xlviii. This is no justification for appalling working conditions, for which there can be no excuse. However, we must be careful in out approach to remedying poor conditions because, carelessly applied, rules to prevent poor working conditions merely drive production to places where the bad conditions can not be seen and may be worse.

xlix. In the UK as a whole there was famine in Ireland after 1846.

l. Eisener, 2003, ONS

li.   See Steven Pinker, *The Better Angels of our Nature* (Viking Penguin, 2011)

lii.   <http://en.wikipedia.org/wiki/The_Lexus_and_the_ Olive_Tree>

liii.   Fire and Steam, Christian Wolmar (Atlantic Books, 2007)

liv.   Only some environmentalists are so extreme, but their effects have sometimes been devastating.

An example is banning the use of DDT as an insecticide from the late 1960s. This led to a huge growth in the incidence of malaria and to millions of deaths as a result. DDT itself is a very safe chemical when not used for whole-area spraying when it causes imbalances in the ecosystem. DDT was once again allowed to be used in controlled circumstances (no whole-area use) following the Stockholm Convention of 2001, organised by the UN Environmental Programme and the World Health Organisation.

At the moment one of the principle avoidable pollutants is the use of insecticide on crops that could be replaced by GM crops that don't need it. This use, and the consequent pollutions and sometimes poisoning, is caused by the Environmentalist belief's objections to the technology of genetic modification, a technology which has been used in all developed countries for major crops for over fifty years without any GM-related problem whatsoever. The first genetically-modified crops were developed in the 1950s and produced by exposing seeds to gamma radiation from Cobalt-60 (see Wikipedia: Mutation Breeding). Such GM plants were and are responsible for much of the world's food including British beer and whisky-making with the genetically-modified Golden Promise Barley variety, launched in 1965.

lv.   This quote is apocryphal but is too good a summary not to use.

lvi.   'The self-drive car is near its ERA point.' This may be technically correct but personal transport could move forward dramatically with the new technologies becoming available. With computer-driven cars, all carefully interlinked and computer controlled, and the roads adapted to improve pedestrian and other vehicle (bikes, etc.) separation, they could speed up cars in heavy traffic as well as move them closer together. At 40kmph, four times as many vehicles can go through the same bit of road in the same time as they can at 10kmph; halve the gaps between them and shrink the vehicle size to half the current length and half the width and (allowing for extra gaps) something like twenty times as many vehicles could use any given road, all travelling at a useful speed.

The degree of cooperation needed at many different scales to make this system work seems unlikely in any foreseeable future. Cars are still on a growth phase, getting larger all the time. Reversing this growth and forcing all into similarly sized small vehicles presents social/psychological challenges that are probably too large.

Well known, as any Internet search will show, but for a good and authoritative description see Papermaking, Dard Hunter (Dover Edition, 1978),

Game Theory

Science of Logical decision making in Humans & Animals.

or

The analysis of Competitive situation (or situation of conflict) in Humans & Animals.

    strategy — A plan of action before the game begins.

    Solution — It is the (Rewards) adaption of strategy that yields a particular outcome